REFRAMING HER

The Bible in the Modern World, 1

REFRAMING HER

Biblical Women in Postcolonial Focus

Judith E. McKinlay

SHEFFIELD PHOENIX PRESS

2004

Copyright © 2004, 2006 Sheffield Phoenix Press

First published in hardback, 2004
First published in paperback, 2006

Published by Sheffield Phoenix Press
Department of Biblical Studies, University of Sheffield
Sheffield S10 2TN

www.sheffieldphoenix.com

A CIP catalogue record for this book
is available from the British Library

Typeset by Forthcoming Publications
Printed by Lightning Source

ISBN 1-905048-00-9 (hardback)
ISBN 1-905048-69-6 (paperback)
ISSN 1747-9630

CONTENTS

PREFACE

Elizabeth Pritchard has written of theology being 'engaged in the construction of a theater of belief'.[1] I have found that a helpful metaphor as I have been exploring the ways of reading biblical characters. It also brought back a memory of sitting in an Indonesian audience some years ago watching a Javanese shadow puppet play. There, gathered at one side, was the collection of puppets waiting for the puppeteer's hand to pick them up and bring them into life across the screen. In the dramatic performance played out in the same way century after century the skill of the puppeteer lay in knowing the repertoire of moves, in how to turn limbs this way and that as the audience gazed, seeing the figures moving as shadows on the screen as the pattern of tradition dictated. And as it watched the audience was lulled into accepting this patterned action and reaction as the natural and appropriate way of playing out the 'big questions' of life and death, good and evil and seeing them resolved once again. I, of course, could not know what each member of that audience was thinking, or how exactly they were processing the drama presented before them, but there was a clear sense of satisfaction at its ending. As I think back and remember this, it seems to me that the biblical storytellers were taking up their characters and moving them across the surface of their scrolls in much the same way, so that each of us, as readers, is being invited to nod acceptance and leave the reading satisfied with the resolution. This is the power of the drama, the power of the scroll. So the question that I have been exploring is whether, or to what extent, I do, and indeed whether I should, nod acceptance of the biblical storytellers' constructions.

On the occasion of the puppet performance I was there as an outsider, looking on at a visual representation of an ancient text selected from the traditions of another culture. What I saw and how I saw it was an outsider's viewing; I was not seeing it through the eyes of that Indonesian audience. So what does it mean for me as I sit in my place at the bottom of the Pacific

---

1. Elizabeth A. Pritchard, 'Feminist Theology and the Politics of Failure', *Journal of Feminist Studies in Religion* 15/2 (1999), pp. 50-72 (62), taking the term 'theatre of belief' from Elaine Scarry, *Resisting Representation* (New York: Oxford University Press, 1994), p. 40.

Ocean, a *Pakeha²* reader in Aotearoa New Zealand, gazing once more at the textual screen with its moving women characters? For, realizing that the 'how' of the storyteller will remain frozen on the paper, lifeless and a lost communication unless I bring it into life, I also recognize that as the reader, my envisaging of these biblical characters will be the envisaging of a reader situated in a particular time and place. My location means that I have interests of my own that I will be bringing into dialogue with those that I will be detecting in the texts, whether I am conscious of this or not. For it is well recognized that while the biblical storytellers, just as the Indonesian puppeteer, were following ancient traditions and using stock patterns and familiar genres, they were commonly employing these for particular purposes, over and above the simple act of entertaining—just as the Indonesian puppet play I watched included overt satirical political comment, although carefully dressed up in humour. So I begin this quest of reading recognizing that questions of interests either overtly displayed or covertly coded within the text need to be asked if the text is to be fully or even partly understood and if I am to avoid being lulled into acceptance of a stance that I might rightly question or even dismiss were I aware of its presence. Robert Carroll's reminder that texts may 'substitute for political action where serious political power is absent',³ both alerts me to the subversive power of a text's agenda and is a further pointer to the need to ask myself whether I am in agreement with the coded standpoint. Interpretation is not a neutral matter, for, once brought to life, texts have the potential to exercise power in the world of their readers. Just as I need to ask of the biblical women, 'Are you who you seem to be and what are you doing in this text?', so I also need to ask whether I wish to applaud and collude with the text, or resist its stance. There is, of course, the added difficulty in asking what is going on within the text in that scholarly views on the historical background of many of the biblical texts are continually being reassessed.

Who, then, was Sarah and what was she doing? And Hagar and Rahab and Jezebel? As a woman reader I am interested not only in texts in which women and feminine imagery feature, but in how the women are being used as characters within their narratives, how they are represented in their roles and how the imagery is being employed. Thus I will be searching this out and reading both consciously and subconsciously with a gender lens, choosing among the many critical tools available for gender analyses, each capable of opening texts up for fresh possibilities of understanding. But I am also a reader situated in a postcolonial context. As Sugirtharajah has noted,

---

2.   The term used for those who are not Maori, and therefore not the indigenous inhabitants of the country.
3.   Robert P. Carroll, 'The Myth of the Empty Land', *Semeia* 59 (1992), pp. 79-93 (79).

postcolonialism has 'a multiplicity of meanings depending on location', and is 'a mental attitude rather than a method'.[4] But, as a critical approach, as Fernando Segovia writes, it is first and foremost one that

> takes the reality of empire—of imperialism, and colonialism—as an omnipresent, inescapable, and overwhelming reality in the world: the world of antiquity...and the world of today.[5]

Here again I will need to choose the critical methods that will best refine the questions that will enable me to hear these narratives speaking in a way that makes connections with my own context. Although postcolonial criticism has largely been an enterprise undertaken from the perspective of the colonized, I shall be attempting this from my position as a settler descendent in the post/colonial world of Aotearoa New Zealand, with the expectation that the task of examining 'how the colonizer constructs and justifies domination of the other in various places and periods of history', which is Musa Dube's description of postcolonial criticism,[6] will bring to life some uncomfortable, disquieting and challenging questions of interpretation and understanding. The double placing of women of the dominant culture in postcolonial countries has now become a truism, as true for me as it is for others. While as a woman I have personally experienced the tactics employed by those with greater influence and more direct access to privilege, as a *Pakeha* woman I have benefited from the power gained and exercised by the dominant culture.[7] An encounter I experienced some years ago made me more sharply aware of this double-placing. The local women's refuge collective of which

4. R.S. Sugirtharajah, 'A Postcolonial Exploration of Collusion and Construction in Biblical Interpretation', in *idem* (ed.), *The Postcolonial Bible* (The Bible and Postcolonialism, 1; Sheffield: Sheffield Academic Press, 1998), pp. 91-116 (93).

5. Fernando F. Segovia, 'Biblical Criticism and Postcolonial Studies: Toward a Postcolonial Optic', in Sugirtharajah (ed.), *The Postcolonial Bible*, pp. 49-65 (56). The additional words are: 'in the world of the Near East or of the Mediterranean Basin; the world of modernity, the world of Western hegemony and expansionism; and the world of today, of postmodernity, the world of postcolonialism on the part of the Two-Thirds World and of neocolonialism on the part of the West'. However, in his article, 'Notes Toward Refining the Postcolonial Optic', *JSNT* 75 (1999), pp. 103-14, Segovia notes the 'problematic' aspect of the term 'postcolonial', and points to the necessary distinction not only between 'imperialism' and 'colonialism', but between the differing 'subdiscourses' resulting from differing time periods and political circumstances.

6. Musa W. Dube and Jeffrey L. Staley, 'Descending from and Ascending into Heaven: A Postcolonial Analysis of Travel, Space and Power in John', in *idem* (eds.), *John and Postcolonialism: Travel, Space and Power* (Bible and Postcolonialism, 7; London and New York: Sheffield Academic Press, 2002), pp. 1-10 (3).

7. See Sharon H. Ringe, 'Places at the Table: Feminist and Postcolonial Biblical Interpretation', in Sugirtharajah (ed.), *The Postcolonial Bible*, pp. 136-51, for a discussion of the challenges this poses for women in dominant cultures.

I was a part was challenged to divide its underfunded resources in order to have two women's refuges in the city, one for Maori women and one for non-Maori. The collective was predominantly *Pakeha* and feelings were strongly divided on the matter; there were many meetings with heated debate. On one occasion a small group of us from the existing collective met with some of the Maori women who had issued the challenge, and as we sat facing each other those of us who were non-Maori were asked, one by one, to state our own personal understanding of the Maori term, *te tino ranga-tiratanga*, that was a key term in understanding the treaty relationship between Maori and *Pakeha* in our land.[8] It was a tense moment for each of us. Did I really understand it? Could I put it into words? We knew something of the gender tensions in our society from the underside, but how acute was our understanding of the ethnic underside when we were all from the more privileged dominant culture?

Therefore, while I am wanting to ask whether, and if so how, the biblical women and feminine images in the texts that I am reading were used to serve certain interests and wished-for realities, I wonder whether I will be able to detect the coded agendas written in as the storytellers tweaked their tales to fit the needs of their own times and placings. Learning to be aware of the danger of not seeing and so colluding with textual tactics and inter-pretations that might reinforce a politics of dominance and discovering ways to counter these is an ongoing process. It is a journey of awakening aware-ness.

This is one reader's account of this journey, as my own encounters with certain biblical women and feminine images have led me to ask sharp and varied questions—of the interests of the biblical texts themselves, of my own personal and contextual responses to these biblical traditions, and of the ways of reading when text and context meet. So I begin, asking not so much 'Who is this person and what is this image?', but 'In whose colours, through whose shaping am I seeing them? And how do they appear in my own eyes, as I open them ever more widely?'

---

8.   See the discussion of the 1840 Treaty of Waitangi in Chapter 2 n. 5, including the meaning and significance of this term. Debates on the location and understanding of sovereignty have continued since 1840. See the call by Annie Mikaere, a Maori lawyer: 'Why not define tino rangitiratanga in terms of Maori self-determination…?' (quoted in Andrew Sharp, *Justice and the Maori: The Philosophy and Practice of Maori Claims in New Zealand Since the 1970s* [Auckland: Oxford University Press, 2nd edn, 1997], p. 302).

ACKNOWLEDGMENTS

This work is very much a personal exploration of reading texts with gender and context as hermeneutical keys, but no work is ever carried out in isolation. I remain grateful for a conversation with David Gunn some years ago in which he urged me to write as a New Zealander; his support and encouragement at subsequent SBL presentations has been important for this work. Paul Trebilco, my colleague and head of the Department of Theology and Religious Studies at the University of Otago, encouraged me to gather some of these pieces together; without that encouragement I suspect that this book would not have been written. The Bible and Critical Theory Seminar meetings in Australia, and Roland Boer in particular, have provided a welcome support and opportunities to try out many of these readings. A special thanks is due to the Friday afternoon Women Writing Theology group in Dunedin, and especially to Mary Huie-Jolly, Kath Rushton, Margaret Eaton and Laurel Lanner, who over the last few years have read a considerable number of pages and offered their good critical advice and encouragement. To my husband Henry, who has had to listen patiently to innumerable conversations about Rahab, Jezebel and the Others, I offer my very warm thanks. Although all of these friends and colleagues have been a part of my journeying with these texts, they are not responsible for the views and interpretive conclusions expressed here; they are my own, reached at this particular time and in this particular place.

To Cheryl Exum and the Sheffield Phoenix Press I would express my thanks for accepting the manuscript and steering it through to publication, and to Duncan Burns for his considerate care in the editing process.

Portions of this book have appeared previously. The Preface includes a small section from 'Foiling Jezebel', published in *SeaChanges, The Journal of Women Scholars of Religion and Theology* 2 (November 2002) (<www.wsrt. com.au/seachanges>). Chapter 1 includes material from 'Reading with Choices and Controls: Genesis 12', *Feminist Theology* 17 (1998), pp. 75-87, and a small section from 'Who's/Whose Sarah? Journeying with Sarah in a Chorus of Voices', in Edgar W. Conrad and Roland Boer (eds.), *Redirected Travel* (JSOTSup, 382; London: T&T Clark International, 2003), pp. 131-43. Chapter 2 is a revised version of 'What do I do with Contexts? A Brief Reflection on Reading Biblical Texts with Israel and Aotearoa

New Zealand in Mind', *Pacifica* 14 (2001), pp. 159-71. Chapter 3 is a lightly revised version of 'Rahab: A Hero/ine?', *BibInt* 7/1 (1999), pp. 44-57 (copyright with Brill Academic Publishers), and 'A Son is Born to Naomi: A Harvest for Israel', in Athalya Brenner (ed.), *Ruth and Esther* (The Feminist Companion to the Bible, Second Series, 3; Sheffield: Sheffield Academic Press, 1999), pp. 151-57. Chapter 4 is a revised version of 'Foiling Jezebel', published in *SeaChanges* 2. Chapter 5 appeared as 'Negotiating the Frame for Viewing the Death of Jezebel', *BibInt* 10 (2002), pp. 305-23 (copyright with Brill Academic Publishers). Chapter 6 is a revised version of 'Framing Jezebel and Others', *SeaChanges* 1 (January 2001) (<www.wsrt.com.au/seachanges/>). Chapter 7 combines material from 'Who's/Whose Sarah? Journeying with Sarah in a Chorus of Voices', with 'Sarah and Hagar: What Have I to Do with Them?', in Caroline Vander Stichele and Todd Penner (eds.), *Her Master's Tools? Feminist Challenges to Historical-Critical Interpretation* (Global Perspectives on Biblical Scholarship; Atlanta: Society of Biblical Literature, 2004). I am grateful to the publishers for their permission to use this material.

ABBREVIATIONS

AB	Anchor Bible
ABD	David Noel Freedman (ed.), *The Anchor Bible Dictionary* (New York: Doubleday, 1992)
BHS	*Biblia hebraica stuttgartensia*
Bib	*Biblica*
BibInt	*Biblical Interpretation: A Journal of Contemporary Approaches*
CBQ	*Catholic Biblical Quarterly*
GNB	The Good News Bible
HAR	*Hebrew Annual Review*
HDR	Harvard Dissertations in Religion
HSS	Harvard Semitic Studies
HTS	Harvard Theological Studies
JAAR	*Journal of the American Academy of Religion*
JB	*Jerusalem Bible*
JPSV	*Jewish Publication Society Version*
JSNT	*Journal for the Study of the New Testament*
JSOT	*Journal for the Study of the Old Testament*
JSOTSup	*Journal for the Study of the Old Testament*, Supplement Series
NovT	*Novum Testamentum*
NRSV	New Revised Standard Version
NTS	*New Testament Studies*
OTG	Old Testament Guides
SBLDS	SBL Dissertation Series
VT	*Vetus Testamentum*
VTSup	*Vetus Testamentum*, Supplements
WBC	Word Biblical Commentary

1

First Step: Moving Off with Wisdom

Feminist scholarship challenges us as critics to become more conscious of—and to state more openly in our work—who we are, what and for whom we work, where our allegiances, commitments and limitations lie, what our experience has been. It challenges us also to make open use of our experience to see and to show that where we stand gives us a valid angle of vision and not the only angle.[1]

My own questioning in response to this challenge began with a study of one aspect of the use of the Wisdom figure in a series of biblical texts. But already in this first foray into asking critical questions of the interests and agendas of these texts I found myself faced with an ambivalence in my own response, an ambivalence that was to become all too familiar. The language of Wisdom sings of her as the tree of life (Prov. 3.18), as the one who rejoices both in heaven and in humankind (Prov. 8.30-31), memory of whom is sweeter than honey (Sir. 24.20). This was, and continues to be for me, a poetry of delight. But my delight was tinged with questions and a certain puzzlement. How did such rich feminine imagery come to have a place in the sacred texts of a culture whose god, for the most part, was hymned and referred to in predominantly male terms? I began asking questions of the origins of such language, knowing that cultures have deep roots, and was soon delving into the ancient texts of Israel's ancestors in the ancient Near East, a world rich in sacred stories and poems of gods both male and female, whose lives and loves and actions directed the lives and loves and actions of the many people, both male and female, who lived within the ambit of their stories. And so many gods—El, Baal, Inanna, Ishtar, Tiamat, to mention only a few—some with names shared with different groups, some particular to certain times and places. Although the origins of Israel and Israel's earliest relationship with its ancient Near East neighbours continue to be debated, it appears that

1. Jane Schaberg, 'A Feminist Experience of Historical-Jesus Scholarship', in William E. Arnal and Michel Desjardins (eds.), *Whose Historical Jesus?* (Canadian Corporation for Studies in Religion/Corporation Canadienne des Sciences Religieuses; Ontario: Wilfrid Laurier University Press, 1997), pp. 146-60 (158-59).

at some point Israel had set limits to this sharing, deciding to separate itself as a self-identified community with a distinctive cultic life, one that moved further and further away from the busy pantheons of its neighbours.[2] As a consequence, it seems that Israel had an urgent need to tell and retell its own life history, both to create a sense of coherence and identity, and to talk itself into an ordering entity in order to differentiate itself from both its ancient Near East ancestors and its contemporary neighbours. For the Israelite asking the question 'who am I?', the answer now became, 'I am the person of my sacred stories, which give me my identity and keep chaos at bay for me'. On this understanding, I saw the storytellers and shapers of sacred traditions working with considerable care at their craft, shaping them to carry particular beliefs and messages to the people at large. My interest now lay in exploring how this was done, how the writers' skills shaped Israel's texts so that they were able to exercise such a power to influence and convey messages capable of affecting the thoughts, values, and actions of their listeners, both overtly and covertly.

Israel, it seemed, had differentiated itself on religious grounds, choosing, even if only gradually, one god from the many of its neighbouring traditions. Where once the people of Israel may have enjoyed a wide-ranging expression of the divine, worshipping different gods for different aspects and times of their lives, this array of gods, male and female, was now to be rejected and left behind. But not entirely forgotten. They were to be used as representing the very powers of chaos itself, now to be confronted, defeated and eradicated. The polemic was sharp. The Deuteronomic texts and particularly the books of Kings repeatedly accused Israel of having 'walked after false gods'. At times the details become explicit: so, in 2 Kgs 17.15-18, 'they made themselves an asherah, worshiped all the host of heaven' (v. 16). And the consequence? 'Therefore Yahweh was very angry with Israel and removed them out of his sight' (v. 18). Those who cut down and burned the altars and sacred pillars devoted to such gods gain the bonus points.

---

2. F.M. Cross's now classic study of the relationship between Canaanite and Israel religious expression, *Canaanite Myth and Hebrew Epic: Essays in the History of the Religion of Israel* (Cambridge, MA: Harvard University Press, 1973), has been followed by a large body of work, including M.S. Smith, *The Early History of God: Yahweh and the Other Deities in Ancient Israel* (San Francisco: Harper & Row, 1990); Susan Niditch, *Ancient Israelite Religion* (Oxford: Oxford University Press, 1997); Robert Karl Gnuse, *No Other Gods: Emergent Monotheism in Israel* (JSOTSup, 241; Sheffield: Sheffield Academic Press, 1997), and 'The Emergence of Monotheism in Ancient Israel: A Survey of Recent Scholarship', *Religion* 29 (1999), pp. 315-36; Bob Becking and Marjo C.A. Korpel (eds.), *The Crisis of Israelite Religion* (Leiden: E.J. Brill, 1999); and Bob Becking *et al.* (eds.), *Only One God? Monotheism in Ancient Israel and the Veneration of the Goddess Asherah* (The Biblical Seminar, 77; Sheffield: Sheffield Academic Press, 2001).

But if the message was clear, the historical reality was less so. I had already been initiated into the ways of reading with a hermeneutic of suspicion,[3] and so had an awareness of the ideologies of texts. I was curious about the asherah in that text. Who or what was she, that even her pillars were to be destroyed? As so many recent studies indicate, she is a teasing figure.[4] Was she the female god, Asherah, who had seemingly strayed in from the supposedly much older Canaanite tradition? Or had she indeed been with Israel all along? Or was the asherah to be read with a lower case 'a', as more simply a type of devotional pillar?[5] According to the biblical texts, however she/it was understood, the asherah/Asherah tended to come and go in line with the prevailing religious viewpoint. King Hezekiah removed her image (2 Kgs 18.4), his son Manasseh replaced it, his grandson Josiah removed it again. And, according to 1 Kgs 15.12-13 King Asa of Judah (913–873 BCE) not only removed 'all the idols that his ancestors had made', but even removed his mother Maacah from her high status position of queen mother 'because she had made an abominable image for Asherah', which he cut down and burned, very much to the approval of the writer(s). Putting the fact that it is Maacah, the queen mother, who is stated as being responsible for this 'abominable image', alongside the mention of women weaving vestments for the asherah in the Jerusalem temple in 2 Kgs 23.7, raises the question of whether there was a special and ongoing place for this goddess or goddess symbol in the lives of Israelite women, perhaps even a cultic women's devotion to Asherah?[6] And are those small Iron Age female figurines that have been uncovered in significant numbers a sign of a particular women's

3.   This term, coined by Paul Ricoeur, asks questions of the vested interests of the text, and is particularly associated with the work of Elisabeth Schüssler Fiorenza in her readings of biblical women.

4.   See Saul M. Olyan, *Asherah and the Cult of Yahweh in Israel* (SBLMS, 34; Atlanta; Scholars Press, 1988), and the recent comprehensive treatment by Judith M. Hadley, *The Cult of Asherah in Ancient Israel and Judah: Evidence for a Hebrew Goddess* (Cambridge: Cambridge University Press, 2000). For the many contributors to the discussion, see the references and bibliography in Olyan and Hadley, as well as the first chapter of my *Gendering Wisdom the Host: Biblical Invitations to Eat and Drink* (JSOTSup, 216; Gender, Culture, Theory, 4; Sheffield: Sheffield Academic Press, 1996).

5.   See Hadley, *The Cult of Asherah*, p. 11: 'it may be determined that "asherah" in the Hebrew Bible usually refers to the wooden symbol of this goddess, but may also refer to the goddess herself'. Note also her conclusion (p. 209), that 'in the biblical record, we can begin to trace how her name "Asherah" gradually evolved into a designation of merely her cultic pole, as the editors of the text attempted to eliminate the evidence of her former worship among the Israelites'.

6.   Susan Ackerman, 'The Queen Mother and the Cult in Ancient Israel', *JBL* 112 (1993), pp. 385-401, has suggested that the queen mothers may have had a quite specific cultic relationship with Asherah.

devotion to Asherah?[7] Sadly, there are no definitive answers here. But even if at times her image had a place in the temple at Jerusalem (2 Kgs 21.7; 23.6), to the writer(s) of the books of Kings she was to be seen as a chaotic force. Worship of Asherah/asherah is included in lists of condemnable practices (2 Kgs 17.16-17), along with the molten images, divination, sorcery, and even child sacrifice. There was no debate: such images were to be destroyed. Whether those responsible were successful in their eradication campaign is, of course, another matter. The inscriptions referring to Yahweh and 'his asherah', found at Kuntillet el-'Ajrud and Khirbet el-Qom and dated respectively c. 800 BCE and between 750 BCE and the end of the eighth century, would imply that they were not, although what is meant by 'his asherah' remains the subject of discussion. Should it be written as 'his Asherah', and understood as his consort, just as she was El's in Canaanite lore? But what was clear from my reading of these texts and my questioning through a hermeneutic of suspicion was that certain elements within Israel had actively countered this feminine representation of the divine, however it was understood. Those responsible for the books of Kings had used the shaping of Israel's historical and sacred narrative as a tool in this would-be eradication programme. But how successful had they been in eradicating the memory?

For I found and continue to find intriguing that, while the books of Kings would have the reader believe that those responsible for guarding Israel's sacred traditions had spent considerable energy combating the feminine representation of the divine, there remains embedded within Israel's accepted and canonical sacred writings another female figure who seemingly not only has divine origins, but who, according to the writers of the book of Proverbs, was present with Israel's male god at creation, even offering the divine gift of life to those who seek her. Naming herself as Wisdom, she assertively gives her own eulogy both in Proverbs 8 and Sirach 24. If the canonical Israelite literature affirms Yahweh as sole deity, for the most part in mighty warrior and male terms, how then is this Wisdom figure to be explained or understood?[8] That was my original question. How did it escape the anti-feminine polemic that was directed against Asherah? One of the more frequent and

---

7. Hadley, *The Cult of Asherah*, pp. 188-205 (Chapter 7), considers that these could be Asherah figures. Others, such as J. Tigay, *You Shall Have No Other Gods: Israelite Religion in the Light of Hebrew Inscriptions* (HSS, 31; Atlanta: Scholars Press, 1986), p. 92, consider it less likely, in Tigay's case on the grounds that there is an 'absence of symbols of divinity' on these figurines.

8. Among the many works on the Wisdom figure, see Claudia V. Camp, *Wisdom and the Feminine in the Book of Proverbs* (Bible and Literature Series, 11; Sheffield: Almond Press, 1985); Stuart Weeks, *Early Israelite Wisdom* (Oxford: Clarendon Press, 1994); Sylvia Schroer, *Wisdom Has Built her House: Studies on the Figure of Sophia in the Bible* (Collegeville, MN: Liturgical Press, 2000).

persuasive explanations is that Wisdom functioned as a metaphor, one of the many in Israel's god-talk.[9] But if this is talk of the divine, which in Israel is largely spoken of in male terms, there is still the surprising point that this figure associated with the divine, albeit metaphorically, is clearly in the guise of a woman. There is, of course, a considerable body of literature on the nature and function of metaphor, but at its simplest, I would see it, following Janet Martin Soskice, as 'that figure of speech whereby we speak about one thing in terms which are seen to be suggestive of another',[10] working much as a lens, 'as though the speaker were saying, "Look through this and see what I have seen, something you would never have noticed without the lens"'.[11] And here is something about the divine that we might never have noticed without looking through this gendered lens! Yet this recognition only led to further questions. Was this language being employed to present female Wisdom as a new dimension of the godhead for Israel, one that was bringing female gender back into Israel's way of talking about the divine? Was this to be understood as the feminine dimension of Israel's male god? Having come to this question by way of the ancient Near Eastern gods, both male and female, I was inclined to agree with those who perceived traces of those ancient Near Eastern goddess roots.[12] For how does one finally eradicate a female deity? One answer seemed to be: turn her into a metaphor where she may be feminine, but now only a feminine expression of one aspect of the acceptable masculine divinity. She who comes with delight, she whom Prov. 8.30 hymns as the delight of God, was now the personified wisdom of Israel's male God. While a significant group in Israel had seen any feminine expression of deity, independent of the male, as a chaotic force to be countered, one scribal tradition had allowed the beauty and the delight of such language, as language and metaphor, to be retained, savoured and valued. But the once-female god was now simply a language ornamentation—nothing more.

And, as metaphor, that language had staying power. This was not the end of goddess-like language. It proved to be a tool that later groups and writers continued to find useful, both in early Judaism and early Christianity. So long as the metaphor remained in use, the repression of the independent female deity was not entirely successful, for metaphor retains a memory of that which it may have been used to repress. Through metaphor's interactive dynamic in which meaning both emerges and is repressed, traces of the now unspeakable are able to remain as part of the 'is not' tension that Ricoeur

9.   See, e.g., Camp, *Wisdom and the Feminine*.

10.   Janet Martin Soskice, *Metaphor and Religious Language* (Oxford: Clarendon Press, 1985), p. 15.

11.   G.B. Caird, *The Language and Imagery of the Bible* (London: Gerald Duckworth, 1980), p. 152.

12.   See Camp, *Wisdom and the Feminine*; Hadley, *The Cult of Asherah*.

and others note.[13] In which case, if the use of this Wisdom metaphor was to
repress the memory of female divinity, as experienced in Asherah and others,
regarded as subversive or worse, it seems that it may not have erased this
completely. For the metaphor itself may have allowed an underlying awareness of female deity to continue, albeit as part of the 'unspeakable' and 'the
repressed', as long as the woman/Wisdom metaphor continued to be employed
in Israel's theology. But if Wisdom herself was a lingering figure still alive in
the later literatures, was such a trace of the female divine only to be viewed
in the Hebrew Bible within the confines of the book of Proverbs? And if she
was brought down to earth and domesticated in the good wife of the poem of
Prov. 31.10-31, as has been suggested of the Wisdom figure,[14] were there
more earthly traces of her elsewhere? Were there traces of her to be detected
in the human women who move through Israel's texts? My questions had
certainly not yet come to an end.

I turned back to view that first woman of the Hebrew Bible, Eve, the taker
of the fruit from the tree of the knowledge of good and evil in the garden of
Eden. Would she provide a link between my first initial foray into the discourse of feminine imagery and my exploration among the 'real' human
women in these texts? Gazing at Eve, however, also meant listening to the
conversation between the snake and the woman, a conversation which led
directly to the taking of the fruit. While this narrative states very clearly that
both woman and snake are creatures of God, created from the dust of the
earth, albeit at a second remove in the case of the woman, once again both
have seemingly travelled a long way to reach this text. For this cluster of
female, tree and snake also has deep roots in the traditions of the ancient
Near East.[15] But there the female was a female god. Was Asherah to be seen
still lurking in the shadows behind this biblical text? If so, in a story that is
itself about boundaries, the female herself had quite literally crossed the
border from divinity to humanity, even while still bearing the title of

13. P. Ricoeur, *The Rule of Metaphor: Multi-Disciplinary Studies of the Creation of
Meaning in Language Texts* (trans. R. Czerny *et al.*; London: Routledge & Kegan Paul,
1978), p. 255. See also Francis Landy, 'On Metaphor, Play and Nonsense', *Semeia*
61 (1993), pp. 219-37, and Mieke Bal, 'Metaphors He Lives By', *Semeia* 61 (1993),
pp. 185-207.

14. E.g. T.P. McCreesh, 'Wisdom as Wife: Proverbs 31:10-31', *RB* 92 (1985),
pp. 25-46.

15. And notably too through the association of Asherah with the goddess Qudshu
who is shown on a plaque and stele holding a snake, and with the term *dt btn* ('Serpent
Lady'). Some of the Late Bronze Age plaque figurines found in many sites are holding
snakes, which, as fertility symbols, are assumed to be symbols of divinity. See Hadley,
The Cult of Asherah, pp. 189-92. See also Othmar Keel, *Goddesses and Trees, New Moon
and Yahweh: Ancient Near Eastern Art and the Hebrew Bible* (JSOTSup, 261; Sheffield:
Sheffield Academic Press, 1998).

'mother of all living'.[16] So, Eve too, it seemed, had been given a role in the task of de-deifying the feminine. And the tree too? In Prov. 3.13-20 it is Wisdom herself, poetically offering gifts of length of days, wealth and honour, who is a tree of life. If there the female was metaphorical divine wisdom personified, now, at the end of the garden story in Genesis 2–3, the *'adam*, both male and female, was like the divine, knowing good and evil, but different in being mortal. It was this mortal female and her ongoing tale in the Hebrew Bible that I now wished to follow, while remaining alert to any signs or traces of a female divine counterpart.

Genesis 2–3, as part of the first eleven chapters of Genesis, was part of the first act of the biblical drama, the biblical curtain-raiser. My gender reading with a Wisdom guidebook had uncovered traces of an Israelite template covering ancient sources, with significant gender implications. What was to be found in the second act? This begins in Genesis 12, as Israel's story of origin with God speaking promise and blessing to Abram in Haran, in a passage set in high relief among the biblical texts by interpreters as the first Call. In the opening prologue of vv. 1-3, it is a Call notably addressed to Abram alone, as the masculine singular pronouns at the beginning and ending of God's speech in v. 1 and continuing into v. 2 make very clear. Yet it is not a solitary Abram; as he acts on this call, he does not go out from Haran alone. Although it is the male blood relationship that is given first mention ('Lot went with him'), v. 5 indicates that Abram 'takes' both wife and nephew, along with all their possessions, both material and human. As I read this verse I paused at the plural verbs; were they indicating joint ownership, that these were the possessions of both Abram, and Sarai, and Lot? Or was Sarai Abram's possession, and the rest a combination belonging equally to Abram and Lot? I was discovering the first hint of a tension in this text.

The land was reached and claimed, with an altar built at Shechem. By now well aware of Asherah's seeming ability to appear behind texts I wondered whether there was yet another hint of her in the mention of the *'elon* of Moreh, which was then explained by the presence of the Canaanites, indicating that this was a place of Canaanite worship. Yet, despite the presence of the tree, it was not Asherah nor any other Canaanite deity who then appeared, but Israel's own god, who, the theophany implied, needed no such symbol, although an altar was then built, after the divine revelation. Again, with Asherah in mind, I wondered whether, as Habel had suggested, 'YHWH

---

16. Asherah was known as 'mother of the gods' and 'procreator of the gods' (KTU 1.4.I.22; 2.31.46). The name *Havva* has also been likened to an Aramaic cognate for snake, suggesting a snake goddess associated with life. James Barr, *The Garden of Eden and the Hope of Immortality* (London: SCM Press, 1992), p. 65, with reference to this, suggests 'the proportions and structure of the story make more sense if at some earlier stage she was something more than that', that is, more than human.

is portrayed as present in the land and one with the God revealed at sacred sites within the land'.[17] In a Canaanite-occupied land, surely Asherah would have been present at such sites. But the land itself was not kind to these new arrivals. Genesis 11.30 had already hinted at the obstacle of human barrenness, a barrenness now to be repeated in the barrenness of the land. While the sevenfold repetition of 'Abram' and 'land' in these verses may have been hinting at their importance, it is the land with its negative fruitlessness that now takes control over Abram's immediate future. And so the move to Egypt where the question that drives the plot is: 'How will Abram and his promise fare in the land of Pharaoh?'—although perhaps there was also a prior question, whether Abram should have been going there at all if Canaan was the promised land as v. 7 had indicated, even if the famine was severe.

Told from Abram's perspective, this is an ancient tale, with ancient understandings of what it is to be a stranger, a *ger*, in someone else's land. Yet Abram's reactions seem strikingly similar to those we nowadays consider the result of 'culture shock', those acute feelings of insecurity, vulnerability, and even paranoia experienced by people removed from their familiar context. Before any Egyptian had even approached Abram, indeed, even before he had entered their territory, he is stating as fact what appears to be only his unsubstantiated fear. While his overriding fear is death itself, the immediate fear is, or so he believes, that his wife will be desired for her beauty and he will therefore be seen as the obstacle, and all too easily disposable. If there was a suspicion that v. 5 regarded Sarai as a possession, the suspicion becomes all the greater here. Abram is afraid that he has what others will want, and so he plots the wife/sister strategy. His pretext is that matters will therefore 'go well' with him, and that his life will be spared; he does not seem at all fearful about his wife being taken by the Canaanites! In effect, he himself has now put both the promise of land and of seed in jeopardy, for he has left the land that he has been shown by God, and he is now about to give away the potential bearer of his seed.

Was this a justifiable fear? Certainly the Egyptians praise Sarai, and she is taken to the house of Pharaoh, the Egyptians, quite naturally, thanks to Abram, believing her to be Abram's sister. Abram has opened up the way for any who so desire to take her and material compensation follows in abundance. It does initially 'go well' for Abram but I am noting that his prosperity comes by giving away a woman. Read with 11.30 in mind, there is an irony, in that such prosperity comes from a barren woman,[18] and also an irony in

17. Norman C. Habel, *The Land is Mine: Six Biblical Land Ideologies* (Minneapolis: Fortress Press, 1995), pp. 130-31.
18. Robert Polzin, '"The Ancestress of Israel in Danger" in Danger', *Semeia* 3 (1975), pp. 81-98 (p. 93), reads Gen. 12 as concerning the possession of wealth which is ill-begotten, so that the giving of progeny is delayed. Abram has failed the test here.

that Abram, who was looking no further than to stay alive, is now even showered with gifts. But soon all is not well, and in particular Pharaoh and his house are far from well. God, who has not been textually present in this episode, intervenes with plagues and Abram's devious plot is revealed. The reason for God's reappearance and action is not given, apart from the rather enigmatic statement that it was 'because of Sarai, Abram's wife' (v. 17).[19] Was it to save the promise? Or because God does not approve of such adultery?[20] What the reader is told is that Sarai is returned to Abram, being now too dangerous for Pharaoh to keep, a nicely ironic reversal.[21] Abram is now ordered out of Egypt, presumably taking all his acquired goods with him, if that is the understanding of v. 20. The formal unit closes at 13.4, with a symmetry and completeness in that the return has been made to the Bethel of v. 8. Abram is back in the land, with Sarai, and Lot, and all their goods and wealth, ready for the next scene in this drama of beginnings.

On the surface this is a simple tale easily read, although the text itself protects certain ambiguities. Did Sarai survive this ordeal sexually unscathed? To be taken into Pharaoh's house is at the very least suggestive of sexual taking. The narrative plot does, of course, have parallels in chs. 20 and 26, but as I am reading the beginnings of Israel's female history, I have chosen to follow the later editors in reading the story of 12.10-20 under the promise of vv. 1-3, only diverging from them in seeing 13.1-4 as its conclusion, my choice being to follow a textual symmetry, where the verb 'going' (*hlk*) both opens and concludes the narrative. But my own interest in this narrative lies with Sarai. If vv. 1-9 focused on Abram, there has been a noticeable shift in this later episode of vv. 10-20. Here again and again the text refers to Sarai, declaring that it is 'because of you, on your account, for her sake'; even God acts 'because of Sarai, Abram's wife' (v. 17).[22] But if Sarai is the focus, she is

19. Fokkelien van Dijk-Hemmes, 'Sarai's Exile: A Gender-Motivated Reading of Genesis 12.20–13.2', in Athalya Brenner (ed.), *A Feminist Companion to Genesis* (The Feminist Companion to the Bible, 2; Sheffield: Sheffield Academic Press, 1993), pp. 222-34 (226), reads 12.10–13.2 as a chiastic structure, with v. 17 at its crux.

20.   There is considerable discussion in the commentaries over whether or not there was an adulterous relationship, frequently focusing on whether or not the verb 'to take' has a sexual connotation here. U. Cassuto, *A Commentary on the Book of Genesis* (trans. L. Abrahams; Jerusalem: Magnes Press, 1964), pp. 357, 362, suggests that the *vav* that introduces the inflicting is antithetic, indicating that God's intervention came in time.

21.   With the further irony that now Pharaoh has good reason to do away with Abram, since he has been the cause of Pharaoh's unwitting violation, or near violation, of another man's property, as J. Cheryl Exum notes in 'Who's Afraid of the "Endangered Ancestress"?', in J. Cheryl Exum and David J. Clines (eds.), *The New Literary Criticism and the Hebrew Bible* (JSOTSup, 143; Sheffield: JSOT Press, 1993), pp. 91-113 (99).

22.   Dijk-Hemmes, 'Sarai's Exile', p. 229, notes that the preposition 'because of you' in v. 13, could also be translated as 'for the price of you'. She also suggests (p. 231), three options for translating 'because of Sarai' (*'l dbr*), the third being 'because of the word of

also the pawn; male fears are notably projected upon her, and through male desire she is used to gain protection and wealth.[23] She herself has no voice; the text seemingly has no interest in any view she might have of the situation, although that does not deter commentators from reading her silence and speaking for her. Not that they all agree. Some interpret her silence at Abram's request to say that she is his sister as her 'agreement to co-operate in the ruse',[24] or as a 'self-sacrifice of the mother',[25] while others read it as an indication of her powerlessness and her 'status as property',[26] or even that speechlessness that is so often the result of sexual violence.[27] But that is to read at the level of the character herself; this, too, is a tale told and crafted with care. Esther Fuchs returns me to the storyteller with her sharp comment, 'the biblical narrative creates women in the image of patriarchal desire'.[28] That is how they were meant to be! There is, of course, another significant silence, or perhaps more correctly, a gap. Where in Abram's words are his concerns for Sarai's fate? Abram's focus remains firmly fixed upon himself. But while Abram, the male, may be fearful, with a fear driven by the fantasy of other men having sex with his wife,[29] it is the woman who discovers the world to be a dangerous and risky place; it is the woman who is subject to the male gaze from those not morally entitled. This is a Sarai in a Lacanian world under the Law of the Father. The final outcome of the story reads as an initial fulfilling of the blessing, perhaps a first instalment. If this has been the goal all along, then Sarai has indeed carried out her part well. But the silencing continues; after her presence has been noted in the first verse of the next chapter (13.1), she immediately returns to her place beneath the text.

This is sobering enough, but I have come to this narrative via the Garden story of chs. 2–3, as the final editors ordered the book of Genesis. Now it is all too possible to see in Sarai the consequences for women of living under the rule of their husbands, if Gen. 3.16 was implying more than a purely

Sarai', implying 'that YHWH is the only one towards whom Sarai does not remain speechless'.

23. Exum, 'Who's Afraid of the "Endangered Ancestress"?', p. 107.

24. V.P. Hamilton, *The Book of Genesis: Chapters 1–17* (The New International Commentary on the Old Testament; Grand Rapids: Eerdmans, 1990), p. 382.

25. Hermann Gunkel, *Genesis* (Göttingen: Vandenhoeck & Ruprecht, 1964), pp. 169-70.

26. Hugh C. White, *Narration and Discourse in the Book of Genesis* (Cambridge: Cambridge University Press, 1991), p. 185.

27. Dijk-Hemmes, 'Sarai's Exile', pp. 222-23.

28. Esther Fuchs, 'The Literary Characterization of Mothers and Sexual Politics in the Hebrew Bible', *Semeia* 46 (1989), pp. 151-66.

29. See Exum, 'Who's Afraid of the "Endangered Ancestress"?', for a psychoanalytical reading of this. 'What is unconsciously desired is also unconsciously feared' (p. 100).

demographic concern.[30] If so, this is the consequence of a societal ordering that did become reality. While the rabbis saw the beauty of Eve in Sarai it may have been more than beauty that Sarai inherited.[31] For although Eve was clearly the one with initiative, enabling her man and, indeed, the human race, to live in the world with discernment and the sagely knowledge of good and evil, and although she was named 'mother of all living' in 3.20, a description that I have already noted resounds with echoes of female deity, that Garden story also allows the reading that 'the woman is created as the man's helper. She is created precisely for him and is derivative from him. The man exercises his authority over her not only after the fruit-eating incident, but also before by naming her in 2.23.'[32] Although other readings may view Eve's role more positively, the fact remains that at the end of ch. 3, after having been brought under the man's naming authority, and clothed together with him by God, Eve slips entirely out of sight. As the *'adam* is sent out and given his agenda for living in the world, there is no further mention of Eve, although she is necessarily present with him at the beginning of ch. 4 when their offspring are needed in turn to enter the world.[33] Women seem to be both necessary and disposable in this narrative biblical world. I am left wondering whether, if the two tales are read in sequence, Eve's silent disappearance, together with the prediction of her being under her man's authority, has given a biblical permission for the later human woman, Sarai, to be moved away in silence.

But I am also discovering that each reading is providing but one of many possibilities. If, instead of reading with an eye on the earlier Genesis story of Eve, one reads Sarai's story in line with the later biblical books, her story also becomes the story of a prototypical ancestor. Read in this way, as Fokkelien van Dijk-Hemmes notes, 'the narrator presents the story about Sarai in Egypt as a prefiguration of the history of the people of Israel in Egypt'.[34] Just as Israel suffered in exile, in a strange land, in Egypt and was

30.   The latter most notably suggested by Carol Meyers, 'Gender Roles and Genesis 3.16 Revisited', in C.L. Meyers and M. O'Connor (eds.), *The Word of the Lord Shall Go Forth: Essays in Honor of David Noel Freedman in Celebration of his Sixtieth Birthday* (Winona Lake, IN: Eisenbrauns 1983), pp. 337-54, and *Discovering Eve: Ancient Israelite Women In Context* (New York and Oxford: Oxford University Press, 1988).

31.   So *Genesis Rabbah* 40.5 where R. Azariah and R. Jonathan in the name of R. Isaac write: 'The model of the beauty of Eve was handed over to the most beautiful woman of the generations to come'.

32.   The conclusion drawn by Beverly J. Stratton, *Out of Eden: Reading, Rhetoric, and Ideology in Genesis 2–3* (JSOTSup, 208; Sheffield: JSOT Press, 1995), p. 101, after due consideration of other views.

33.   She does, of course, make the strong but enigmatic and much discussed statement in 4.1 that she has 'produced a man with the help of the Lord' (NRSV).

34.   Dijk-Hemmes, 'Sarai in Exile', p. 233.

exploited, and just as their plight was noticed by their god who intervened on their behalf, so it was with Sarai, who had experienced all before them, as their mother in that land. Another intratextual connection is more sobering: Gen. 12.1 is notably similar to 22.2, with the blessing of 12.2-3 echoing elements of 22.17-18. Many commentators pair the father's call to leave Haran with the later order to take the son to Moriah, but I cannot help wondering whether there is not an anticipating hint of that later near sacrifice in the handing over of Sarai in Genesis 12.

Reading the commentators I note that Brueggemann, like the rabbis, talks of 'the irresistible beauty of mother Sarah', and suggests that 'the story offers humor' in 'the shrewdness of father Abraham'.[35] I wonder about his choice of the word 'shrewd'. Vawter couples it with sagacity![36] If this is applause for Abram, then it follows traditional choices, for the rabbis long ago exonerated Abram. R. Phineas in the name of R. Reuben, in *Genesis Rabbah* (40.4), considered that in addressing Sarai and giving her the role of his sister, Abram was denying himself his own principal role, and thus deliberately and humbly treating himself as subordinate. Luther notes that many thought Abraham at fault because he 'willingly and knowingly...exposes his wife to the danger of adultery...for [he] values his own life more highly than the chastity of his wife and the welfare of others', with which I agree, but then he goes on to point out how mistaken is this view! Abraham exposes his wife to danger 'in order to glorify God...whatever is done to the glory of God... deserves to be praised'. Nor does Luther stop there, but continues:

> In this passage the Holy Spirit provides instruction about home life when he relates that Abraham spoke so amicably to Sarah. In the first place, he entreats her; in the second place, he adds those words about her beauty. Here you hear nothing tyrannical, nothing dictatorial; everything is affectionate and lovely, the way it ought to be among those who are well-matched.[37]

What can I say in response? In more recent twentieth-century times, Cassuto too has made a case for an honouring and therefore honourable Abram,

> If he wishes to represent Sarai as his sister, it is only because he thinks that in this way he would be able to protect her honour more successfully than if he had to risk combat with the local inhabitants in a foreign land, or even a series of combats, which could only result in his death without his wife's honour being saved.[38]

Abram has convinced Cassuto!

35. Walter Brueggemann, *Genesis* (; Atlanta: John Knox Press, 1982), p. 128.

36. Bruce Vawter, *On Genesis: A New Reading* (Garden City, NY: Doubleday, 1977), p. 180. Gunkel, *Genesis*, similarly talks of the intelligence of the patriarch.

37. Martin Luther, *Lectures on Genesis: Chapters 6–14*, in Jaroslav Pelikan (ed.), *Luther's Works* (St Louis: Concordia, 1960), II, pp. 291-96.

38. Cassuto, *Genesis*, p. 350.

Yet the Sarai who is my interest in this narrative has been shown as a Sarai who waits on the sideline while God has delivered promise and blessing to Abram in vv. 1-3, and who remains there in vv. 4-9 while all is well in the land. But once the land failed, she too became vulnerable. Does the intervention of Israel's god redeem this reading? I note the lack of any word of celebration on her return; she is simply taken back and departs once more as part of Abram's retinue, to slip out of sight again while Abram and Lot discuss important matters of land distribution. Her story continues later, with some markedly different family dynamics, but it begins in Genesis 12, and beginnings subtly exercise control. This is not a good beginning.

During the time I had been following Sarai, noting some of the subtle and not so subtle gender dynamics in this text, I had also been reading Jane Tompkins' essay, 'Me and My Shadow', where she talked of the conditioned embarrassment at talking 'personally in a professional context' and of the 'straitjacket[ing]' effect of writing with the emotions kept at a careful distance.[39] My own reaction to her essay was one of relief, for it gave me permission to own that however much I tried, I could not avoid responding emotionally to stories such as Sarai's in Genesis 12. Although I was working with this text 'professionally' as a biblical reader, I was finding that I could not compartmentalize this work from other aspects of my life. My interest in the ways in which women are presented and portrayed in the texts of the biblical tradition owes much to my experience some years ago as a member of a local Women's Refuge Collective, so I did feel emotionally angry at the way Sarai was treated, even though I was working with this text 'professionally'. I needed to ask, 'If she is the archetypal woman biblical ancestor, what are we meant to read from this as contemporary women?' Nor did I want someone to say, 'Well, look at how she treated Hagar a few chapters on'. I know very well how abuse can lead to further abuse. Having worked my way through to the expectation of a well reasoned conclusion, I was left with uneasy questions: about the story itself, about the ways in which it had so often been read and about the ways in which we hear it today.

I returned to this text some time later, realizing that there was even more at stake here. For this is not simply a story of two individuals, a Sarai and an Abram—Genesis 12 is essentially an origin story for Israel. I had been reading the narrative as narrative, alert to the dynamics of the gender codings, with little attention to any historical mooring. History is, of course, a slippery category. For whose history is one to seek? If Sarai's, then this assumes a historical period behind the text, an assumption that some are reluctant to make. Even for those who do, setting a time frame for that is problematic.

---

39. In Linda Kauffman (ed.), *Gender and Theory: Dialogues on Feminist Criticism* (Oxford: Basil Blackwell, 1989), pp. 121-39 (123, 138).

Sarai/Sarah, it would seem, has been journeying through time, indeed running quite breathlessly in recent years, to span a timeline from c. 2500 to
200 BCE! My first readings as a student in search of her historical roots were
in John Bright's classic history, where she was, if not a wandering nomad, at
least a wandering 'semi-nomad', travelling 'in search of seasonal pasture…in
the early centuries of the second millennium B.C.',[40] although, as Bright
himself admitted, no contemporary text had managed to capture this journeying in print. The anachronism of 'Ur of the Chaldeans' (Gen. 11.31)[41]
alone raises suspicions of the historicity of this text. So it was not too
surprising to find Sarai soon located in a much later Babylon, penned there
by a scribe who in all probability was keen to exploit an Ur/Babylon link in
an effort to persuade sixth-century Judaean exiles that they were not in an
alien land at all, but in the very place from which their ancestors had come,
that they were virtually at home among their own kin.[42] Whether that scribe
was the creator or reviser of the narrative remains an open question, for it
may have been that 'another large-scale literary revision of the patriarchal
tradition was undertaken during the exile'. Its purpose would, of course, have
been similar: despairing exiles were to hear these traditions afresh and
recognize the ancestors as 'bearers of unconditional promises which had still
not gone out of date and as models by which they could orientate themselves
in their own time'.[43] But this was not yet the end of my search for Sarai or
Sarah's origins, for a fresh trail led out once again from Babylon, but this
time to a diminished Yehud, reduced to a province under Persian rule.[44]

---

40.   John Bright, *A History of Israel* (London: SCM Press, 2nd edn, 1972), pp. 94-95.

41.   As Gösta W. Ahlström, *The History of Ancient Palestine from the Palaeolithic Period
to Alexander's Conquest* (ed. Diana V. Edelman; JSOTSup, 146; Sheffield: Sheffield
Academic Press, 1993), p. 182, notes, 'the Chaldeans do not appear on the historical
stage until the ninth century BCE… This phrase does not occur again in the Old Testament before Neh. 9.7, thus it may point to a late date for the origin of the Abraham
narrative and for the "promise of the land".'

42.   Habel, *The Land is Mine*, pp. 117-18.

43.   Rainer Albertz, *History of Israelite Religion in the Old Testament Period. II. From the
Exile to the Maccabees* (trans. J. Bowden; London: SCM Press. 1994), pp. 405-406. Others,
such as Michael C.M. Prior, *The Bible and Colonialism: A Moral Critique* (The Biblical
Seminar, 48; Sheffield: Sheffield Academic Press, 1997), p. 219, hold the view that 'The
fact that Abraham is referred to as an individual only in the exilic texts (Isa. 51.2; Ezek.
33.24), and that, with the exception of Josh. 12.3-4, 12, the pre-exilic parts of the Old
Testament make no mention of the incidents associated with Abraham, Isaac or Jacob
suggests that the stories used by the author of Genesis may be no earlier than the period
of the Babylonian exile'.

44.   R. Christopher Heard, *Dynamics of Diselection: Ambiguity in Genesis 12–36 and
Ethnic Boundaries in Post-Exilic Judah* (Atlanta: Society of Biblical Literature, 2001), p. 9,
follows a body of other scholars who suggest that in contrast to the circumstances of a
deported people, 'the imperially-sponsored, temple-centred culture of Yehud will have

Here I could hear the scribe shaping his narrative of a family 'called' to stake a divine right to the land on behalf of those returnees from Babylon who had arrived back in 'the land' only to find themselves embroiled in bitter land claims. In this scenario, the land 'that I will show you' (Gen. 12.1) once again had its own quite particular interpretation.[45] By now I was pausing in scholarly breathlessness to consider these varying biblical contexts. I was realizing that while it is clear that 'When biblical writers sought to describe the past, they built the picture around a particular idea, or a systematic, coherent set of ideas',[46] it is nonetheless quite possible to change the suggested context and see the contours of the story change accordingly. Sarai, wife of the ancestor promised land, descendents, and a dynastic great nation would be welcomed by Israelites in exilic Babylon, but the move to pen an origin story significantly different to that of Exodus would make equally good political sense for a scribe in Yehud; overlords cast into the sea might not have gone down too well with the Persian leadership. What remained clear was that this was no real-life, met-in-history Sarai, but a scroll-captured character, carefully drawn to suit her writer's/writers' interest(s). But while I recognized her now as a Sarai, a pawn of the biblical storytellers, the challenge for me, as for all readers, was not only to tease out and analyze her narrative but to make my own considered choices of how she might enter and speak to the concerns of my own world and context. For if texts read differently according to the suggested positioning of their scribal narrators, they also interpret differently according to the context of their readers. It was time for me to take this into account.

provided precisely the sort of material context' required for the production of the final form of Genesis. Those responsible were Yehud's 'immigrant elite' whose concerns were ethnic definition and corresponding land claims. Heard's thesis argues for a 'high degree of correspondence between the interest promoted in the books of Ezra and Nehemiah and in the book of Genesis' (p. 22).

45.   Ahlström, *The History of Ancient Palestine*, p. 182. As he notes (pp. 846-47), a promise of land 'has no function to fill for people living in the country'. While this could apply to the Babylonian exiles, he sees the argument used in the context of a contest for land rights between the returnees and the indigenous people.

46.   Yairah Amit, *History and Ideology: An Introduction to Historiography in the Hebrew Bible* (trans. Yael Lotan; The Biblical Seminar, 60; Sheffield: Sheffield Academic Press, 1999), p. 34.

2

A MATTER OF DIFFERENCE

We cannot afford to ignore the activity of reading, for it is here that literature
is realized as *praxis*. Literature acts on the world by acting on its readers.[1]

If, as I suggested at the end of the last chapter, texts are interpreted differently according to the context of their readers, then perhaps I need to state a
little more about myself and my context, for who I am and where I do my
work will inevitably determine my angle of vision. Both consciously and
subconsciously it influences the way in which I read and understand all texts,
including the texts of the Hebrew Bible. Although immediately there is a
further complexity, in that while I may write about myself I will inevitably
be choosing what I tell, there will be other aspects of myself affecting how I
read, and which are part of my context, that I will quite deliberately choose
not to write about or of which I may not even be aware. Any form of auto-
biographical writing is always selective; it is yet another case of the reader be
wary.

   Geographically I am a New Zealander, living at the south of the Pacific.
But if I expand that to say that I live in Aotearoa New Zealand that already
hints at more to be said.[2] For I am a *Pakeha*, non-Maori, living in a country
originally settled by Maori, but subsequently entered by Europeans, first
arriving in significant numbers in the nineteenth century, as whalers, traders
and settlers. On my father's side my roots in this land go back four generations. My ancestors left Scotland under the leadership of a somewhat charis-
matic religious figure, Norman McLeod, who had had a number of disputes
with his church authorities, and had decided to emigrate to Nova Scotia in

---

   1.   Patrocinio P. Schweickart, 'Reading Ourselves: Toward a Feminist Theory of
Reading', in Elizabeth A. Flynn and Patrocinio P. Schweickart (eds.), *Gender and Reading: Essays on Readers, Texts, and Contexts* (Baltimore: The Johns Hopkins University
Press, 1986), pp. 31-62 (39).
   2.   Aotearoa is the Maori name for this country. Certain institutions such as the Presbyterian church to which I belong, acknowledge this in their title, the Presbyterian
Church of Aotearoa New Zealand, although officially the country tends to be known only
as New Zealand, a sign in itself, of the continuing colonial mindset.

Canada. There they settled and formed a self-identified Presbyterian community. Then, in the 1850s, a significant number, including McLeod, left Nova Scotia and travelled on again to New Zealand. The family history that has been passed down to my generation begins with the highland clearances and the enforced landlessness of dispossessed crofters, followed both by the failing herring trade in Scotland and divisive church disputes. Those that set sail again from Nova Scotia arrived in New Zealand as settlers with the land-buying power of a self-contained Gaelic speaking community, an identity that was carefully maintained for a generation or two and still remembered in Waipu, the original area of settlement, which celebrates this tradition with Highland Games each January. On my mother's side, however, I claim Yorkshire ancestry, my mother having arrived here in the 1920s with her parents, who were looking for better business opportunities. This mix of early and more recent arrivals is a typically New Zealand heritage.

Nowadays New Zealand is an independent state within the Commonwealth,[3] but it was formerly a country under colonial rule, so that as one of the many with deep family roots in its settler colonial past I am very much part of a postcolonial society. One of the questions that continues to challenge societies with such a history is how far the 'post' of postcolonial reflects the present reality of the political orderings. Anne McClintock includes New Zealand among the countries she describes as

> breakaway settler colonies…distinguished by their formal independence from the founding metropolitan country, along with continued control over the appropriated colony (thus displacing colonial control from the metropolis to the colony itself).[4]

While her conclusion that such countries 'have not undergone decolonisation' is well argued, it is also provocative. For many would strongly deny that there is a 'continued control' exercised by the settler descendents and their more recent counterparts and would point to the fact that the term 'New Zealander' includes all now living in this country. According to this view the 'all' includes settler descendents, recent immigrants as well as Maori, who are the 'people of the land' (in Maori, the *tangata whenua*); all have equal opportunity and equal share in what the land offers. There is, however, a particular dimension to life in this country, for New Zealand has a foundational document, the Treaty of Waitangi signed in 1840 by the crown and a significant number of Maori chiefs. But if written texts carry within them the potential for disagreement over interpretation, this is particularly so for a written treaty between two quite different cultures. In this case, beside the

3.   And, as such, recognizes Queen Elizabeth as Head of State.
4.   Anne McClintock, 'The Angel of Progress: Pitfalls of the Term "Postcolonialism"', in Francis Barker, Peter Hulme and Margaret Iversen (eds.), *Colonial Discourse/Postcolonial Theory* (Manchester: Manchester University Press, 1994), pp. 253-66 (257-58).

added complication that not all the Maori chiefs and tribes were party to the treaty, there were misunderstandings from its very beginnings. Not only was the treaty written in two languages, Maori and English, but each version contained significant differences, with quite varying understandings and interpretations, which have not been resolved even yet.[5] Not surprisingly, behind the contested words lie different perceptions of the orderings of power, so that any study of the Treaty is a study in power relations and power discourse. The fact that the Bible had a part to play in the interpretation of the crucial terms and the ensuing confusion is an indication of the influence of the missionary background. For example, the term *rangatiratanga* used in the Maori version of the Treaty to express the guarantee of possession was also used in translations of the Lord's Prayer for 'kingdom', and therefore implied a 'sovereign' right, far more reaching than the English translators had meant. The durability of the Crown's claim to hold to its own understanding and interpretation of sovereignty even today is an indication of the effectiveness of its own quite particular sovereignty discourse. As Claudia Orange notes, the result has been that 'the European record in the last century and a half has shown a determination to dominate. In many respects New Zealand, in spite of the treaty, has been merely a variation in the pattern of colonial domination of indigenous races.'[6] Jane Kelsey makes the even stronger comment that this 'durability...suggests that colonial leopards do not change their spots; they just stalk their prey in different ways'.[7]

5.   The Treaty was signed in 1840 between Queen Victoria and the Chiefs and Tribes of New Zealand, whereby the Chiefs ceded to the Queen 'absolutely and without reservation all the rights and powers of Sovereignty (in the English version). In the Maori version sovereignty was translated as *kawanatanga* meaning simply governorship. In Article Two of the English version, the chiefs and tribes were guaranteed 'the full exclusive and undisturbed possession of their Lands and Estates, Forests, Fisheries and other properties which they may collectively or individually possess so long as it is their wish and desire to retain the same in their possession'. In the Maori version, which left out the condition of collective or individual possession, the guarantee of possession was expressed as *te tino rangatiratanga*, and covered only lands, dwelling places and property of all kinds. The term *te tino rangatiratanga*, literally meaning chieftainship, conveyed more than a simple possession, and was, as Claudia Orange, *The Treaty of Waitangi* (Wellington: Allen & Unwin New Zealand, 1987), p. 41, comments 'a better approximation to sovereignty than kawanatanga' so that 'Maori might well have assumed, therefore, that their sovereign rights were actually being confirmed in return for a limited concession of power in kawanatanga'. Article Two also stated that if Maori wished to sell land, then they were to sell it to the Crown, but again the translation by the word *hokonga* 'did not stress the absolute and exclusive right granted to the Crown' (p. 42). Not all chiefs signed the documents.

6.   Orange, *The Treaty of Waitangi*, p. 5.

7.   Jane Kelsey, 'From Flagpoles to Pine Trees: Tino Rangatiratanga and Treaty Policy Today', in Paul Spoonley, David Pearson and Cluny Macpherson (eds.), *Nga Patai:*

It is that suggestion of 'different ways' that interests me. It brings the task of reading with the hermeneutic of suspicion into the foreground again on two levels. It requires a reading of the present political dynamics and their consequences in this country in which I live, which, in turn, requires a searching analysis of the rhetoric which drives political policies. In concrete terms this means reading the political discourses alongside the statistics of the daily realities. It means asking why those whose rhetoric is about one people and equal opportunities are seemingly unaware of, or choose to be silent about, the poverty, health and prison statistics which are an indication that all is not well in the balance between Maori and non-Maori. But, as New Zealand historians point out, the colonial discourse was from the beginning an 'interested' text, intended to persuade rather than reflect or portray the political realities. This became particularly marked when the balance originally held between settler and Maori erupted into violent land wars, which continued from 1845 to 1872. As Fleras and Spoonley note, 'Racial stereotypes of the Maori provided the moral justification for armed conquest in Aotearoa/New Zealand, and obfuscated the actual economic rationale for war—the shortage of land for settlement'.[8] For Maori, of course, it was a matter of 'resistance to European expansion' and all that that implied.[9] It was the imbalance between reality and discourse that led me back to read Israel's texts. For Israel's history as it is recorded in the Hebrew Bible is also a quite particular discourse, a history as the writers would have us read it. So if I, as the descendent of a settler community within a colonial world, and consequently one of those whom present statistics reveal as having, even today, better access to education and health care, and enjoying better economic wellbeing, am on the lookout for signs of the stalking leopards in my own context, I also need to be on the lookout for similar signs in the discourses of the biblical texts. For both, I need to read with a sharply refined hermeneutic of suspicion. But it is not simply a matter of two parallel exercises using the same tools. For the Bible not only holds a unique position in communities of Jewish and Christian faith, it is also part of the cultural heritage of European and other traditions, and therefore has a continuing role in the present world, which includes Aotearoa New Zealand. Therefore

Racism and Ethnic Relations in Aotearoa/New Zealand (Palmerston North: The Dunmore Press, 1996), pp. 177-201 (178).

8. Melanie Wall, 'Stereotypical Constructions of the Maori "Race" in the Media', *New Zealand Geographer* 53.2 (1997), pp. 40-45 (41), quoted by Augie Fleras and Paul Spoonley, *Recalling Aotearoa: Indigenous Politics and Ethnic Relations in New Zealand* (Auckland: Oxford University Press, 1999), p. 71.

9. James Belich, *The New Zealand Wars and the Victorian Interpretation of Racial Conflict* (Auckland: Auckland University Press, 1986), p. 15. 'They were...bitter and bloody struggles, as important to New Zealand as were the Civil Wars to England and the United States'.

if there is a significant discourse within the biblical texts that might reinforce a continuing colonizing mindset in the reader, this becomes a matter of contemporary ethical and political concern in this country as in others.

Identifying some of the realities of my own context and recognizing that there are connections to be made between aspects of its discourse and that of the Hebrew Bible is the first step. The next is choosing the appropriate critical approach. If Aotearoa New Zealand is to be identified as a post-colonial country, and if there are detectable similarities between its discourses and those of the Bible, then it seems most likely that postcolonial theory will provide some of the most appropriate analytical tools. As tools of a 'critical enterprise aimed at unmasking the link between ideas and power',[10] these will complement and further refine my use of the hermeneutic of suspicion, as I ask questions of both discourses, mine and the biblical texts'. Some connections come immediately into view. For a significant move within the discourse strategies that powerful peoples employ to maintain their ascendancy, and which are shared by ancient and contemporary peoples alike, is the construction of a myth of 'ethnic origins'.[11] What frequently accompanies this move is an equally carefully constructed representation of those considered 'other'. The very terminology here is already posing a problem. For the term 'ethnic' is itself an anachronism, together with those other related alternatives, 'ethnicity' and 'ethnic identity'. Yet they are useful in describing a feature of community living that is virtually as old as time, in that they are simply denoting

> an identity that sets a group of people apart from other groups with whom they interact or coexist in terms of some distinctive criteria, which can include language, religion, history, or any other aspect of culture. Such identities involve processes of labelling and the formation of implicit and explicit contrasts between cultural traditions.[12]

Here the word 'processes' is an important key, for identity formation is a continuous process. People are continually negotiating and re-negotiating

10.   R.S. Sugirtharajah, 'Textual Cleansing: A Move from the Colonial to the Post-colonial Version', *Semeia* 76 (1996), pp. 7-19 (13): 'It is a discursive resistance against imperialism, imperial ideologies, imperial attitudes and their continued incarnations among such wide-ranging fields as politics, economics and history, and theological and biblical studies'.

11.   Daiva Stasiulis and Nira Yuval-Davis, 'Introduction: Beyond Dichotomies—Gender, Race, Ethnicity and Class in Settler Societies', in *idem* (eds.), *Unsettling Settler Societies: Articulations of Gender, Race, Ethnicity and Class* (London: Sage Publications, 1995), pp. 1-38 (19).

12.   Siân Jones, 'Identities in Practice: Towards an Archaeological Perspective on Jewish Identity in Antiquity', in Siân Jones and Sarah Pearce (eds.), *Jewish Local Patriotism and Self-Identification in the Graeco-Roman Period* (JSPSup, 31; Sheffield: Sheffield Academic Press, 1998), pp. 29-49 (34).

what it is that allows them to identify themselves as an 'us' and then maintain that self-identity in the midst of changing circumstances. Diana Edelman's reminder that societies are 'not static units that remain unchanged over time' needs to be kept in mind. So too her sharp comment that it 'is methodologically unsound to presume that premonarchic Israel would have been coterminus with monarchic Israel in its boundaries or its population composition'.[13] While we know relatively little about premonarchic Israel, one can assume that at some time in its early history there would have been a move to understand itself as 'a collectivity' which was 'trans-clan and transtribal'.[14] This very changing and changeable nature of societies makes the task of maintaining a sense of identity all the more necessary. But how to do that? 'On most occasions', as K.L. Noll notes, 'the two topics of discussion are (1) shared stories about the past and (2) shared values in the present'.[15] These stories allow the sense of a 'perceived biological descent',[16] perceived because it is the perception that is all important, not simply the matter of a historical biological ancestry, which is but one possible factor among others in the continuing community maintenance. The shared values for Israel were underpinned by the belief that this was a people chosen by God.[17]

But the additional factor that was all important for Israel, and which continues to be important for indigenous colonized peoples, was the relationship with the land. So, I would want to set beside Siân Jones' definition, Steven Grosby's inclusion of the importance of land in his discussion of nationality, seeing this as 'a configuration of traditions that are pervaded by vital life and that have as their referents territorially specific beliefs about the processes of the generation, maintenance, and protection of life'.[18] The shared stories of the past include stories of the gaining of land which for Israel was quite specifically the story of the divine promise of a land. Israel was a people chosen to live in this particular land. For Israel this was not a matter of debate: the land was Israel's through divine gift and through the

13. Diana Edelman, 'Ethnicity and Early Israel', in Mark G. Brett (ed.), *Ethnicity and The Bible* (Leiden: E.J. Brill, 1996), pp. 25-55 (41).

14. Steven Grosby, *Biblical Ideas of Nationality Ancient and Modern* (Winona Lake, IN: Eisenbrauns, 2002), pp. 15-16, refers to Josh. 3 and 4 and the use of 'all Israel' throughout the book of Joshua.

15. K.L. Noll, *Canaan and Israel in Antiquity: An Introduction* (The Biblical Seminar, 83; London: Sheffield Academic Press, 2001), p. 140.

16. Noll, *Canaan and Israel in Antiquity*, p. 142.

17. See Grosby, *Biblical Ideas of Nationality Ancient and Modern*, p. 102, who suggests that there was 'a homology between Yahweh and Israel', with Israel being given 'the promise of life by the creator of life...the origin and transmission of the life of the national lineage is seen as being directly linked to the divinity, hence to the order and even the creation of the world'.

18. Grosby, *Biblical Ideas of Nationality*, pp. 111-12.

presence of God there with them in the land (Num. 35.34). The *torah*, which set out how Israel was to live as a people, was specifically a *torah* for living in the land, according to the Deuteronomic code. 'As the only law of the land, it unified both the inhabitants of the land into the people of Israel and the land itself into the land of Israel.'[19] To be Israelite was to know oneself as chosen and gifted by God, and therefore as covenanted with God.

Unfortunately, the matter of who one is so often tends to bring with it the flip side of who one is not. Others, best identified through the capital 'O' as 'Others', then become a necessary factor as they are to be the ones over against whom the 'we' identify themselves. Identifying or constructing 'Others' then becomes a crucial task. For the community's writers it becomes 'a political and linguistic project, a matter of rhetoric and judgment'.[20] It has frequently been observed that the most problematic social transactions occur precisely at the boundary, between 'us' and those who are most 'like us'.[21] In the Bible this can be seen, as Mark Brett notes, in the laws of warfare in Deut. 20.10-18, which reserve the most violent treatment for the cities which are 'near' rather than those which are 'far'.[22] But this example has to be set against the general strategy of an 'othering' discourse developed by Israel, whereby, because Israel and Canaan had seemingly shared an earlier history,[23] Israel was specifically Israel because it was not Canaan and must not be Canaan. This is markedly different, of course, from the situation in New Zealand where there was initially a clear distinction between European and Maori. It does, however, probably explain the move by New Zealand

19.   Grosby, *Biblical Ideas of Nationality*, pp. 25-26.

20.   J.Z. Smith, 'What a Difference a Difference Makes', in J. Neusner and E.S. Frerichs (eds.), *'To See Ourselves as Others See Us': Christians, Jews, 'Others' in Late Antiquity* (Chico: Scholars Press, 1985), p. 46, quoted in Mark G. Brett, 'Interpreting Ethnicity: Method, Hermeneutics, Ethics', in *idem* (ed.), *Ethnicity and the Bible*, pp. 3-22 (10). See also L. Daniel Hawk, 'The Problem with Pagans', in Timothy K. Beal and David M. Gunn (eds.), *Reading Bibles, Writing Bodies: Identity and the Book* (London/New York: Routledge, 1997), pp. 153-63 (161-62), regarding the story of Achan in Josh. 7: 'Outsiders may become insiders, but transit in the opposite direction will not be tolerated: *Israelites* may not cross the boundaries that differentiate Israel from Canaan. Canaanites may find a space among the people of YHWH, but the people of YHWH must not take to themselves anything of Canaan.'

21.   Brett, 'Interpreting Ethnicity', p. 6.

22.   Brett, 'Interpreting Ethnicity', p. 10.

23.   See, e.g., J.C. de Moor, 'Ugarit and Israelite Origins', in J.A. Emerton (ed.), *Congress Volume: Paris, 1992* (Leiden: E.J. Brill, 1995), pp. 205-38 (205-206): 'both archaeological and linguistic data are nowadays converging to the conclusion that broadly speaking, the ancient Israelites may be regarded as Canaanites in every respect...' And, as Diana Edelman ('Ethnicity and Early Israel') points out, if it is difficult telling a Canaanite pot from an Israelite one, or a Canaanite house from an Israelite house, it is surely no less difficult to recognize the differences in ancient religious practice.

missionaries in the late 1830s to advocate 'a Protestant colony or protector-
ate that would keep out the papist French, control the agents of vice and
facilitate mission work', by which was meant, of course, their own particular
mission work.[24]

Reading the rhetoric against the background of the political realities of
the time is all the more difficult for later readers of the biblical texts in that
the Hebrew Bible consistently looks at its world from the perspective of
Israel. Added to which, as Noll notes, 'Iron Age 1 Palestine has left us almost
no writings and a relatively uniform material culture' so that 'the challenge
of finding one ethnic group, the Israelites, is daunting'.[25] Details of the
'Other'ed, in particular of the ancient Canaanite culture, are, therefore,
either missing or worked over with an Israelite favouring pen. This latter is a
practice not peculiar to the biblical writers; it is one that also provides a connection with my own context. For it is one of the characteristics of settler
history that it 'effaces and distorts the complex histories and societies of
indigenous peoples which existed prior to and during prolonged periods of
contact with Europeans'.[26] The further complication when the European
history includes a significant missionary enterprise is that the missionary
documents that record much of the early days of settlement also view these
through their own eyes.[27]

There is, however, a further concern with the biblical material, for while
the anti-Canaanite polemic in itself might simply be noted as an antiquarian
interest, as a political and linguistic project or strategy it had notable staying
power, giving biblical warrant over centuries for the polemic to 'be deployed
against whatever "Canaanites" people wanted to loathe, conquer, or exile'.[28]
These are texts still posing a quite particular challenge to interpreters in
contexts where there is a potential for violence, whether verbal, institutional
or physical. Yet, as I was reading these texts, I was easily able to imagine
myself listening in on a sequence of ancient conversations, that continued
over centuries, as the politics of succeeding times threw Israel's self-under-
standing into question again and again causing them to ask: 'What is it that
makes us distinct as this people, Israel?'

24. James Belich, Making Peoples: A History of the New Zealanders from Polynesian
Settlement to the End of the Nineteenth Century (Auckland: Penguin Books New Zealand,
1996), p. 182.

25. Noll, Canaan and Israel in Antiquity, p. 145. See also Niels Peter Lemche, Ancient
Israel: A New History of Israelite Society (The Biblical Seminar, 5; Sheffield: JSOT Press,
1988), and The Canaanites and their Land: The Tradition of the Canaanites (JSOTSup, 110;
Sheffield: JSOT Press, 1990).

26. Stasiulis and Yuval-Davis, 'Introduction: Beyond Dichotomies', p. 4.

27. Belich, Making Peoples, pp. 136-37.

28. Regina M. Schwartz, The Curse of Cain: The Violent Legacy of Monotheism
(Chicago: University of Chicago Press, 1997), p. x.

Yet, the same time, Israel's attitude to those it considered Other was both nuanced and ambivalent. For a body of texts that range widely in their datings and source backgrounds, this was, perhaps, not too surprising.[29] There are texts where Israel clearly has a concern for *gerim*, those considered either outsiders in some sense or more particularly 'resident aliens'. So Exod. 23.9, which commands that 'You shall not oppress a resident alien; you know the heart of an alien for you were aliens in the land of Egypt', or Lev. 19.34, which notably declares that 'the alien (*ger*) who resides with you shall be to you as the citizen among you; you shall love the alien as yourself, for you were aliens (*gerim*) in the land of Egypt'. This is then heavily underlined with the divine formula, 'I am Yahweh, your God', for a key to Israel's self-identity was the God-factor. The question was always, 'Who are we and who is our God and what does that mean for us?', the understood sub-text being: 'Who is not our God?' In both these texts Israel was acknowledging and recognizing its own historical and contextual memory of being 'other' among strangers. It was to be read with a further added layer of meaning for later Israel, for whereas the texts themselves were referring to the bitter experience of slavery in Egypt, for later readers Israel as *gerim* spoke of the traumatic experience of exile in Babylon. If, in fact, as Kidd suggests in his discussion of Deut. 10.19b, such texts are post-exilic, at least in their written form, then the connection between the narrated context and Israel's later experience provides a key to this doubled layer of meaning in that 'it was the new awareness of being themselves *gerim* which created a new sensitivity to the non-Jewish *ger*'.[30] In effect, this awareness becomes part of Israel's very self-identity, which therefore creates a bond with these sojourning strangers, whom Israel must love as themselves.

Just as the process of self-identity is always ongoing and never static, so the term *ger* changed over time, being used with different understandings in different periods. In Christiana van Houten's study she concluded that 'The laws dealing with the alien developed and became more inclusive. What began as an appeal for justice for the alien in the Covenant Code (Exod. 23.9), comes to be understood as a legal principle in the Priestly laws.'[31] José

---

29. As Jon D. Levenson ('The Universal Horizon of Biblical Particularism', in Brett [ed.], *Ethnicity and the Bible*, pp. 143-69 [145]) notes in the context of the universality of God, 'there is no one "biblical" position on this or on most other great theological issues'.

30. José Ramírez Kidd, *Alterity and Identity in Israel* (Berlin: W. de Gruyter, 1999), p. 83. He further suggests (p. 84) as a 'likely' explanation, that '*Diaspora oriented* theologians' were responsible for this text, 'with the intention to challenge the nationalistic circles of the Palestinian community, to accept *all* those who had newly joined the community'. See also Rolf Rendtorff, 'The *Ger* in the Priestly Laws of the Pentateuch', in Brett (ed.), *Ethnicity and the Bible*, pp. 77-87.

31. Christiana van Houten, *The Alien in Israelite Law: A Study of the Changing Legal Status of Strangers in Ancient Israel* (JSOTSup, 107; Sheffield: JSOT Press, 1991), p. 175:

Ramírez Kidd also detects a move over time from *ger* referring to non-Israelites simply living or sojourning within Israel and for whom Israel acts as a host of the needy, to the term covering those who are non-Israelite but who are nonetheless recognized as being a part of the Jewish religious community, and therefore needing to be covered within the legal system in order to preserve the holiness required by the community living in the land.[32] Saul Olyan's study of cultic representation points to the distinction between the understanding of a *ger* in the Holiness and Deuteronomistic texts. The boundary between *ger* and Israelite in the Holiness texts, with their concern for maintaining a separation from anything defiling or polluting, depends on whether or not the person is circumcised, as is explicit in Exod. 12.43-49. The Deuteronomistic texts are more difficult to categorize, but Olyan suggests that there is a key client factor in operation, any incorporation of a *ger* is by way of a patron through a 'strategy of subordination', although incorporation does not extend to absorption, since in these texts the implication is that a *ger* will always remain outside the lineage–patrimony system.[33] A radical departure comes into view in Ezekiel's vision of the redistribution of land in Ezek. 47.22-23, where the *ger* who has fathered children is to receive an allotment as an inheritance, which, as Olyan notes, 'effectively eliminates all difference between him and the native, fully assimilating him into the lineage and inheritance structure of the society'.[34]

In whichever sense of the term, and however much the *ger* as an incorporated foreign resident outsider is or is not considered a problem, such a person is to be viewed very differently from one categorized as a *zar*, *ben nekar*, or *nokri* who is not an insider in any sense at all. Rarely does such a person, variously viewed as a foreigner, an outsider, or a non-belonger in some significant category, receive a good biblical press.[35] I began this work with a

---

'This then opened the door for the inclusion of the alien into all the rights and privileges of Israelite society...the inclusive tendency is the working out, in the legal tradition, of God's purpose to include and save all'. There are notably debatable issues of redaction and dating in her discussion.

32. Kidd, *Alterity and Identity*, pp. 71, 117-18. So Num. 15.14-16.

33. Saul M. Olyan, *Rites and Rank: Hierarchy in Biblical Representations of Cult* (Princeton, NJ: Princeton University Press, 2000), pp. 79-80.

34. Olyan, *Rites and Rank*, p. 73, noting that this text 'appears to be a gloss...using language reminiscent of the Holiness materials'. He suggests that it 'may have been intended as a challenge to the limited integration program characteristic of late Holiness materials found in the Pentateuch'.

35. Claudia V. Camp, *Wise, Strange and Holy: The Strange Woman and the Making of the Bible* (JSOTSup, 320; Gender, Culture, Theory, 9; Sheffield: Sheffield Academic Press, 2000), pp. 40-41, notes four usages: persons of foreign nationality, persons outside one's own family household, persons not members of the priestly caste, and deities or practices outside the covenant relationship. See also Christopher T. Begg's useful summary under 'Foreigner', in *ABD*, II, pp. 829-30.

discussion of the Wisdom figure of Proverbs, so I am mindful here of that other womanly personification *Kesilut* (Prov. 9.13-18) whom the scribes seemingly fused with the *'ishah zarah/nokriyyah* of 2.16-19; 5.3-6; 6.24-25; 7.10-23. Such women are a danger, warn the sages. Yet at first glance these women, presented as posing sinister threats to the naïve youth of Israel, seem to share only the terminology with the ethnic outsiders. There is no internal evidence for their being specifically foreign in terms of ethnicity. For all that the youth are left in no doubt that these are women to be resisted and avoided with the same care as if they were 'foreign', these appear to be women who are crossing insider and not external boundaries. What causes the confusion, as Claudia Camp notes, is the Hebrew Bible's 'collapsing of language for illicit sex, illicit worship and intermarriage with foreigners, especially foreign women'.[36] What is particularly disturbing for the woman reader is this scribal strategy of setting women as symbols of the threatening powers of disordered chaos.

Certain biblical figures, however, who are explicitly non-Israelite and therefore presumably to be understood as *zarim*, such as Jethro (Exod. 18) and the poignant Uriah the Hittite, although he may have been more *ger* than *zar*, are presented without apology or excuse as having positive roles in Israel's narrative. Others, such as Balaam (Num. 22–24), Rahab (Josh. 2) and Naaman (2 Kgs 5), make their point precisely through being non-Israel-ites who come to acknowledge the pre-eminence of Yahweh. But set such texts beside others referring to the peoples who are listed as occupying the land before Israel, and a contradiction is clearly visible. Exodus 34.24 declares 'for I will cast out nations before you, and enlarge your borders', with the 'I' presented as the divine voice, and the promise wholly for Israel's benefit. The directive is sharp in Num. 33.55, 'If you do not drive out the inhabitants of the land from before you, then those whom you let remain shall be as barbs in your eyes and thorns in your sides', and the thought even sharper in Lev. 18.24-30, 'the land will vomit you out' if you commit the abominations which were practised by 'the inhabitants of the land who were before you.'[37] The land itself acknowledges Israel as both a people and their territory, with dire consequences for those who fail to recognize this, even inadvertently by being in the land before Israel's supposed entrance. Often the lists of such people are quite specific, as in Exod. 34.11: 'See, I will drive out before you the Amorites, the Canaanites, the Hittites, the Perizzites, the Hivites, and the Jebusites'. Deuteronomy takes this even further: when such peoples are

---

36. Camp, *Wise, Strange and Holy*, p. 17. See also Gail Corrington Streete, *The Strange Woman: Power and Sex in the Bible* (Louisville, KY: Westminster/John Knox Press, 1997), and my own work, *Gendering Wisdom the Host*, pp. 81-99.

37. See also Num. 21–25; 31; 33.50-56; Deut. 7.1-11; 9.1-5; 11.23; 18.9-14; 20.16-18; Lev. 20.22-24; Pss. 78.54-55; 80.8.

delivered by God into Israel's hands, Israel must 'utterly destroy them... show[ing] them no mercy' (Deut. 7.2). The concern also has a domestic edge, for if you let your children marry among these people, then (Exod. 34.16) 'their daughters who prostitute themselves to their gods will make your sons also prostitute themselves to their gods'. Here, again, the matter of self-identity can be heard for the question 'Who is our god?' had the flip side: 'Who is not our god?' The result of not asking the question or not observing this boundary line was dire: 'Then the anger of YHWH would be kindled against you...and destroy you quickly' (Deut. 7.4). But there is a certain ambivalence about foreign women. Where the texts have a concern for the circumcised status, this clearly does not apply to women! And where there is a concern for lineage the importance of patrilineal descent meant a lesser concern regarding the potential mothers. So, in the war against Midian, Moses says to the people in Num. 31.18 that of the captured Midian women, 'all the young women who have not known a man by sleeping with him, keep alive for yourselves'. At times it seems as if the Bible wants to turn a blind eye to the matter altogether and allow romance a free hand. Joseph may marry Asenath (Gen. 41.45) and Moses himself chooses a Midianite, Zipporah, romantically met by a well (Exod. 2.21).

The more intense concern over intermarriage is, of course, to be found in the texts of Ezra and Nehemiah (Ezra 9 and 10; Neh. 13.23-30), where all such *nokriyyot* wives are to be sent away, together with their children. What is particularly disturbing about this Ezra–Nehemiah stand is that it seems that in all likelihood the returnees from Babylon and the people they found in the land on their return were not entirely of different stock but could trace their roots to common Israelite ancestors. Yet in the eyes of the returnees, according to the writers of Ezra and Nehemiah, these surviving inhabitants of the land, referred to now as 'the peoples of the land' to distinguish them from those who had experienced the purifying ordeal of exile, were not a part of the true Israel. But not only were they not a part of the Israelite community, they were now considered pollutants, and regarded as virtual Canaanites.[38] The language is explicit: those Israelites who are partners in mixed marriages with these people have 'forsaken' God's commandment, for their wives belong to a people who have made the land 'unclean with the pollutions of the peoples of the lands, with their abomination' (Ezra 9.11). What is equally explicit is the concern for the outcome of such marriages, the danger to the 'holy seed' (v. 2). This sharp division which created foreigners

38. Robert P. Carroll, 'The Myth of the Empty Land', *Semeia* 59 (1992), pp. 79-93 (85): 'That is to say, they were to be avoided at all costs and could not be regarded as part of the holy enclave focused on the rebuilt temple (cf. Ezra 4.1-5; 10.1-5)'. He suggests that there is an echo of 2 Kgs 17 behind Ezra 4.2, with its insinuation of wrongful worship practices.

out of a people who shared an Israelite ancestry, was, as Robert Carroll suggests, 'an ideological construction' which simply glossed over the historical realities.[39]

An interesting question, however, is whether this ruling was ever carried out. For, as is well recognized, there is no external evidence for such a drastic move having taken place. As with the origin accounts that would see Israelites and Canaanites as ethnically and historically separate, so here the account of the divorcing of the foreign wives may belong solely to the discourse.[40] As a boundary marker this would simply be a repeat of that discursive division of Israelite and Canaanite, that is, a feature both of the Deuteronomistic History and texts such as Lev. 18.24-30, and which is now reinterpreted to refer to all intermarriage.[41] That such anti-Canaanite language had an ongoing power can also be seen in the late tale of Susanna, with its abusive insult, 'You son of Canaanites!' (Sus. 56), written at a time when the term 'Canaanite' no longer had any political reality.[42]

Yet among the later sections of the Isaiah scroll there is a very different attitude to foreigners, as Isa. 56.6-7 and 66.20 demonstrate. In 56.6-7, not only will God bring the *bene hannekar* who love the name of Yahweh to the 'holy mountain', but their burnt offerings and sacrifices will be accepted on the altar. This presents a very different attitude to that of Ezra and Nehemiah, although its language echoes some of the very texts, such as Deut. 23.2-9, which appear to underline their exclusionary stand. The echoes, however, are now part of a challenging reversal.[43] Although it may be, as Smith-

---

39.   Carroll, 'The Myth of the Empty Land', p. 85.

40.   As Daniel L. Smith-Christopher comments in 'The Mixed Marriage Crisis in Ezra 9–10 and Nehemiah 13: A Study of the Sociology or the Post-Exilic Judaean Community', in Tamara C. Eskenazi and Kent H. Richards (eds.), *Second Temple Studies 2: Temple and Community in the Persian Period* (JSOTSup, 175; Sheffield: JSOT Press, 1994), pp. 243-65 (247), 'the possibility remains that these "mixed-marriages" were considered "mixed" *only* by Ezra and his supporters, and in the first case not by the married persons themselves'. The named peoples are not so much ethnic labels of the time but 'old terms that almost surely have become stereotypically pejorative slurs' (p. 257).

41.   As Olyan comments (*Rites and Rank*, p. 82), this 'innovative' move was 'justified through exegetical elaboration of earlier texts such as Lev. 18.24-30, which urges Israel to avoid the polluting acts…of its Canaanite predecessors'. It takes this concern one step further as Camp, *Wise, Strange and Holy*, p. 56, acknowledges: 'this tale of mass divorce of women construed as foreign consolidates the rhetoric against exogamy with the rhetoric of uncleanness in a new and powerful way'. Olyan (*Rites and Rank*, pp. 88-89) also notes the use and extension of Deut. 7.3-4 and 23.4-9 by both Ezra and Nehemiah.

42.   See also *Jub.* 25.1-9.

43.   See Olyan, *Rites and Rank*, p. 92, where he also notes the shared use of the term *ben nekar* by Isaiah and Nehemiah (Neh. 9.2) and concludes that 'it is certainly plausible to see Isa. 56.3-7, if not Isa. 56.1-8, as a composition of the fifth century, a response to the exclusionary program described in Ezra–Nehemiah'.

Christopher observes, that 'in most periods of Israelite history…exclusionary attitudes co-existed with idealistic laws',[44] it can equally be suggested that in most periods the matter was under discussion, if not sharp debate. The points at issue continued to centre on the very definition of 'foreigner', and what might constitute the danger of incorporating such a person into the community.

It is one thing to recognize the exclusionary polemic as polemic, to be aware that the very notion of 'foreigner' is largely a social construct, and to appreciate the fact that Ezra and Nehemiah were not Israel's only or last word on the matter, it is another to decide how to interpret such anti-foreign texts when they are encountered in their own canonical context. It is easier to tease this out with specific texts as examples. I had been reading the Elijah and Elisha stories and had been trying to imagine the task facing that ancient Israelite scribe responsible for gathering together the traditional material that was to be set down on the scroll of the books of the Kings. I had been trying to imagine him sitting there, with tale after tale spread out before him telling of the miraculous power of the God of Israel as revealed through these 'men of God', the prophets.[45] I assume that he was aware that the final arrangement was to be part of a much more complex work which was to carry some quite particular messages to its immediate audience, and that he, or the team of which he was a part, was to convince the people that there was one god to be worshipped in Israel, and that God was not the god of the neighbouring peoples. This I understood as the narratives' undergirding theme, particularly, for example, in the accounts of Jezebel and Ahab's clashes with Elijah and Elisha. The vital question here was: 'Who were the people of Israel going to worship, Yahweh or Baal?' If any ties of a history shared with Baal worshippers still lingered, this was where they faltered. Difference had become important, and practices, such as the worship and devotion to gods like Baal and Asherah, which appear to have been an accepted feature of Israelite religious practice, at least among a section of Israel, were now used in this narrative as the boundary markers, to indicate the point at which people were labelled 'Us' or 'Other'. Underlying the moves and counter-moves of the prophets and their royal adversaries was the question of which god held the power over life and death, and therefore over the forces of creation. So, the scribe in his gathering task had also become a player in the boundary setting, placing the textual markers in what was at

44.   Daniel L. Smith-Christopher, 'Ezra and Isaiah: Exclusion, Transformation, and Inclusion of the "Foreigner" in Post-Exilic Biblical Theology', in Brett (ed.), *Ethnicity and the Bible*, pp. 117-42 (119).

45.   Taking the view, with Burke O. Long, *1 Kings with an Introduction to Historical Literature* (Grand Rapids: Eerdmans, 1984), p. 175: 'that this block of material consists of a number of originally separate stories and fragments of tradition'.

one and the same time a religious and an ethnic struggle. If an earlier shared history meant that Canaanites and Phoenicians were not markedly different from Israelites, then one of his first tasks was to make sure that the people were able to differentiate the one from the other.[46] A plotted literary distinction was crucial. Other traditions such as Ezra and Nehemiah may have used other terms such as 'peoples of the land' with their abominations (Ezra 9.11), but the issue remains the same. As Regina Schwartz suggests, there were two interrelated questions at the top of the scribal writer's task sheet, 'how to identify her (i.e. the foreigner) and what to do with her'.[47]

I note the 'her' for, as a woman, I have a particular interest in 'her' factors. But a focus on the 'her' factor brings in further difficulties. If I wanted to test the textual reality against its historical background, there is the matter of not having sufficient access to the history behind the text. While, as I have already noted, this is true for much of the biblical material, it is particularly so of women's history as women historians have long recognized. As Bernadette Brooten wrote some years ago of early Christian material, 'the lack of sources on women is part of the history of women'.[48] So, when 'otherness' includes being female as well as being ethnically different, the difficulty is compounded. All too frequently the writings of those who record what the dominant groupings wish recorded carry the signs of 'masculinized memory, masculinized humiliation and masculinized hope'.[49] The 'what to do with her' takes me back to the matter of the linguistic and rhetorical projects. Clearly one rhetorical strategy was to create a stock figure, a female embodiment of evil 'Otherness' that could be used again and again, almost as a *leitmotif*. This was a gender strategy that the sages used well, bringing in the motif of the death-bringing 'outsider' woman, the *'ishah zarah*, to stalk the

---

46.   As A.R.C. Leaney, *The Jewish and Christian World 200BC to AD200* (Cambridge Commentaries on Writings of the Jewish and Christian World 200 BC to AD 200, 7; Cambridge: Cambridge University Press, 1984), p. 80, notes, 'The term Phoenicians does not occur in the Hebrew Old Testament… They belong to the amalgam of nations which the Bible calls Canaanites.'

47.   Schwartz, *The Curse of Cain*, p. 79.

48.   Bernadette J. Brooten, 'Early Christian Women and their Cultural Context: Issues of Method in Historical Reconstruction', in Adela Yarbro Collins (ed.), *Feminist Perspectives on Biblical Scholarship* (Atlanta: Scholars Press, 1985), pp. 65-91 (66).

49.   Cynthia Enloe, *Bananas, Beaches and Bases: Making Feminist Sense of International Politics* (Berkeley: University of California Press, 1989), p. 44. There has been a considerable body of work exploring the power of male discourse and how that has affected women, but work relating this to the power of colonial discourse has been relatively recent. Many of these also include a class analysis. Stasiulis and Yuval-Davis ('Introduction: Beyond Dichotomies', pp. 31-32), note that the current focus on gender, race, ethnicity and class 'in no way implies that there are not other significant social relations and identities (pertaining to, for example, sexuality, religion and language through which power and resistance are constituted)'.

first chapters of Proverbs (Prov. 2.16-19; 5.3-6, 20; 7.5). But it is fleshed out further in other texts. Jezebel, for example, appears not only as the 'bad' wife of one of the kings of Israel, primarily on the grounds that she is a Baal- and Asherah-worshipping Phoenician, but she is visibly a prime example of that very stock figure of 'foreign' evilness, whose seductive and sinister powers are inevitably deathly. The project worked so well that she has never been forgotten. The name Jezebel, with all the pejorative understandings that go with it, lives on to be used and reused at will. But it is not only the name, Jezebel, which connects the ways of the biblical writers with those of today. The linguistic and rhetorical strategy itself is alive and well. Fleras and Spoonley note the disturbing consequences of such 'othering' in their discussion of the use of negative stereotyping in New Zealand film:

> to the extent that individual and collective identities are shaped by being recognised and misrecognised by others, damage can be inflicted through demeaning or contemptible images.[50]

Repeat such demeaning and pejorative images often enough and they will be accepted as 'truthful' rather than questioned and recognized as the polemical tools that they are. So, the then Bishop of Salisbury could state in an address to the Palestine Exploration Fund in 1903,

> Nothing, I think, that has been discovered makes us feel any regret at the suppression of Canaanite civilisation by Israelite civilisation...the Bible has not misrepresented at all the abomination of the Canaanite culture which was superseded by the Israelite culture.[51]

Such a reading according to the grain of the text is both disturbing and an indication of the success of the Israelite discourse. Jezebel, depicted as the killer of God's prophets, as well as the murderer of Naboth, the faithful Israelite, had a part in this, being a 'her factor' that provided a convenient ploy for the writer's project. One might ask what were Phoenicians and Canaanites meant to do! One of the biblical writers' answers was 'be a Rahab'. For although she was a Canaanite and openly a prostitute, whereas Jezebel was only accused of harlotry, because Rahab came to acknowledge the power of Israel's god she was saved from Jericho's destruction, and her family rewarded with a place in Israel (Josh. 6.23-25). The contrast is sharp: Jezebel held to her Phoenician cultural habit and was virtually demonized, while Rahab seemingly took hers off and was saved. The concern is not too different, if at all, to that expressed by Samuel Marsden to Thomas Kendell

---

50. Fleras and Spoonley, *Recalling Aotearoa*, p. 65.

51. Quoted by Edward W. Said, 'Zionism from the Standpoint of its Victims', in David Theo Goldberg (ed.), *Anatomy of Racism* (Minneapolis: University of Minnesota Press, 1990), pp. 210-46 (221).

as he was planning a visit back to England while leaving his children behind in New Zealand, 'at an Age when they in a very special manner require the Eye of the Parent, to prevent them from mingling amongst the Heathens and learning their ways'.[52] It is clear that the Rahab and Jezebel narratives are texts needing to be reread through a postcolonial lens.

Yet before I attempt this, there is a further complicating fact that needs to be noted; texts can look quite different, depending on the 'where' of the reading. Exodus, for example, Israel's 'salvation' story of stories, has not only had a long and established place in faith communities over the centuries, but has been and continues to be a linchpin in many contemporary liberation theologies. It also has its own history of interpretation in the reading from the 'where' of Aotearoa New Zealand. The way in which soon after the Bible had been brought to this country Maori peoples applied the Exodus event to themselves has been well documented. In 1845, for example, Heke, one of the tribal leaders, is recorded as 'addressing the people, comparing themselves to the persecuted children of Israel'.[53] During the 1860s, the belief grew that the Maori race was, in fact, descended from the Israelites, being one of the lost tribes of Israel, which made the identification with their situation all the stronger. So, the *Pai Marire* called themselves *Tiu* ('Jews'), while others used the term *Morehu* ('Survivors' or 'Remnant').[54] The land was the 'New Canaan', and therefore in the eyes of the *Pai Marire* movement there would be a restoration of Maori control, 'they would be delivered from bondage from their Pakeha overlords'.[55] Very similar language was used by the great prophet and warrior leader Te Kooti, the founder of the *Ringatu* faith, on his return from exile in the Chatham Islands in 1868. As he landed on the beach at Whareongaonga he too presented himself as a Moses figure called to deliver his people from bondage. The contemporary novelist Witi Ihimaera draws upon this and brings it up to date in his novel *The Matriarch*, where the grandmother tells her grandson,

> And so I begin your journey, e mokopuna,[56] at the time of your awakening, by pushing you out into the universe... This the mother of Moses did when she

52. Quoted by Belich, *Making Peoples*, p. 136. Samuel Marsden, described by one historian as the 'Saint Augustine of New Zealand', was the founder of the first mission station in the Bay of Islands in 1814.

53. R. Burrows, 'Journal, 27 April 1845' in *Extracts from a Diary kept by the Rev. R. Burrows During Heke's War in the North, in 1845* (Auckland: Upton & Co., 1886), p. 32, quoted by Bronwyn Elsmore, *Mana from Heaven: A Century of Maori Prophets in New Zealand* (Tauranga: Moana Press, 1989), p. 167.

54. Elsmore, *Mana from Heaven*, p. 177. The *Pai Marire* was one of several prophetic movements. As a 'Good and Peaceful' movement, it emerged in 1862, led by Te Ua Haumene. See also Belich, *Making Peoples*, p. 220.

55. Witi Ihimaera, *The Matriarch* (Auckland: Heinemann, 1986), p. 79.

56. *Mokopuna* is the Maori word for grandchild.

placed her sacred son into a tiny woven vessel and consigned him to the Nile... And the child was guided to the daughter of Pharaoh and lived in Pharaoh's palace...until the time came when he said to Pharaoh, 'E hoa, let my people go'. And in our own country, these were the words said by your ancestors also. By Te Kooti on the dark side, and by Wi Pere in the parliament of the Pakeha. And these were the words which have come down to me, and which I now pass on to you... Go into the world of the white man. Say to him, as Moses did, 'Let my people go'. Say to him again, 'Take no more of our land, and let us go into our own land of Canaan'.[57]

These are all examples of quite particular and very positive adaptations from a Maori perspective. At the same time, shifting the focus from Christ to the God of the Hebrew Bible, served to 'distance the new Maori religion from its European cousin',[58] as illustrated by Chief Tiopira Te Hukiki's greeting the missionary Leonard Williams in 1878 with the statement, 'You have not visited us for years, and now that you have come to us again you find that we have given up the way of the Son and have adopted instead the way of the Father'.[59]

But what happens when those who read the Exodus account realize they are not so much the suffering Israelites in Egypt as the Israelites who overrode the Canaanites? Or, alternatively, what happens when the text is read from that other underside, from the viewpoint of the displaced Canaanites, as Robert Warrior, an indigenous scholar from North America, has done in a much-quoted article?[60] Once a postcolonial lens is applied, the similarities between the Israelite account of the settlement in Canaan, with its taking of the land already occupied by others, and our own history as *Pakeha* (non-Maori) in this land of Aotearoa New Zealand are disturbingly clear. Land is a shared factor, for colonialism involves a struggle for scarce resources— namely, land—and the Crown's primary reason for establishing its sovereignty and signing the Treaty was to ensure exclusive control over the land trade.[61]

---

57. Ihimaera, *The Matriarch*, pp. 294, 297. Wi Pere Halbert was a Maori member of parliament from 1884–87 and 1894–1905 who repeatedly spoke against the loss of Maori land.

58. Belich, *Making Peoples*, p. 221.

59. Judith Binney, *Redemption Songs: A Life of Te Kooti Arikirangi Te Turuki* (Auckland: Auckland University Press, 1995), p. 296.

60. R.A. Warrior, 'Canaanites, Cowboys and Indians', *Christianity and Crisis* 29 (1989), pp. 261-65.

61. Fleras and Spoonley, *Recalling Aotearoa*, p. 13. As Wendy Larner and Paul Spoonley note in 'Post-Colonial Politics in Aotearoa/New Zealand', in Stasiulis and Yuval-Davis (eds.), *Unsettling Settler Societies*, pp. 39-64 (42-43), 'Differences in attitude towards land ownership were to leave a legacy of bitterness and hurt. Individual and private ownership of land, and its exchange as a commodity were not Maori concepts.'

The saying is recorded that

> The missionaries were sent to break in the Maoris as men break in a wild
> horse; to rub them quietly down the face to keep them quiet, while the land
> was being taken away.[62]

Although it was, of course, not quite as simple as this. Belich quotes a Maori
chief in the early 1840s declaring

> It is the Pakeha we want here. The Pakeha himself will be ample payment for
> our land, because we commonly expect to become prosperous through him.[63]

In fact, Belich suggests that it was not land per se that was the cause of the
wars that erupted after the 1840 Treaty, but that in the mindset of the
imperialist times of the nineteenth century 'there was something unnatural,
unEuropean, about white communities living in equal partnership with
blacks'. He goes as far as to suggest that 'if New Zealand had contained no
land at all, and Pakeha and Maori had both been societies of boat people,
these ideologies (i.e. the myths of empire and hardening racial ideologies)
might still have pressured the former to assert their sway over the latter'.[64]
That, of course, is one historian's supposition, but it does indicate the historical complexity. A further complexity is the fact that not all *Pakeha* were
of one mind. Just as in the Second Temple period there were differing
groupings with differing viewpoints, so there were differing *Pakeha* narratives
in early colonial New Zealand. If the settlers' narrative was not of a mythical
empty land, it was of an 'under-utilized' one. But it also contained the
polemic of 'Maori being misled by missionary inter-meddling', whereas the
missionary or 'Church Party' narrative

> included the existence of a fallen but redeemable portion of humanity
> (Maori) and the efforts and success of conversion continually being hampered
> by the incursions, distractions and oppositions of the 'ravenous and blood-
> thirsty' settler.[65]

62. Bronwyn Elsmore, *Like Them that Dream: The Maori and the Old Testament*
(Tauranga: Tauranga Moana, 1985), p. 33. I am indebted to Mary Huie-Jolly for this
quote from her article, 'Maori "Jews" and a Resistant Reading of John 5.10-47', in Musa
W. Dube and Jeffrey L. Staley (eds.), *John and Postcolonialism: Travel, Space and Power*
(The Bible and Postcolonialism, 7; London: Sheffield Academic Press, 2002), pp. 94-110
(102).

63. Belich, *Making Peoples*, p. 201, quoting from Mary Boyd, *City of the Plains: A
History of Hastings* (Wellington, NZ: Victoria University Press for Hastings City Council,
1984), pp. 5-6.

64. Belich, *Making Peoples*, p. 231.

65. M.P. Grimshaw, '"Fouling the Nest": The Conflict between the "Church Party"
and Settler Society during the New Zealand Wars 1860–1865' (unpublished PhD dissertation, University of Otago, Dunedin, New Zealand, 1999), p. 114.

The outbreak of war in the 1860s only exacerbated this, as the churches and missionaries were caught in a conflict of interests.[66] Bishop Selwyn's opposition to the surveying of the Waitara land block is well known; among the reasons he gave for this stand was

> That inasmuch as this Colony was avowedly formed, not for the acquisition of territory for the English race, but for the protection of the New Zealanders, this primary object shall not be sacrificed to the aggrandizement of the English Provinces.[67]

This advocacy was not the winning voice. After the resulting conflict one politician reflected that

> By refusing to buy [Waitara], the evil might have been postponed, but it was sure to break out at some time & in some form & I do not think a better case or a more timely opportunity could have been selected.[68]

So, despite the opposition, a dominant *Pakeha* will prevailed. And while the motivating causes are complex and may be debated, the question that quite naturally follows and which all settler peoples have to answer is 'By what authority and on what grounds can they justify to themselves either their own moves or those of their parents, grandparents or great-grandparents to gain and preserve authority over land and the people of the land?'[69] The master narratives which cultures provide offer later generations a convenient and powerful way of addressing such questions. Belich points to 'the old Pakeha myth of origin' which has it that the colonizing enterprise began on the initiative of Edward Gibbon Wakefield, the New Zealand Company and its affiliates in the 1840s. According to this narrative, 'Pakeha New Zealand was peopled in a single process by a "better stock", by which was meant, at minimum, better than the convict Australians'.[70] But as Belich notes, what makes this myth rather than reality is the fact that the European pioneers

---

66. See Allan K. Davidson and Peter J. Lineham, *Transplanted Christianity: Documents Illustrating Aspects of New Zealand Church History* (Palmerston North: Department of History, Massey University, 3rd edn, 1995), pp. 115-38. As they note, not all missionary groups took the same stand. While Bishop Selwyn opposed the settlers in Taranaki in 1855 over land purchases, considering them too greedy, 'the Wesleyan missionaries tended to identify more closely with the settler cause' as they also had pastoral concern 'for the growing settler community' (p. 116).

67. Quoted from Davidson and Lineham, *Transplanted Christianity*, p. 120.

68. Belich, *Making Peoples*, p. 235, giving the reference as Henry Sewell, *Journal 1859-65* (Canterbury Museum, Christchurch, New Zealand), 23 April 1860.

69. As Fleras and Spoonley, *Recalling Aotearoa*, p. 14, note, 'Traditionally, three explanations were used to justify the settlement and appropriation of indigenous lands: (a) the doctrine of *terra nullius* (empty or under-utilised lands)…(b) conquests…and (c) voluntary consent through treaty or legislation'.

70. Belich, *Making Peoples*, p. 279.

came before the 1840s, many *were* convict Australians, and the companies contributed only about four per cent of the founding population. However, as he adds, 'myths do not become unimportant merely because they are false, and the myth was not entirely false'. Following his thesis that 'the peopling of Pakeha New Zealand and its cultural construction…were two interlocked processes,'[71] what is very clear is that the origin narratives of both ancient Israel and Aotearoa New Zealand played an important role in shaping their people's sense of identity. Reading the discourses of Israel's ethnic identity, and being alert for the signs and traces of those ancient negotiations, is necessarily a critically reflective enterprise. It demands an alertness both to one's own interests as reader and those of the text. It means that as a reader I need to be on the look out for any potential connections that these texts might be making with my own context. Aware that this might be an uneasy or even uncomfortable and disquieting task, I am tempted to ask, 'Why bother?' The words of Patrocinio Schweikart heading this chapter point to the power of literature:

> We cannot afford to ignore the activity of reading, for it is here that literature is realized as *praxis*. Literature acts on the world by acting on its readers.[72]

If I was in any doubt, an incident that occurred in a class in which I was participating brought this home to me with a sobering reality. It was a course where students for Christian ministry were learning something of Maori culture, and the Maori elder, who was also an ordained Christian minister, was outlining the genealogy of the gods, telling how Rangi, the sky father, and Papatuanuku, the earth mother, produced many offspring including Rongo the *atua* of peace, Tangaroa of the sea, Tane of the forest, and Tuma-tauenga of anger. One of the class, who were for the most part ethnically *Pakeha*, objected to a presentation that suggested 'other gods' were being honoured, and refused to accept the explanation that these represented elements of life of continuing relevance, with a lasting and valued place in the spirituality of Maori, the people of the land, the *tangata whenua* of Aotearoa New Zealand. I, as the Maori elder's *Pakeha* colleague, was embarrassed but recognized that the student in this reformed tradition was able to draw upon texts to argue his case. Texts such as Lev. 18.25, 28, with its talk of the land vomiting out those committing abominations, defined as the practices of the inhabitants of the land, make the point very sharply. The fit with my own context began to feel uncomfortably close.

---

71. Belich, *Making Peoples*, p. 279.
72. Schweickart, 'Reading Ourselves', p. 39.

3

READING RAHAB AND RUTH

Cultural recall is not merely something of which you happen to be a bearer
but something that you actually *perform*.[1]

The Rahab of Joshua ch. 2 and 6.22-25 is one of the biblical 'Others', one of
those condemnable Canaanites. Yet, as the catalyst of the conquest of
Jericho, she became an Israelite hero/ine.[2] Remembered as a paradigm of
faith for Israel, she lived on in Christian tradition to be listed in the Gospel
of Matthew (Mt. 1.5) as an ancestor of Jesus and hymned for her faithfulness
in the letter to the Hebrews (Heb. 11.31). But as I began thinking and writing about this long-famed Rahab, I recognized an ambivalence about this
hero/ine. There were questions I wanted to ask about the way in which the
story portrayed her, questions that became more insistent at each rereading
of the text. This chapter is an exploration of that ambivalence, as I returned
to the biblical story, and watched as the 'I' of my reading gained entry into
the narrative world of Rahab.

As I began this rereading I reminded myself once again that I was from
another world, another community, and that my questions and my observations would be coming from the twentieth-century context of Aotearoa
New Zealand. I needed to remember that I, like Rahab, live in a society
where there are certain culturally prescribed gender roles and expectations,[3]
and that my own interest comes equally from my being, as I have already
stated, of white European descent and living in a Pacific country to which
my ancestors sailed assuming a place that was theirs to settle. My expectation was that just as I would be entering into Rahab's story, so, as I read, her
world would intrude into and speak to mine. Land and its possession would

1. Mieke Bal, 'Introduction', in Mieke Bal, Jonathan Crewe and Leo Spitzer (eds.),
Acts of Memory: Cultural Recall in the Present (Hanover and London: Dartmouth College,
University Press of New England, 1999), pp. i-xvii (i).
2. The spelling indicates the difference the English would make between a male and
female 'hero'.
3. See Bev James and Kay Saville Smith, *Gender, Culture and Power: Challenging New
Zealand's Gendered Society* (Auckland: Oxford University Press, 1989).

be interests in common, interests which would be disturbing and which I already realized were bringing me some unease. I was not entering this narrative as a naïve reader, just as I was not coming as an Israelite.

So I turned back to the text and reread Rahab's story as it was told there in the book of Joshua, mostly in ch. 2, but with a short sequel in ch. 6. Rahab may be the central character in ch. 2, but it is notably Joshua, the Israelite leader, who sets the action in train. And while the focus may be on the action of sending out the spies in the first verse of the first chapter, with the verb coming first in this opening sentence, the lineage tag, 'son of Nun', highlights the importance of Joshua, its subject. Would I have expected such a mission, this secret sending out of two men, coming as it does after the strong promise command of Yahweh in 1.2 to cross into the land? They, however, are immediately designated 'spies', giving notice that this is to be a conflict text. And, as all good spies should, they are to infiltrate secretly and view the land. And so they go.

As it is told, however, they intrude not so much to view the land, as to view the woman of the land. And, indeed, if the taking of the land seems immediately to be by way of the taking of woman, the description, or explanation, of Rahab as a *zona* further underlines this.[4] I notice that she is introduced first as a *zona*, and secondly as one whose name is Rahab, the '*broad*', a name which allows a *double entendre* that spans the languages.[5] If Exod. 34.15-16 warned against Canaanite women, among others, leading Israelite men to 'prostitute' themselves to the 'other' gods of the Canaanites, here is one such woman, clearly labelled *zona*. Reading intertextually, Daniel Hawk may well be right in suggesting that highlighting her ancient trade may be an instance of prostitution serving 'as a metaphor for the violation of Yahweh's covenant…a peril personified by this person who shelters the spies'.[6] In any

4. Frank Moore Cross, 'A Response to Zakovitch's "Successful Failure of Israelite Intelligence"', in Susan Niditch (ed.), *Text and Tradition: The Hebrew Bible and Folklore* (Atlanta: Scholars Press, 1990), pp. 99-104 (102), attempts to exonerate the spies by suggesting that a brothel is the best place for getting local information and protecting one's anonymity.

5. H.M. Barstad, in an unpublished paper ('The O.T. Feminine Personal Name Rahab: An Onomastic Note', mentioned by Magnus Ottoson in his article 'Rahab and the Spies', in Herman Behrens *et al.* [eds.], *Dumu-E2-Dub-Ba-A: Studies in Honor of Ake W. Sjöberg* [Philadelphia: Occasional Publications of the Samuel Noah Kramer Fund, 1989], pp. 419-27 [p. 420 n. 4]), argues from the Ugaritic *rhbt* that the word refers to the female organ, so that it is 'not a "real" personal name but a "nickname" bluntly indicating the woman's métier'.

6. L. Daniel Hawk, *Every Promise Fulfilled: Contesting Plots in Joshua* (Louisville, KY: Westminster/John Knox Press, 1991), pp. 61-62, with reference to Exod. 34.14-16; Deut. 31.16-18; Judg. 2.17. As Phyllis Bird demonstrates in Phyllis A. Bird, '"To Play the Harlot": An Inquiry into an Old Testament Metaphor', in Peggy L. Day (ed.), *Gender and*

case, the message clearly comes across that in this land sexuality is available and can be bought. Two verbs together gain the men entry into her house. Rahab is syntactically passive, enclosed within the spies' purposeful entry, as the sentence closes with the two words that complete the task so far, *vayyishkebu-shammah* ('and slept there').[7] This paid taking of the woman will lead to taking of the land. Rahab's name may, in fact, be doing triple duty in also serving to link woman and land, in that in Exod. 3.8, in the promise given by God to Moses, the place of the Canaanites, the Hittites and others is described as *tobah* and *rehabah*, 'a good and broad land' (NRSV). If she is the only character in the story to be named, apart from Joshua who lies more behind the action than within it, this was clearly with good reason.

But in v. 2 there is a hitch. Is Daniel Hawk right in suggesting that there may be a more ominous note in this connection between woman and land, that it may be hinting at 'the land's darker side—the land as seductress'?[8] Suddenly there is no active subject; neither Joshua nor his spies are any longer in control, and this on the first night of their mission! If the spies were meant to be acting secretly, the passive verb, 'was told', now covers over the secret act of another. Could it have been Rahab? The reader is not told, but another power is now revealed: Jericho has a king who knows about the searching of the land. Does the text imply that he also knows about the connection of women and land? For his order to Rahab to bring forth the men who have come, with the repetition of the verb of 'coming', with its two objects, 'you' and 'your house', heightens the *double entendre* of the act of entry. But can such entry be reversed? The verb of entering, which has dominated this sentence, now closes it. The Israelites have come; they have effected their entry.

Verse 4 opens with an active feminine verb. The woman moves into action on behalf of the men, taking them and hiding them. The Israelites have entered and she now seems programmed with an Israelite agenda; physical entry seems also to have been ideological. Can Rahab be considered Canaanite any longer, for it is she, and not the Israelite spies, who is effectively working secretly? And so she answers the king's interrogators, admitting their

---

Difference in Ancient Israel (Minneapolis: Fortress Press, 1989), pp. 75-94 (76), the root meaning of *znh*/*zonah* is 'to engage in sexual relations outside of or apart from marriage', and therefore wider in implication than the common English understanding of prostitution. Rahab's trade is, however, most likely the latter. Carole R. Fontaine, *Smooth Words: Women, Proverbs and Performance in Biblical Wisdom* (JSOTSup, 356; London: Sheffield Academic Press, 2002), pp. 85-86, sees Rahab in the tradition of the Mesopotamian 'ale-wives' who notably provided more than ale, but who were also understood as having insight into the human heart, 'a kind of wisdom all its own'.

7. The sexual *double entendre* of *shkb* highlights the manner of the stay.
8. Hawk, *Every Promise Fulfilled*, p. 62.

entry. Did she or did she not know their ethnic identity? The Septuagint solves the question by erasing her denial, but the flow of words continues with v. 5 standing as witness to her lying. She cannot 'bring forth' these men for they have gone and there is now no question about the 'I do not know'. It is truth that has gone out and not the men. With falsehood comes assertion; imperatives follow. It is the woman who gives the orders now, and to the king's messengers no less, just as she continues as the active agent in v. 6. The men, now grammatically reduced to suffixes, are tucked away among the flax stalks, like children tucked up in bed by their all-commanding mother. Verse 7 rounds off the scene. The king's men do as she commands; as Trent Butler nicely puts it: 'She is so persuasive the royal messengers are transformed into pursuers'.[9] And there is the final ironic touch; the city gates are closed behind them and the reader savours the knowledge that the enemy is shut within instead of being kept out.

Verse 8 returns the focus to the spies, whose concern is all with sleep, but even that they cannot control, for up comes Rahab onto the roof, and in full voice. This time there is no doubt about her 'knowing'. Yet what she knows is the Hebrew scriptural tradition. One wonders whether it is Rahab or a *rediviva* Miriam speaking in v. 10, as she speaks the language of Holy War.[10] Although her speech is of fear and melting hearts and dread 'of you', it is addressed ironically to these two hapless and seemingly incompetent spies, before concluding in v. 11 with the remarkable affirmation that Yahweh *your* God is the God of heaven above and earth below. Perhaps the spies have not been so incompetent after all, but have given her a crash course in Deuteronomic theology!

But the 'now then' signals that this is not the end of her speech. The one who spoke in imperatives to the king's envoys or lackeys now turns them upon the two, so desperate for sleep among the flax. Is this the *zona* exacting her fee, her cost? Is there a veiled threat in her words?[11] And yet again the language that follows is strangely familiar. The spies are to swear by Yahweh that they will reciprocate the *hesed* she has shown them. If Yahweh and *hesed* are joined syntactically by her actions, *hesed* and the also requested *'emet* are terms that come with strong Israelite covenantal associations. The practical details follow the theological justification: father, mother, brothers, sisters, in gendered order, and all their dependents, are to be saved from death. This is the rescue on her mind; no talk yet of rescue for

9.   Trent C. Butler, *Joshua* (WBC, 7; Waco, TX: Word Books, 1983), p. 32.

10.   For a discussion of the parallel with Exod. 15, see Yair Zakovitch, 'Humor and Theology or the Successful Failure of Israelite Intelligence: A Literary-Folkloric Approach to Joshua 2', in Niditch (ed.), *Text and Tradition*, pp. 75-98 (89).

11.   Suggested by Robert Culley, 'Stories of the Conquest: Joshua 2, 6, 7 and 8', *HAR* 8 (1984), pp. 25-44.

the spies. They meekly agree, 'our lives for yours, to death'. But if Rahab has been reading Deuteronomy, the spies obviously have not, or they would have remembered that Deut. 7.2 and 20.16-18 categorically forbid any such arrangements. In Holy War there were to be no survivors at all. The story allows no problem, however, and simply carries on.[12]

At last she lets them escape. The detail of her house within the wall is in keeping with the 'entering in' motif of vv. 1-4. From that inner space she sets them down by a cord in a vulnerable descent to an outside world where they must flee for their lives to the mountains. Now at last the men find their voice. And it is 'at last', for they are now on the ground, and should be fast on their way instead of standing there shouting back up to Rahab. As Yair Zakovitch points out, they are once again 'flagrantly' disregarding the basic rules of spying.[13] If they now have the courage to stipulate conditions there is a visual humour in these conditions having to be called out to Rahab who is high above—and, for the moment, secure—in her window in the wall. The spies' reference to the oath as 'which you have made us swear' is recognition of their erstwhile passivity; now on the ground outside they can afford to be more assertive. While there may be convincing philological reasons for the use of the masculine forms of the verbs in vv. 17, 18, and 20, it would seem that if bargaining is bad enough in this situation, then bargaining with a woman is beyond the pale, and so there is resort to a formal denial. In v. 18, however, they are back in control and full voice—'behold, when we are coming'—and so they lay down their conditions for Rahab and her family's survival with considerable emphasis on their own blamelessness if these are not met. The final order is the insistence on her silence (v. 20).[14] All is agreed. Finally the spies return to Joshua with their report, which is, in fact, Rahab's—but all is now ascribed to Yahweh. The part of the woman, whose words and acts protected them and allowed them to survive, is glossed over. The gift, magnified as 'all' the land, is attributed to Yahweh alone. Do the two boastfully include themselves in the success? The final word 'before/ because of us' has a final ironic ring. As an echo of Rahab's words, it surely refers to the Israelites as a whole but spoken by the spies it can equally be read as hinting at the terror they inspired—from underneath the flax!

Has this reading been the story of a great hero/ine? In its setting in the book of Joshua this is the prelude of the conquest. But it is to be read not

12. Some commentators suggest that her speech has convinced them that she is now a Yahweh confessor and that therefore the ban no longer applies.

13. Zakovitch, 'Humor and Theology', p. 93.

14. Danna Nolan Fewell and David M. Gunn, in *Gender, Power and Promise: The Subject of the Bible's First Story* (Nashville: Abingdon Press, 1993), p. 120, suggest that the impression given is 'that they hope she will fail to adhere their conditions'. Then their indiscretion will certainly not be disclosed.

only in the context of the book of Joshua, but of the whole Deuteronomistic History, if one follows the classic work of Martin Noth in this regard.[15] Widen the lens a step further and Rahab stands at that pivotal point where the Pentateuch meets its canonical sequel. She is a most significant person in Israel's narrative memory. This is not to deny a long pre-history; Noth himself used the term 'etiological sagas' to define such narratives.[16] The announcement in 6.25 that Rahab's family lived in Israel 'to this day' might well be understood as explaining the presence of a group sensed as in some way different, although it might just as likely be a storyteller's 'happy-ever-after' ending that sends the audience away satisfied and content. But certainly the voice of a storyteller weaving a tale from the stuff of folklore is not difficult to hear. With Zakovitch, it is easy to detect echoes of the 'woman who rescues a man' stories, with a stock motif in the descent from the window, beside which there is, and always has been, a popular and universal appeal of spy stories. In so many respects these are 'comic-book characters— a clever, calculating Canaanite harlot and two bungling spies'.[17] Others have pointed to the possibility of the motif of the trickster here, frequently found in myth, where, as Carole Fontaine notes, 'the deceiver paradoxically becomes Helper and Donor by reasons of her deception, and humanity profits

---

15. Martin Noth, *Überlieferungsgeschichtliche Studien* (Tübingen: Niemeyer Verlag, 1943). Noth's hypothesis has long been debated, some, such as R.G. Kratz, *Die Komposition der erzählenden Bücher des Alten Testaments. Grundwissen der Bibelkritik* (UTB 2157 M; Vandenhoeck & Ruprecht, 2000), suggesting that it is no longer useful and does not do justice to the complexity of the redactional process behind the corpus of Genesis to 2 Kings. Where Noll, *Canaan and Israel in Antiquity*, p. 233, states that with the current differences of opinion among scholars, over both dating and the redactional activity, to refer to Deuteronomy, Joshua to 2 Kings as though these were unquestionably the Deuteronomistic History is 'methodologically inexcusable', Raymond F. Person, Jr, *The Deuteronomic School: History, Social Setting and Literature* (Studies in Biblical Literature, 2; Atlanta: Society of Biblical Literature, 2002), p. 1, introduces his work with the statement that 'research on the Deuteronomic History is clearly in a state of flux'. Ralph W. Klein, in a review published in *RBL* 4 (2003) of Antony F. Campbell and Mark A. O'Brien's recent work in the field (*Unfolding the Deuteronomistic History: Origins, Ugrades, Present Text* [Minneapolis: Augsburg Fortress, 2000]), perhaps sums up the present situation, writing that 'the vast majority of scholars subscribe to the idea of some kind of DH, although there are notable exceptions' (cited at <www.bookreviews.org/subscribe. asp> on 5 April 2003). Whether or not one accepts the hypothesis in either its earlier or variant later versions, canonically the book of Joshua begins a new phase in Israel's narrative.

16. See the discussion and partial agreement by Gene M. Tucker, 'The Rahab Saga (Joshua 2)', in James M. Efird (ed.), *The Use of the Old Testament in the New and Other Essays: Studies in Honor of William Franklin Stinespring* (Durham, NC: Duke University Press, 1972), pp. 66-86.

17. Zakovitch, 'Humor and Theology', p. 96.

from the redistribution of power thereby accomplished'.[18] One needs, of course, to ask who is helped, and if, first and foremost, it is Israel, which in this case has power and land transferred from Canaan, then in Israelite terms Rahab is indeed a Helper and Donor; heard in Canaan, there would be markedly different words used to describe her role. As Kathleen Ashley notes of the dynamics of trickster tales, much depends 'upon the interpretive community in which they are told'.[19]

I, of course, am not reading this in ancient Israel. So, if different interpretive communities inevitably read the power plays of trickster tales in quite different ways, as indeed the text itself permits, how am I, and the readers in my context, to read Rahab in this tale? Do we need to ask again whether she was the saviour, or the traitor, or the victim, of the story? Was she manipulated and exploited, or did she see an opportunity and take advantage of it?[20] In the story she saved two men—but only two. She gave away no vital information nor made any strategic plans to help the Israelite invasion, and yet she gained for herself the prize of life, if not as a pseudo-Israelite, at least on Israelite soil in the land promised to Israel by Israel's all-powerful God. If this is a text of the mighty works of that god, who has been seen as the human power holder and wielder, acting as the agent of the deity? Rahab? As the story progressed she certainly had power over the lives of the spies. But as a marginalized woman of a group that was about to be routed and killed, that power surely appears as the power of the last gasp, of the desperate underside. Told over generations in Israel, with the outcome already known, there is no question: the power is Israel's. But if this is so, then, as Danna Fewell and David Gunn have suggested, the very 'foreignness' of Rahab would appear to undermine that Israelite perspective, for 'when foreigners can quote Deuteronomy with more facility than Israelites', that would seem to raise questions in itself about the 'grand theological ideas of chosenness and exclusivity'.[21] Polzin, too, suggests that Rahab herself is a living critique who turns the ideology back against Israel, with her very survival due to 'the wickedness and lack of faith of Israel'.[22] The power interplays are complex indeed. What is unquestionable is that in the narrative as it is told, Rahab can be heard

18. Carole R. Fontaine, 'The Deceptive Goddess in Ancient Near Eastern Myth: Inanna and Inaras', *Semeia* 42 (1988), pp. 84-102 (99). See other essays in this issue.

19. Kathleen M. Ashley, 'Interrogating Biblical Deception and Trickster Theories: Narratives of Patriarchy or Possibility?', *Semeia* 42 (1988), pp. 103-15 (113).

20. As Fewell and Gunn, *Gender, Power and Promise*, p. 120, note: 'Should Israel destroy Jericho (and if they keep their word), then she is in good stead. If they fail…no-one in Jericho is any the wiser.'

21. Fewell and Gunn, *Gender, Power and Promise*, p. 120.

22. Robert Polzin, *Moses and the Deuteronomist: A Literary Study of the Deuteronomic History* (New York: Seabury Press, 1980), p. 88.

voicing the Deuteronomistic theology and language and using it to her own advantage, to gain her own life and the lives of her family.

I am now suspicious. It seems that once again Israel has taken what was once a folk tale and reshaped it as a tool of its own political ideology. Evidence of the hand of a writer or editor adding material in order to provide clues to aid the Israelite listeners in their response is there in text. If one looks at the chapter form-critically, the narrative can easily be divided into various sections. After Joshua's introductory order in the first verse, there is the hiding episode (vv. 2-7), then Rahab's deal (vv. 8-14), then the escape with further stipulations (vv. 15-22), and finally the reporting back to Joshua (vv. 23-24). Together they make what at first reading appears to be a coherent narrative, but on closer scrutiny questions of this coherence arise. Gene Tucker, for instance, finds an inconsistency in the two reports of Rahab's hiding of the spies (vv. 4a and 6), although there is the possibility that the reader is meant to understand that Rahab immediately pushed them into a temporary hiding place before later taking them up onto the roof. As so often, much depends on the reader's interpretive decision-making.[23] But what is more significant is that Rahab's long speech and its response in vv. 8-14, and also that of the spies and her response in vv. 17-21 could be removed, leaving the essential elements of a rescue/spy tale intact, a long-accepted ground for suspecting the hand of an editor.

It is these speeches, and particularly Rahab's, that raise pressing questions for me. For whose voice is it that I am hearing? Is this really a Canaanite Rahab? As I noted above, it stretches credibility to have a Canaanite who is more than 'rather well read in the Deuteronomistic traditions of the exodus and the wilderness'.[24] Indeed, she is far too well read. Sihon and Og traditions, Song of the Sea traditions, Holy War language, she has it all. In story terms she may save only two very mediocre spies, but her words, which form the gist of the spies' report to Joshua in v. 24, are heard as the very guarantee of Israelite success. This is the theological affirmation that needs to be heard—by the spies, by Joshua, and by each succeeding Israelite audience. This is not to pass over the careful voicing of the spies who in their report of v. 24 carefully reinterpret 'the land' as 'all the land'. For could they have possibly thought that Jericho was the whole of the promised land?! But it is after the Holy War formula has been delivered that the conquest begins, and that formula begins here with Rahab.

23.   Many translators make use of the pluperfects 'had hidden' and 'had brought' as solutions.

24.   John L. McKenzie, *The World of the Judges* (Englewood Cliffs: Prentice–Hall, 1966), p. 48, emphasis added. Tucker, 'The Rahab Saga', follows Noth in identifying Deut. 2.30–3.7, 4.39 and 11.25 underlying the speech.

Why were these words put into her mouth? I find that a teasing question. Was she chosen because such a person, a Canaanite prostitute, was the least likely to believe in the power of the Israelite God? The story then shows that apparent enemies could not only 'melt in fear' before that God, but could 'melt' into potential aids and agents of Israel itself. That is one possibility. I can imagine Deuteronomistic writers thinking 'We have the Rahab tradition to slot in here, and a Canaanite woman whose faith was so strong that she put her own life in danger to help the Israelites enter her land will be ideal narrative device for our History'. And if it was a team of writers, I can further imagine one of them offering to write a long speech for Rahab, so she could be heard by generations of later Israelite readers expressing faith in Israel's God and using the very words of the Holy War formula. From Israel's perspective, Rahab's words, coming from the mouth of a Canaanite, would not only be crucially affirming, but they would also seem miraculous and a witness both to their God's power and particular care for Israel.

Rahab's narrative, of course, does not end with ch. 2, but continues with a short sequel in Josh. 6.22-25. Robert Polzin sees the writers using this to make yet another point. He detects an underlying challenge here to the theology of Deut. 9.4-5, where Moses warns the people not to attribute the gift of land to any righteousness on their part; on the contrary, 'it is because of the wickedness of these nations that Yahweh is driving them out before you'.[25] This, of course, neatly justifies the dispossession of the land, but, as Polzin notes, not all of these peoples were dispossessed. Apply the same rationale, and, as Polzin expresses it, 'it is not because of Rahab's merit that she and her household will continue to occupy the land, but because of the wickedness and lack of faith of Israel'.[26] For, as I noted above, Joshua's act in sending out the spies could be read as signalling not only a timidity and a lack of faith in God's promise, but a disobedience of the divine order given in 1.2. This is over and above the later matter of the disregarded ban, although once a binding oath had been made in the name of Yahweh, and its conditions kept, the divine *ḥesed* had to be shown. If this is not quite such good news from an Israelite perspective, it does explain an otherwise dissonant note in this conquest account.

However I or other readers might hear these Deuteronomistic messages, the tale is not good news for the majority of the inhabitants of the land, which brings me back to my earlier question of whether Rahab can be understood as a hero/ine. Can one who hands over her own people and land to another power really be regarded as such? Or is there an assumption that readers will always back and cheer a winner, particularly if the reader belongs

25. Polzin, *Moses and the Deuteronomist*, pp. 88-91.
26. Polzin, *Moses and the Deuteronomist*, p. 88.

to the group that benefits from the prize that winners necessarily receive, in this case the prize of land? Musa Dube makes a strong case for this tale fitting the 'literary type-scene of land possession in the rhetoric of God, gold, glory, and gender'.[27] And of course, when couched in Holy War terms and waged under a Sacred Canopy, who can argue or read against this? But was Rahab, in fact, a winner? Certainly at the beginning of the story she appears as triply disadvantaged from the perspective of Israel, not only as a woman, but as a *zonah*, a marginalized woman, and then a Canaanite to boot.[28] While as a *zonah* she may have had a certain independence, and, apparently from this text, her own house, as Phyllis Bird notes, such women were 'tolerated but despised' with the 'social status... of an outcast'.[29] So, while on an individual level she may have had a certain ambivalent independence, in societal terms she was the vulnerable underside of a patriarchal world. Such marginal characters are society's weak points in several senses, and one might imagine Rahab quickly deciding that being a virtual foreign agent was a better bet than remaining an outcast. Yet I tend to agree with Phyllis Bird that there is a 'plausibility' problem in reading the story in this way.[30] How likely would it have been for such a marginal woman to have had the background information on which to base such a decision? How could she have known that the Israelites were going to be the winners? How could she trust them? The spies themselves had doubts about her, as seen in their concern that she speak to no-one about this affair. If, however, this is a Deuteronomistic text, such questions are irrelevant. This is an Israelite view. No-one is required to wonder how Rahab slept at night remembering fellow Canaanites now dead, or to ponder how she lived in Israel as an ex-Canaanite, and whether it was in that curious half-world where so many past spies and agents spend their days in everlasting exile. Rahab chose Israel: therefore Rahab is a winner.

Although the text leaves me with this assumption that Rahab is a winner, living happily ever after and free from danger, it has also left me with the message that not only is it dangerous to enter the home of a foreign/outsider woman, but that such women can eventually be bought, that foreign women are sexually available, just as their land lies there for the taking, with the further implication that morally 'loose' equates with 'loose tongued', as seen

27. Musa W. Dube, *Postcolonial Feminist Interpretation of the Bible* (St Louis, MI: Chalice Press, 2000), p. 76. Other examples that she gives on p. 119 are the stories of Pharaoh's daughter, Zipporah, Dido, Pocahontas, and the African woman in Joseph Conrad's *Heart of Darkness*.

28. As Fewell and Gunn (*Gender, Power and Promise*, p. 119) note: 'She is the quintessential Other'.

29. Phyllis A. Bird, 'The Harlot as Heroine: Narrative Art and Social Presupposition in Three Old Testament Texts', *Semeia* 46 (1989), pp. 119-39 (119-20).

30. Bird, 'The Harlot as Heroine', p. 132.

in the spies' concern that she tell no-one.[31] Far from inviting me, as the reader, to question any of these assumptions, the text's strategy has been to lead me, almost unawares, to accept its values and interests as the story itself is accepted. In this the textual Rahab has virtually become the model, for as I have followed her progress through this narrative, I have been watching her reading the situation virtually as an Israelite, entering their ideological world and seeing the future lying in the power of the Israelite God. I am now left wondering whether she has fallen in line even to the extent of assuming the wickedness of her own people, according to Deut. 9.4-5.[32] Reading as the Other has uncomfortable requirements; the text certainly does not offer the expectation that she will retain or regain her dignity as a Canaanite.

The ethnic/land issue in this text is perhaps all the more disturbing in that the clear distinctions set out in Deuteronomy, and which hold true for Joshua, are categories that in all likelihood belong to the discourse rather than the reality. As already noted in the previous chapters, it seems more and more probable that the Israelites were not a group ethnically distinct from the Canaanites at all. The conquest narratives, therefore, may very well be the quite deliberate ideological discourses that put the stamp of dis- tinctive Israelite identity upon those who would differentiate themselves from others. If this is so, no wonder Rahab sounds like an Israelite, for she is an Israelite construct and constructed as a pawn of the text which makes her into the all-important Other, and so a significant part of the justifica- tion for the dispossession of her people's land.[33] She thus has a very necessary place in the 'semiotic economy' of Israel.[34] This is the making of Rahab the hero/ine. Rahab was created 'Other' in order to provide the 'Us' of Israel with an identity. Questioning Rahab turns out to be an uncovering of double agents.

31.   Dube, *Postcolonial Feminist Interpretation*, p. 76, observes the frequency of this pattern, where once the woman 'is met, her affections won, then the land she represents will also be entered and domesticated by the colonizer, or it is at least available for the taking of the colonizer, if so desired'. Dube (p. 144) sees this as belonging to an ideology 'of presenting the targeted groups as womenlike people who require and beseech domi- nation'.

32.   See Polzin, *Moses and the Deuteronomist*, pp. 88-91. Although there is also the possibility that, in asking for the ban to be defied, she is boldly holding that very theology up for scrutiny.

33.   Note the emphasis on land, mentioned in vv. 9, 14, 24. See also Lori Rowlett, 'Inclusion, Exclusion and Marginality in the Book of Joshua', *JSOT* 55 (1992), pp. 15-23, for a similar discussion of the ideology behind Rahab's move from Other to Insider, and her voluntary submission to the Israelite and Yahwistic structures of control.

34.   A helpfully descriptive term used by Esther Fuchs in the context of a discussion of patriarchal ideology in 'For I Have the Way of Women: Deception, Gender, and Ideology in Biblical Narrative', *Semeia* 42 (1988), pp. 68-83 (68).

These twists take some unravelling, for the subtlety with which the text would claim my tacit agreement means that it is not easy to stand aside and recognize my complicity. Yet I cannot simply dismiss the co-opting of Rahab as an ancient once-upon-a-time, long ago tactic. Chandra Mohanty, for example, writes of how written material in her Asian context becomes part of the 'basis of the exercise of power and domination', used to provide 'the context through which new political identities are forged'.[35] A reminder of the universal and timeless nature of such strategies. So too Renita Weems has pointed to the way in which the contemporary American reading system requires the reader of prescribed texts to 'surrender herself to the experiences, world view, values, and assumptions embedded in the work', which may be the very counter to her own. There is little other choice.[36] In Aotearoa New Zealand the novelist Patricia Grace, of Ngati Raukawa, Ngati Toa and Te Ati Awa descent, has one of her characters talk of the need of her people 'to know that our truth does not appear on pages of books unless it is there between the lines'.[37] The history of race relations here as elsewhere is complex and multi-faceted, but a report from one F.E. Maning in 1873 is chilling in its statement that 'if all your schools are going on as well as that of Wirinake there will soon be no Maoris in New Zealand'.[38] The cost of remaining Other in Aotearoa New Zealand is all too clearly described by Patricia Grace: 'those who had learned to look at who they were in distorted mirrors, had seen awry reflections of themselves and had become traumatised. And their stories of self-hated were told in their…self-defacement, their maiming and their havoc…in the dreamless, frightened eyes.'[39] As Susan Stanford Friedman writes, 'the cultural narratives in which we think about race and ethnicity not only reflect but also shape the material realities of racism' and such discourse circulates both 'overtly and covertly'.[40] For Bible readers, Rahab's story is overtly one of the many narratives that shape our thinking, whether we are conscious of this or not; more covertly, as a biblical narrative, it has become part of our Western cultural heritage.

---

35. Chandra Talpade Mohanty, 'Introduction: Cartographies of Struggle. Third World Women and the Politics of Feminism', in Chandra Talpade Mohanty *et al.* (eds.), *Third World Women and the Politics of Feminism* (Bloomington: Indiana University Press, 1991), pp. 1-47 (34-35).

36. Renita J. Weems, 'Reading *Her Way* through the Struggle: African American Women and the Bible', in Cain Hope Felder (ed.), *Stony the Road We Trod: African American Biblical Interpretation* (Minneapolis: Fortress Press, 1991), pp. 57-77 (65).

37. Patricia Grace, *Cousins* (Auckland: Penguin Books New Zealand, 1992), p. 208.

38. Quoted in the publication *Gospel and Cultures* (Auckland: Conference of Churches in Aotearoa New Zealand, 1996), p. 7.

39. Grace, *Cousins*, p. 215.

40. Susan Stanford Friedman, 'Beyond White and Other: Relationality and Narratives of Race in Feminist Discourse', *Signs* 21/1 (1995), pp. 1-49 (6).

What is all the more disturbing is the realization that the effectiveness of such narratives is due in part to the seeming invisibility of the textual strategy, which, of course, is an integral part of the strategy. David Penchanksy sums it up: 'The Deuteronomic Template is meant to be an invisible strategy, shaping the reading of the later stories while the reader remains unaware that she is being manipulated'.[41] While in biblical studies we frequently talk about the shaping of the material, we talk far less about such covert shaping of the reader. So if Rahab is a hero/ine, it is not only ancient Canaanites who are in danger. Follow her speechwriter into this text and there is an ongoing danger that other dominant cultures, such as mine, will find it all too easy to identify with the dominant voice, which justifies the taking of land, on the assumption that Canaanites are inherently wicked. But an even more disturbing danger is that such a voice may also lead those who have lost their land to Christian invaders and settlers to read against their own history and identity.[42] They will then be reading with this Israelite agent Rahab, surrendering themselves unquestioningly to this worldview. The effect of such counter or anti-identity reading, has been well, if soberingly, described as 'bleeding without knowing one has been cut and hooked without seeing a ripple in the water'.[43]

So, as I struggle with these issues, I no longer wish to ask whether Rahab was a hero/ine. That description of the victimized reader 'bleeding without knowing one has been cut', finally forces me to revise my question, and to face the costliness of such co-opting. As a reader from a dominant culture I find this an uncomfortable challenge. Pierre Bourdieu uses the term 'symbolic violence', meaning 'that gentle, invisible form of violence, which is never recognised as such, and is not so much undergone as chosen…the "cultural capital" which those wanting to advance in the material terms of the dominant culture need to acquire'.[44] As he and Terry Eagleton comment, resistance to this form of institutional colonialism is 'more difficult, since it is everywhere and nowhere, and to escape from that is very difficult'.[45] As I have been writing this I have been remembering a conversation

41. David Penchansky, 'Up for Grabs: A Tentative Proposal for Doing Ideological Criticism', *Semeia* 59 (1992), pp. 35-41 (38).

42. Cain Hope Felder's definition of 'sacralization' (in 'Race, Racism, and the Biblical Narratives', in *idem* [ed.], *Stony the Road We Trod*, pp. 127-45 [128-29]), as 'the transposing of an ideological concept into a tenet of religious faith (or a theological justification) in order to serve the vested interests of a particular ethnic/racial group' needs to be considered seriously.

43. William Myers, 'The Hermeneutical Dilemma of the African American Biblical Student', in Felder (ed.), *Stony the Road We Trod*, pp. 40-56 (42).

44. Pierre Bourdieu, *Outline of a Theory of Practice* (Cambridge: Cambridge University Press, 1977), p. 192.

45. Pierre Bourdieu and Terry Eagleton, 'Doxa and the Common Life', in Slavoj Žižek (ed.), *Mapping Ideology* (London/New York: Verso, 1994), pp. 265-77 (270).

with a woman friend, one of the *tangata whenua*, the people of the land in Aotearoa New Zealand, talking about the costliness of choosing to enter the *Pakeha* or European culturally determined world, which leads to gains and promotions in what my society regards as a successful career path, and the consequent pain and sense of alienation from her own community that it caused. So now I would ask not whether Rahab was a hero/ine but whether Rahab the Canaanite survived without bleeding, and whether she came to realize that she bled. The fact that the narrative is not interested in such a question does not matter, nor whether or not this Rahab belongs only to the text, for throughout the years there will have been many Rahabs in Israel and elsewhere, some even perhaps persuaded by this very tale.

The Deuteronomists used Others against whom their community could assert and define themselves, even if those Others, like Rahab, were in reality their own ethnic grouping, now set apart and stigmatized. Different readers will continue to hear this text differently, but those whose own cultural experiences bring to the fore a jangling recognition of this co-opting but polarizing strategy may be moved to ask to what extent our readings and our narratives contribute to this silent bleeding in our own contexts. The conflict narratives of the conquest are indeed dangerous tales. If Rahab is a hero/ine, then let the reader read again.

This was my original conclusion to reading Rahab. Musa Dube has recently proposed that the Rahab story could, in effect, become a critical template, or what she calls 'a reading prism', through which other texts could be viewed with an eye to seeing 'whether a text is imperializing or anti-imperial', and so both warn and 'assist postcolonial readers to read against imperial and patriarchal forms of oppression'.[46] Certainly Rahab is not the only biblical non-Israelite who is seen crossing the Us/Others border. The story of Ruth reads almost as a hymn to boundary crossing—in the right direction; right, of course, being defined again by the storyteller. Was Ruth, then, to be read through the Rahab reading prism? I had, in fact, read it with such questions in mind at the SBL Annual Meeting in 1997, where, after a brief mention of this being an idyllic tale of love and devotion, I began by asking such questions as, 'Who was this tale told by, told to, told for?' Not waiting for a reply—these were, of course, rhetorical questions—I suggested that if one took these questions seriously, the resulting reading would soon discover a sharpness not only in the tale/tail of Ruth but in the very body. So I imagined the storyteller beginning and the listeners settling down. I imagined that it might gone like this:

> Listen carefully. Do you remember 'the days when the judges ruled'? Have you been to Egypt, Gerar perhaps, with Abraham, and Isaac, and the brothers of Joseph when there was a 'famine in the land'? Then this is your story. But

46. Dube, *Postcolonial Feminist Interpretation*, p. 201.

listen further: 'a certain man of Bethlehem' called Elimelech is forced to flee, not to Egypt, not to Gerar, but to Moab.[47] But you, as Israelites, remember a Mosaic instruction that no Moabite, even down to the tenth generation, is to be admitted to the assembly of God (Deut. 23.3). (What is this storyteller up to? Ask 'What is an Israelite?', and the biblical answer is not a Moabite.) But settle down again. Moab for these God-fearing, life-seeking Israelites is deathly, only a woman is left as survivor. Listen as the storyline is replayed in reverse: in the days when there was death in the land, of Moab, a woman sets out, but now to Bethlehem, where there will bread from God for God's people. And for Moabite daughters-in-law? Can they be included? But Naomi attempts to dissuade them. The phrase 'your mother's house' (v. 8) points to the crux of the matter; these are not Naomi's daughters, these women have Moabite mothers. One Moabite listens, weeps, kisses Naomi and leaves the narrative, the other weeps, but clings, and edges forward into the storyline. Naomi the Israelite now names the hurdle, which is the matter not only of kinship but of the divine. 'Your sister-in-law has gone back to her people and to her gods.' Can a Moabite Ruth enter this Israelite story with integrity?

That is the question. The audience waits—will they be reassured by her speech, 'your people shall be my people and your God my God'? I do not think that this confession 'blunt[s]' the issue of Ruth's foreignness as Katrina Larkin suggests.[48] On the contrary, I see its implications setting the basis for what follows. Read from the Israelite point of view it is, of course, a significant border-crossing, the moment of transformation. Naomi may be resoundingly silent now, but there is certainly more to be said. For the Moabite herself there will be no return; her bones will not lie in the soil of Moab. 'And so the two of them went on' (v. 19)—the two of them. Naomi returns; Bethlehem, 'home of plenty', is home to Naomi, but Ruth, despite her speech, is explicitly Ruth the Moabite, daughter-*in-law* (v. 22). No recognition yet of the Israelite transformation; tension remains for the Israelite audience at the end of this first chapter, relieved only by the final sentence that tells of the beginning of the barley harvest with its hint of gathered blessing in the plural 'they came'—the two of them.

Talk of Naomi's wealthy kinsman in ch. 2 keeps 'the Moabite who came back with Naomi from the country of Moab' (v. 6) as the outsider. The audience stirs. Ruth's question, 'why have I found favour in your sight… when I am a foreigner' (v. 10), is theirs. They listen for the answer. She has 'left her father and mother, and her native land', therefore, she may justifiably hope for a 'full reward' from the God of Israel, 'under whose wings' (v. 12) she has sought refuge, a wing somewhat fused with that of Boaz in

47. For a discussion of the significance of this setting, see Danna Nolan Fewell and David M. Gunn, '"A Son is Born to Naomi!": Literary Allusions and Interpretation in the Book of Ruth', *JSOT* 40 (1988), pp. 99-108 (103).

48. Katrina J.A. Larkin, *Ruth and Esther* (OTG; Sheffield: Sheffield Academic Press, 1996), p. 53.

ch. 3. The redeeming Israelite God and the solidly human Israelite redeemer, Boaz, are apparently acting together. The Moabite, however, is not yet fully gathered, so in ch. 4 the Bethlehem elders sit in the town gate to sort out publicly the redemption rights—of property, of family name and of the outsider woman now part of an Israelite inheritance. Once acquired with the land rights, she is no longer Ruth the Moabite, but the woman 'coming into the house' of Boaz (v. 11). The prayer of all the people announces to the audience—in case they have missed the full significance of this insider/outsider dealing—that Ruth is joining the line of Rachel, Leah and Tamar, to become, like them, a mother in Israel. But does Ruth perhaps still have something of the Moabite about her, that not even the exaggerated perfection of the seven can wholly eradicate? The storyteller reassures with the cry 'a son has been born to Naomi' (v. 17). Ruth may be allotted an Israelite husband but not his child. The Israelites stretch with satisfaction. All is well. The story that began with famine and death to Israelites has ended with birth; promise leads not only to hope for Israel but to that archetypal Israelite, David. It is good to be Israelite in the storyteller's world, good to have one's cultural identity so warmly affirmed.

Yet textual clues are not so much decoded as teased out for their fit by readers who not only bring, but are enfleshed and enmeshed in their own cultural assumptions. If I apply Musa Dube's reading prism, I cannot avoid noting the pivotal place that acquiring Israelite land occupies in this story. I am now in a familiar world, for land rights signify a crux of bicultural relationships and conflict in Aotearoa New Zealand.[49] But again, as with the Rahab narrative, this is double-edged: acquiring woman goes with acquiring the land. Is it my reading lens or the story itself that has become much shadier? I go back to the very beginning of the tale, and look for tell-tale signs of an ideology of domination, for the contradictions that flag the cover up of asymmetrical power relations. And so I return to the opening sentence 'in the days when the judges ruled'. At first reading this is a simple matter of fact context-providing statement. But who were these judges? Surely none other than those military deliverers raised up both to deliver the would-be Israelites from the resisting onslaught of peoples of the land, and from the rule of Moab (Judg. 3.12-30), and to retain the land that they had taken. So, this is a tale told in the context of land wars. I know such a history well, and its ways of telling. In my childhood education the land wars in my country were called the Maori Wars and the telling was all from one side. As the

---

49. While significant tribal claims for compensation have been settled, others have yet to be heard. As I am writing, considerable tension has arisen concerning rights and ownership of the foreshore and seabed. Maori maintain that they hold customary title, while others argue for the Crown's ownership. The present Government is currently attempting to find a mediating course.

historian James Belich has noted, the New Zealand Wars of 1845–72 'were…bitter and bloody struggles, as important to New Zealand as were the Civil Wars to England and the United States…they were examples of that widespread phenomenon: resistance to European expansion'.[50] The beginning of the book of Ruth signals: be alert to what is afoot in this text.

I now note the curious God ambiguity in ch. 1; Naomi may recognize a difference in kinship but she clearly does not afford religious difference the same respect. Ruth herself later chooses to leave her Moabite gods, but as early as v. 8 Naomi is heard invoking the Israelite Divine Name for daughterly blessing. But read the whole tale again and ask that most basic of questions: Who is this Ruth to whom we are introduced? Isn't she the Moabite who speaks the language of Israelite covenant theology, the Moabite who knows the requirements of Israelite family law, the Moabite who knows that the 'covering wing' (*kanap*) of the god of Israel (2.12) can materialize in the 'covering wing' (*kanap*) of the worthy Israelite benefactor (3.9), the Moabite who acts not so much for herself but for the promise to Israel, the Moabite who will bear the son anticipating the golden age of David? This is Ruth who once was Moabite but now is Israelite, denying her own language, denying her own spirituality, denying her own kinship claims. Even burial on home ground, for the land acquired with Ruth is not her land at all. The choice of returning home or going forward with Naomi posed by the storyteller turns out to have been no choice at all but a textual strategy to promote the model of Israelite faith; Orpah was the literary foil. This is an Israelite metamorphosis framed by intertextual allusion. Not only does Ruth *cleave* to Naomi (1.14), but she is directed by Boaz in ch. 2 to *cleave* to his Israelite women workers; the language of Gen. 2.24 transformed from marriage relations to ethnic. But can a Moabite Ruth be a model Israelite heroine? This is the crux question. Again, the text shows its ideological colours. Ruth on the threshing floor is a questionable adventuress; a chorus of intertextual allusions to other sexually questionable foreign or outsider women can be all too clearly heard, including that to the ancestral daughter of Lot responsible for the birth of Moab himself.[51] Boaz, on the contrary, is, of course, an honourable redeemer.

And who is Naomi? While on the surface level she may be seen working to provide husband, security, and Israelite identity for Ruth, is she not, on another level, more significantly serving the 'hidden transcript'[52] of the text,

50. James Belich, *The New Zealand Wars and the Victorian Interpretation of Racial Conflict* (Auckland: Auckland University Press, 1989), p. 15.

51. Noted by Danna Nolan Fewell and David M. Gunn, 'Boaz, Pillar of Society: Measures of Worth in the Book of Ruth', *JSOT* 45 (1989), pp. 45-59 (48).

52. A phrase used by James C. Scott, *Domination and the Arts of Resistance: Hidden Transcripts* (New Haven: Yale University Press, 1990).

the underlying goal of assimilation, transforming Moabite into Israelite? Can one trust a woman who has shown such ambivalence to her daughter-in-law, who both incites her to resistance and yet exposes her to danger and the charge of cultural dishonour? Is it not a case now of daughter beware, and daughter be on guard against this power-wielding Israelite woman? The Israelite Naomi, playing her set role, is uncomfortable for a *Pakeha* reader in Aotearoa New Zealand. And yet, I am not sure. Perhaps Naomi did respect difference. Perhaps Naomi and the narrator had different views. Perhaps she genuinely wanted both her daughters-in-law to return home because that was culturally appropriate, so that Orpah's action followed Naomi's wish. But what can a mere character achieve against the powerful ideology of a narrator's text? Do I wish to be reminded yet again of the powerlessness of those whose views are silenced by the overwriting of the public text? I look again at that final scene: is it a powerfully silent or powerlessly silenced Naomi who takes and nurses the child, born by Ruth? If read through the lens of traditional Maori custom whereby the first grandchild was commonly claimed for its upbringing by the grandparents, this might be heard as Naomi's formal recognition of Ruth as her daughter. Or is it the Moabite producing the child for the Israelite, as a *rediviva* Hagar? For the consequence is that the Moabite's child is now truly Israelite, assimilation complete, with Israel the winner.[53] Musa Dube's description of Rahab as an example of the 'text-ual fantasies of colonizers', in that it fulfils 'the colonizer's ideal dream…that the colonized will proclaim the colonizer's superiority, pledge absolute loy-alty, and surrender all their rights voluntarily', might equally be applied to Ruth.[54] The Bethlehem women almost pre-empt the final ideological climax, or does the text waver under the weight of its claims? They have already given the child a name before the narrator sets the text firmly in the direc-tion of Israel's Davidic history, adding the Israelite genealogy, the authen-ticating *whakapapa*,[55] the ancestral authority, with its final erasure of Moabite maternity. The covenant vow of Ruth so memorized, quoted and sung over centuries as a model of devotion and faith, but now heard as a speech of ethnic and religious rejection, was a significant hint of the direction ahead.

   Not a good story for Moabites! While I cannot read as an ethnic Moabite, although colonizers have a long history of presuming to be surrogate read-ers, women of dominant races know at least a little of the effects of being 'Other'ed. Mothers, and mothers in the political tradition of the biblical

---

53.   Ellen van Wolde, 'Texts in Dialogue with Texts: Intertextuality in the Ruth and Tamar Narratives', *BibInt* 5.1 (1997), pp. 1-28, and Laura Donaldson, 'The Sign of Orpah: Reading Ruth Through Native Eyes', in Brenner (ed.), *Ruth and Esther*, pp. 130-44, also note the requirement of assimilation in this text.

54.   Dube, *Postcolonial Feminist Interpretation*, p. 78.

55.   The Maori term for genealogy.

Moabite mothers even more so, know of daughters taken off by the powerful and they know the consequences of that. Young women creeping among the gleanings, in danger of rape, promised rewards by older power-holding men who may or may not deliver, and who, if they do, will make sure the deed is done secretly at night, with all that that implies —this is not a story, this is known experience. And yes, I know that according to the text it is Naomi who suggests the threshing floor strategy, but I am reading with suspicion even here. I want to give the warning: Moabite mothers beware!

I am aware that many marginalized women's voices tell this story, and tell it differently. There are those who tell this as a story of successful resistance, as the story of an outsider woman who infiltrates for gain under cover of darkness. Some tell it as a model story of women who survive against the odds.[56] But it is also the story of a woman heard through submissive speech ('I am Ruth your servant'), through male validated relationship ('and now my daughter'), through marriage, through male property rights, through the birth of a male heir. Such voices resist the invitation to enter the narrative world for warm embraces with role-modelling biblical ancestors. I ask myself what has happened to that idyllic tale of love and devotion that I have treasured for so long? Am I only to read it that way under the bedclothes at night? For my own mental and emotional health, and perhaps even for the strength to confront the truths presented in these other readings, I need to hear Ruth in more than one key. I need to hear of Ruth and Naomi as strong women, as part of the scriptural blessings. But a text that begins in Moab and whose last word is 'David' (cf. 2 Sam. 8.2) raises issues that not only concern women; its canonical setting in the Septuagint-Christian tradition after the book of Judges and before 1 Samuel, only serves to make its political agenda the more overt.[57] As I have reread the book of Ruth, I have become fearful of its place as sacred scripture in my country, for racial politics are alive and well in Aotearoa New Zealand, with an unspoken assumption of assimilation revealed in the praise given to 'other' groupings when they have achieved well in the ways of the dominant culture, which in this situation means achieving well in what is for the most part a European education system, speaking a fluent English, and living according to norms that are *Pakeha*, as my friend knew well to her own cost. The attitudes to those who hold to

56. See Sarojini Nadar, 'A South African Indian Womanist Reading of the Character of Ruth', in Musa W. Dube (ed.), *Other Ways of Reading: African Women and the Bible* (Atlanta: Society of Biblical Literature; Geneva: WCC Publications, 2001), pp. 159-75 (172): 'Ruth emerges as a woman who takes control of her destiny... She is a survivor, not a victim of circumstances, waiting for a man to change her fate.'

57. See the comments made by David Jobling in 'Ruth Finds a Home: Canon, Politics, Method', in Exum and Clines (eds.), *The New Literary Criticism*, pp. 125-39 (139).

their own ways, to their own cultural or ethnic identity, even when this means poorer living conditions without the benefits that dominant cultures grant to their own, are provocatively articulated by the journalist Rosemary McLeod:

> if they won't get on with living our way of life, whose fault's that? It's their own fault that they fail in the education system, that they're dying from Third World diseases, that they fill our prisons and live in a cycle of welfare dependency—so we can uphold the democratic cause with a clear conscience.[58]

This is the contemporary 'Us' and 'Them' discourse, which I, like Israel in Canaan, recognize and hear as one of the dominant. I am mindful of the point made by Victor Matthews and Don Benjamin that 'culture is always a delicate blend of story and daily living, of mythos and ethos'.[59] My fear is that there is a seemingly coherent insider mythos in the books of Joshua and Ruth that all too easily reinforces a sadly persisting and pervading colonial ethos.

If these are texts that give resounding applause to Canaanite and Moabite women for serving the Israelite cause, despite their opening Israel up to an 'ineffaceable strangeness',[60] what happens to women who refuse to do that? Many, of course, will not make the text at all, silenced forever by the pens of the scribes. Memory, including narrative memory, is always selective, repressing what it does not want remembered.[61] But what of those whom the scribes did remember and who remained keeping to their own ways and culture within Israel rather than choosing to stay outside with Orpah? I was curious to know how the textual re-membering process might have proceeded, my suspicion being that the result of 're-'membering may have been to introduce a very different woman than the one known by her own friends and family. Could that woman be glimpsed at all? Knowing that the likelihood of that was very slight, I wanted to keep the question in my mind as I explored the Israelite, and now the biblical, version. And who better to view than the biblical Jezebel?

58.   Rosemary McLeod, 'We're all right, mate', *Sunday Star Times* (4 June 2000), p. A9.

59.   Victor H. Matthews and Don C. Benjamin, 'Introduction: Social Sciences and Biblical Studies', *Semeia* 68 (1994), pp. 7-21 (19).

60.   Julia Kristeva in Catherine Clément and Julia Kristeva, *The Feminine and the Sacred* (trans. Jane Marie Todd; New York: Columbia University Press, 2001), p. 102, sees it as matter for praise that Ruth 'opens royal security to a permanent inquietude and spurs the dynamic of its drive for perfection'.

61.   See the essays in Bal, Crewe and Spitzer (eds.), *Acts of Memory*.

4

READING JEZEBEL

Who should the narrator, the patriarchal Subject, blame for causing his fellow men to walk in the wrong path, if not that most disturbing of Others, the alien woman?[1]

As might be expected, in 1 Kgs 16.31 Jezebel is first introduced in the context of her marriage to King Ahab, whose own introduction in the two preceding verses is telling, as one who 'did evil in the sight of Yahweh more than all who were before him'. The marriage notice in v. 31 then serves as evidence of this, 'and as if it had been a light thing for him to walk in the sins of Jereboam son of Nebat, he took as his wife Jezebel daughter of King Ethbaal of the Sidonians', a name meaning 'with Baal'.[2] Is the naming of the Sidonian king more than a lineage tag? If, as it appears, it is included as part of an anti-Jezebel introduction, it is interesting to remember that Saul and Jonathan had earlier named sons Eshbaal and Meribbaal respectively (1 Chron. 8.33, 34; 9.39, 40), although the writers of 2 Samuel (chs. 2–4) had apparently found that an ideological challenge and made 'shameful' changes to Ishbosheth and Mephibosheth.[3] I now only await the dire

---

1. Fewell and Gunn, *Gender, Power and Promise*, p. 167.
2. There are clear questions about the historicity of the Jezebel tales. Claudia V. Camp, '1 and 2 Kings', in Carol A. Newsom and Sharon H. Ringe (eds.), *The Women's Bible Commentary* (London: SPCK; Louisville, KY: Westminster/John Knox Press, 1992), pp. 96-109 (103), suggests that, 'it is unlikely that her polytheistic religion would have motivated her to eliminate the prophets of Yahweh unless these presented a political threat. If anything, the reverse would have been the case: the exclusivistic nature of prophetic Yahwism might have induced some of its adherents to adopt a crusade mentality against worshipers of other deities.' As others have noted, Ahab is introduced in 21.1 as *king of Samaria* although the political unit of Samaria only came into being after 722 BCE. As Iain W. Provan, *1 and 2 Kings* (OTG, 11; Sheffield: Sheffield Academic Press, 1997), p. 23, states, 'Those who take the book of Kings seriously must pay as much attention to its character as story as they do to its character as historiography'.
3. Mark S. Smith, *The Early History of God: Yahweh and the Other Deities in Ancient Israel* (San Francisco: Harper & Row, 1990), comments (p. 14) that 'In Saul's family, either *ba'al* was a title for Yahweh, or Baal was acceptable in royal, Yahwistic circles, or

consequences that must follow such a Baalist boundary-crossing marriage. I do not have to wait long. Immediately following the marriage announcement the writer states that Ahab went and served Baal and worshipped him and set up an asherah pole.[4] This implies that it is Jezebel who is responsible for Ahab worshipping what the writer would have me understand as 'other' gods.[5] The implication would appear to be that Jezebel was an *'ishah zarah*, one of these archetypal dangerously outsider women against whom the sages of Israel took such care to warn their students. As if to underline such a malign influence, he has the text move to Hiel of Bethel's building programme at Jericho, which cost the sacrificial deaths of his firstborn and youngest sons, Abiram and Segun (16.34). Guilt by association! With this dangerous Phoenician Jezebel now resident in Israel, the scene moves out from considerations of marriage to the much graver issue of Israel's religious identity. The concern is carefully plotted leading to no less than a contest between the gods of Israel and Phoenicia, with the question already hovering: can Jezebel's Baal be foiled? Imagining myself as a first time reader, I am now prepared for the dramatic tension ahead.

Israel's prophet makes the first move, staking the claim of Yahweh over the elements (1 Kgs 17.1). Round one: Israel's god sends a drought and Elijah is marked out for special mention and protection. The next sequence of seven verses in good folktale style ends with a problem; there is a lack and a need: Elijah needs drinking water (v. 7). And so the unexpected, and even daring, move to Baal's own province, Sidon, where another Sidonian woman just happens to appear in his path (v. 10). Coincidence? No. Israel's god is responsible for this too, as I, and Elijah, have been told (v. 9). The actors, Elijah and the woman, play out their appointed roles, but not without the twists that good stories demand. Elijah, the prophet of Yahweh, requests

---

both'. Although he concludes (p. 15) that while 'in Israel during the Judges period…Baal was probably no more a threat than El', this changed in the ninth century, a view largely based on the Ahab/Jezebel texts. He notes the inscriptions on the Samaria ostraca (ninth or eighth centuries) with *ba'al* type names, which 'have prompted some scholarly speculation about the widespread acceptance of Baal from the period of the Judges down through the fall of the northern kingdom in 722, especially in the north'.

4. See the discussion of asherah/Asherah in Chapter 1.

5. Smith, *The Early History of God*, p. 7, suggests that in the period of the judges, 'Israelite and Canaanite cultures shared a great deal in common, and religion was no exception'. See Provan, *1 and 2 Kings*, p. 70: 'The Deuteronomistic vision of religion is increasingly presented, in fact, as a later retrospection and an imposition on an earlier, very different reality'—although Provan himself remains cautious on this issue. What is not highlighted in these chapters is that Jezebel apparently allowed Ahab to honour Yahweh by naming their own children, Ahaziah, Jehoram and Athaliah. See also F.C. Fenshaw, 'A Few Observations on the Polarisation Between Yahweh and Baal in 1 Kings 17–19', *ZAW* 92 (1980), pp. 227-37 (234).

drinking water and then bread as well, but the woman cannot produce even the morsel of bread he begs; she and her son have so little they are near death. Again the tension: will Elijah's god permit all three to die of starvation? Can Israel's god act in Sidon? Elijah announces the 'do not fear' cue (v. 13) and I imagine the scroll writer's audience relaxing, already anticipating the divine command: the woman's morsel will be made into a cake and a divine oracle announces a continuous supply of meal and oil, until Yahweh sends the rains. As I now pause to take in the idyllic scene of the woman and her son and the prophet eating together, I realize why the story has been told: to signal the winner of the godly contest. Yahweh, the god of Israel can order food and rain, even in the land of Baal.

But there is more. Throughout these chapters there is the overarching question: who is the god of life and death, is it Baal or Yahweh? Producing food is one thing, but which god can command power over life itself? I can almost anticipate the next move: the woman's son falls ill. Again I imagine that Israelite audience watching as the child's breath fails and death itself is present. The tension is sharp: is Yahweh a god of death or life (v. 20)? For they have been persuaded both by the woman and by the prophet that Yahweh has something to do with this death (vv. 18, 20). But have they got it right? Relief flows as the prophet's threefold prayer and action brings the child back to life. This whole chain of events in Sidon has been framed by life, from the oath sworn before Ahab in v. 1 to the statement to the mother in v. 23. And yet the climax awaits one more verse, the response of the woman: she, the Sidonian, the Phoenician, recognizing the word of the Israelite god Yahweh spoken through the prophet as the truly life-giving divine word, finally declares that the word of Yahweh is truth.[6] Baal has been foiled on home territory. The small tale of the Sidonian widow is the larger Deuteronomistic narrative in miniature.[7]

But what has this to do with Jezebel back in Israel? She may have moved out of sight after that ominous introduction, but allusions, asides and reports have kept her in the readers' minds. The widow's accusation that Elijah has

---

6. Jopie Siebert-Hommes, 'The Widow of Zarephath and the Great Woman of Shunem: A Comparative Analysis of Two Stories', in Bob Becking and Meindert Dijkstra (eds.), *On Reading Prophetic Texts: Gender-Specific and Related Studies in Memory of Fokkelien van Dijk-Hemmes* (Leiden: E.J. Brill, 1996), pp. 231-50 (234-35), charts the repeated significant placing of the term 'the word of YHWH' in this narrative. As Phyllis Trible, 'Exegesis for Storytellers and Other Strangers', *JBL* 114 (1995), pp. 3-19 (6), expresses it, 'This Phoenician woman also does what Jezebel will not. She affirms Elijah and his god.'

7. Although, as Camp, '1 and 2 Kings', p. 106, notes, the two parts of the widow's tale may originally have circulated independently, as the woman in the second episode seems 'more well-to-do than the widow of the first'.

'come against me to bring my sin to remembrance, and to cause the death of my son' (v. 18) finds echoes in the later narrative of Jezebel and her sons.[8] But although Jezebel returns in the immediate wake of Elijah the life-giver, and life-restorer of ch. 17, I need move only a few verses on from the confession of the 'good' Sidonian to discover that dark deeds have been afoot in Samaria. For when Jezebel appears next in ch. 18, 'Death…seems to be on the brink of seizing all of Yahweh's prophets' (18.4, 13).[9] In this third year of drought, motifs of life and death are foremost. So once more the dramatic tension: who will provide food? Surely it cannot be Jezebel! For although Jezebel has been on a deathly prophet-killing spree, her own four hundred prophets are reported safe and eating well at her table (v. 19). In fact, in ominous contrast to the idyllic threesome dining at Zarephath, she has been hosting no less than four hundred and fifty prophets of Baal and four hundred prophets of Asherah.[10] If the question of who will be revealed as the giver of life is still hovering, perhaps the text is here allowing the death-dealer to be seen as a life-giver after all. But with the implication that Asherah worship is part of the Baal cult, a human queen and a divine queen are spelling double danger. The word *nabi'*, used both for Yahweh's prophets and for Baal's, heightens the tension. The message is: be careful! The reader must look twice to see which is which. Jezebel's Baal has yet to be foiled in Israel.

The contest, however, is not yet over; the familiar scene of the test by fire at Mt Carmel follows. Fire comes down and burns the watered offering and wet wood, the drought ends, the rains fall, and Israel's god is undisputed winner. But the drama continues; Jezebel, so clearly the 'bad' Phoenician, is stalking Elijah. Reversals and repetitions abound; with his god's divine warrant Elijah is now the killer of Baal's prophets (18.40). But if Elijah runs in triumph to Jezreel at the end of the chapter, he is also running in the direction of Jezebel, for in the next verse (19.1) she reappears, and, as Hauser expresses it, 'Singlehandedly,…dramatically alters the course of events. Elijah…is transformed by Jezebel into a whimpering defeatist…Jezebel serves

---

8. So K.A.D. Smelik, 'The Literary Function of 1 Kings 17.8-24', in C. Brekelmans and J. Lust (eds.), *Pentateuchal and Deuteronomistic Studies* (Leuven: Leuven University Press, 1990), pp. 239-43 (242).

9. Alan J. Hauser, 'Yahweh Versus Death—The Real Struggle in 1 Kings 17–19', in Alan J. Hauser and Russell Gregory (eds.), *From Carmel to Horeb: Elijah in Crisis* (JSOTSup, 85; Sheffield: Almond Press, 1990), pp. 11-89 (28).

10. I find it interesting that certain earlier commentators, such as James A. Montgomery, *The Books of Kings* (Edinburgh: T. & T. Clark, 1951), p. 310, and the editor of *BHS*, suggest that the mention of the four hundred prophets of Asherah should be deleted from the text. Although these four hundred are not mentioned again in the Mt Carmel contest, it is, as Gwilym H. Jones (*1 and 2 Kings* [2 vols.; Grand Rapids: Eerdmans, 1984], II, p. 317) comments, plausible for both Baal and Asherah (Astarte) to be mentioned as 16.32-33 implied that both were Jezebel's deities.

once again…as a powerful agent of death.'[11] The later Masoretes appear to have had some trouble depicting Elijah in this way, and pointed the verb in 19.3 as 'he saw', against the earlier versions 'he was afraid'. If Jezebel was death personified, then well might Elijah have been afraid. The Septuagint has a significant addition to Jezebel's threat of death to Elijah (19.2), with the words 'if you are Elijah and I am Jezebel', their very names spelling out the contrast in their divine allegiances.[12] Is Jezebel winning the contest on the human level? For Elijah is cowering. Again the irony: the one who could say so authoritatively to the widow 'do not fear' is now fearful for himself, a fugitive fleeing for his life and sharing the stage not with a life-giving Phoenician widow, but a dangerous death-dealing Phoenician queen. In the space of three verbs he is off to the wilderness.

In the context of Jezebel's threat, earlier delivered by a messenger, it seems he should be very wary of the messenger (the same word, *mal'ak*) who now appears before him, but the tensions, the apparent slippages, are soon resolved. This is a messenger from Yahweh, who once again provides the wherewithal of life with yet another spread of food (1 Kgs 19.6-8). It would seem that Jezebel, Baal's agent, has been foiled. Another small tale reinforces this. In contrast to Elijah's miracle of life for the widow's son in her upper chamber, in 2 Kgs 1.2 Jezebel's son Ahaziah falls out of his upper chamber to his eventual death, after sending to the god Baalzebub for help, the very name of the god acting as a reminder that this is Jezebel's son,[13] although the concluding verses of 1 Kings have already announced that this king did 'what was evil in the sight of Yahweh, and walked in the way of his father and mother'.

Yet before Jezebel makes her own fateful exit in 2 Kings 9, two more women appear in 2 Kings 4 in an apparent retake of that first scene in Zarephath, but with variations. It is these, of course, that are telling. The Naboth's vineyard episode has been placed between these doublets, but I decide to follow the women storyline and return to Naboth later. Both these later women are Israelites; no doubts can be cast on the religious credentials of the first, introduced as part of the prophetic community. Once again it is a matter of life and death and once again much-needed oil flows freely. Desperation leads to a flow of conversation but it is only the woman who

11.   Hauser, 'Yahweh Versus Death', p. 60, reads the text with Ugaritic motifs in the foreground. See Rick Dale Moore, *God Saves: Lessons from the Elisha Stories* (JSOTSup, 95; Sheffield: JSOT Press, 1990), pp. 117-21, for a strong rebuttal of such a reading, although directed at the work of Leah Bronner.

12.   Elijah means 'Yah(weh) is my God', and Jezebel is a distortion of 'Where is the Prince?', that is Baal. *Zebul*, the title of Baal, has seemingly been changed to *zebel* meaning 'dung'.

13.   This appears to be another negative misnomer—*zebub*, rendered as 'flies' in the Septuagint and Josephus, is a pejorative variant of *zebul* (prince).

mentions Yahweh; this time the miracle is attributed to Elijah's successor, Elisha, who makes no mention of his god at all.[14]

The text moves swiftly to the longer second tale (vv. 8-37), with its focus on the 'great' woman of Shunem,[15] the story of the oil having functioned, as David Jobling so nicely puts it, as 'a warm-up for the main event'.[16] This time it is her son who dies, with Elisha providing the miracle of life. But why tell these tales twice over? Yahweh clearly foiled Baal chapters ago; Jezebel has dropped out of sight, although there was an uneasy echo of Hiel's sacrifice (1 Kgs 16.34) in the Moabite king's sacrifice of his firstborn immediately before the entrance of these two women (2 Kgs 3.27). But the differences in the replays are notable. Now it is the women who call out or invite the prophet, and whereas the earlier Phoenician mother only gradually came to recognize the prophet as a man of god, the Shunammite recognizes this from the start (2 Kgs 4.9). It is the prophet himself who needs convincing! Elisha even has difficulty in responding, for although he is so grateful for the Shunammite's generosity that he wants to do something for her, he is seemingly so patronisingly patriarchal that she refuses his offer to speak for her in the high places with a dignified dismissal.[17] He, of course, is not put off, but, as it would appear, has to consult with his servant Gehazi in order to decide what it is that she needs. There is a nice irony here in the echo of Yahweh's announcement of Isaac's birth in Gen. 18.4; with Elisha a divine birth announcement requires Gehazi's prompting![18] Although, as Mary

---

14. This episode also reads as a tale from the underside, critiquing the economic disparities in Israel, with its added detail that the woman is at the mercy of an oppressive economic system, with creditors virtually hammering at her door and her children at risk of being taken as economic hostages.

15. The word can apply to both status and wealth. Clearly her building plans indicate a certain wealth, but the inherent ambiguity allows both meanings to be heard.

16. David Jobling, 'A Bettered Woman: Elisha and the Shunammite in the Deuteronomic Work', in Fiona C. Black, Roland Boer and Erin Runions (eds.), *The Labour of Reading: Desire, Alienation, and Biblical Interpretation* (Atlanta: Scholars Press, 1999), pp. 177-92 (191).

17. Mark Roncace, 'Elisha and the Woman of Shunem: 2 Kings 4.8-37 and 8.1-6 Read in Conjunction', *JSOT* 91 (2000), pp. 109-27 (114), points out quite rightly that 'it is difficult to say what her response meant' and that in the three-way conversation between Elisha, Gehazi and the woman 'who is speaking to whom and who means what is not easy to determine'.

18. Mary Shields, 'Subverting a Man of God, Elevating a Woman: Role and Power Reversals in 2 Kings 4', *JSOT* 58 (1993), pp. 59-69 (63), describes this as 'a parody of the annunciation-type scene'. Roncace, 'Elisha and the Woman of Shunem', p. 115, uses the word 'subverts'. Fokkelien van Dijk-Hemmes, 'The Great Woman of Shunem and the Man of God: A Dual Interpretation of 2 Kings 4.8-37', in Athalya Brenner (ed.), *A Feminist Companion to Samuel and Kings* (The Feminist Companion to the Bible, 5; Sheffield: Sheffield Academic Press, 1994), pp. 218-30 (229), notes other parallels between

Shields comments, 'No one thinks to ask whether a child is really the woman of Shunem's greatest desire'.[19] The story then moves to the replayed scene of the child's death and miraculous revival. But, again ironically, when the child dies the prophet proves incapable of reading the situation. If Jezebel was bent on destroying the prophets, even the great prophet Elijah, this woman of Shunem has to entice Elisha to be Yahweh's life-giving channel.[20]

As the reader, I find myself sharing the mother's frustration as she clasps the prophet's feet and blames him for what has happened, and then watches the failing attempt of Gehazi, which she has astutely anticipated in her insistence that Elisha himself accompany her home. The outcome, of course, is inevitable: Elisha at last follows the moves of Elijah, the miraculous takes place once more, the child lives, and the woman falls at the prophet's feet, this time bowing to the ground in worship. Once again the tale has ended with a woman's recognition of the prophet as a man of God, but the Shunammite has had to work hard for this result. Whereas the widow of Zarephath quite simply allowed Elijah to demonstrate his prophetic powers, this Shunammite woman has had to prod Elisha into prophetic action. If she leaves without a word, that doesn't matter; there is no need for a final affirmation of faith, as in the earlier episode, for this Shunammite woman has not only been a believing Israelite from the beginning, recognizing Elisha as a holy man of God, she has been pivotal in his acting as one. It is she who has demonstrated the power of Yahweh. David Jobling has suggested that the Shunammite is Jezebel's alias, on the grounds that '*any* strong woman is *every* strong woman'.[21] But I am wondering whether she, as Yahweh's agent, has been quite deliberately introduced as another foil to Jezebel. If one woman has been attempting to counter the prophet, the man of God, the other has been working with him. The contrast is stark: once again, it is a matter of the good and the bad woman.

There is, of course, a sequel to the Shunammite's tale. As the sequence has been read so far, the story of Jezebel, the Phoenician who crossed from Sidon to Israel but refused to acknowledge Yahweh as God, has been interwoven with those of the Phoenician, who became a believer in Israel's god even in Zarephath, and the faithful Shunammite. I am now wondering whether the sequel in 2 Kgs 8.1-6 is a quite deliberate move to reintroduce the boundary-crossing theme. For, read within the larger Jezebel Ahab

the Shunammite and Sarah. Jobling, 'A Bettered Woman', p. 180, sees parallels with Hannah.

19. Shields, 'Subverting a Man of God', p. 67.

20. Siebert-Hommes, 'The Widow of Zarephath and the Great Woman of Shunem', pp. 239-40, notes the ironic repetition of the phrase 'man of God' in vv. 21-27.

21. Jobling, 'A Bettered Woman', p. 190.

narrative, it is as if the writer is asking what is to be expected of an Israelite woman who is moved across the borders of Israel to live in 'foreign' territory? Will she maintain her faithfulness to Yahweh? So test her by sending her off to the land of the Philistines for seven years, then see what she will do on her return. The dynamics are interesting. As ch. 8 continues, once back in Israel the Shunammite moves into action in order to reclaim her land, but is immediately subsumed into a narrative eulogy of Elisha. Four times the text refers to the miraculous raising to life of her son, although attributed solely to Elisha, without mention of Yahweh. Gehazi tells this to the king, who ironically is none other than the son of Jezebel, although the text delicately refrains from giving his name. Here, too, there is a subtle contrast, a further poignancy, for this son will soon be dead, shot by the murderous but Yahwistic Jehu, while the Shunammite's son is present as a living symbol of Yahweh's gift of life (v. 5). The focus may be on the prophet, but once again this is a tale of blessing for the woman, who has returned to her both her land and revenue owed from the day she left.[22] Life and blessing come from the true God.[23] By way of contrast, the next chapter has the unbelieving Jezebel, unbelieving that is in Israelite terms for she too was faithful to her god even on foreign soil, thrown out of her window to her death, her body left to the dogs. Read together, life contrasts with death, and return of land with the denial of burial in the land for Jezebel whose remains are to have no lasting place in Israel.

If I were reading chs. 4 and 8 on their own, I would be delighting in the strength and initiative of the Shunammite, and rejoicing in the blessings that finally came to her. She is a Hebrew Bible hero/ine, a true 'woman of worth'.[24] But reading her story with what has preceded, I am aware of other

---

22. As so often, there are details of the story of which we are not told. For example, if the famine was so severe that she had to leave, how is it that there is any revenue from the fields to be returned to her? And why does she have to plead for her lands? As Mordechai Cogan and Hayim Tadmor, *II Kings* (New York: Doubleday, 1988), p. 87, comment, there is no way to determine this. John Gray, *I and II Kings* (London: SCM Press, 1977), p. 527, sees a parallel with the story of Naomi's land in the book of Ruth.

23. Albeit in this case through the agency of the king's official. Roncace, 'Elisha and the Woman of Shunem', pp. 125-27, argues that, being absent from the scene, Elisha 'has nothing to do with the woman regaining her land', that 'the woman did not need her husband, Elisha, or her son… She appealed to the king on her own'. The repetition of Elisha's name, however, does not allow him or the god he represents to slip out of mind, and indeed, Jobling suggests that the prophet has finally 'bettered' the woman, and that the 'diminishment' of a strong woman, as in the case of the Shunammite, inevitably 'takes precedence over other textual programs' ('A Bettered Woman', p. 190).

24. The use of the adjective *gedolah*, if understood to indicate her ability and worthiness rather than wealth or size, as Jobling, 'A Bettered Woman', p. 179, and Shields, 'Subverting a Man of God', p. 60, propose, echoes the 'worth' *(hayil)* of Ruth 3.11.

dynamics. She and the other believing women of 1 Kgs 17.8-24 and 2 Kgs 4.1-7 are nameless; only Jezebel, their would-be foil, is given her distinguishing name. They have been ciphers in the prophets' stories, no names required. For these have, after all, been prophets' stories, with the focus primarily on Elijah and Elisha, male prophets, and on the male gods, Baal and Yahweh. Reading these texts has allowed me a scrutiny of the writer's, or writers', ways of persuading the readers of their ideological rightness. Jonathan Smith's phrase, 'a political and linguistic project, a matter of rhetoric and judgement', describes this strategy well.[25] For I am now aware that once again I have been watching an ancient Israelite editor ordering texts where issues of ethnic and cultural identity have been a key concern, and where the identifying feature of the women has primarily been the religious factor, the god(s) they worship. This has been the boundary marker above all else. It is this that has justified the textual discrimination against Jezebel; it is this that has brought the Shunammite to the forefront of Israel's story. She has briefly emerged from the shadowy female underside of Israel to be a key figure in the confession of Yahweh, the god with power over life and death, which has been at the same time the story of the foiling of Jezebel, that Phoenician marker of 'otherness'. As I have been following the narrative thread I have been watching Jezebel, the boundary crosser, foiled not only by prophets but by women set up against her, the 'good' Sidonian against the 'bad', two Israelite Yahwistic believers against the lone Phoenician adherent of Asherah and Baal. The strategy has indeed been the foiling of Jezebel.

But this has only been one ploy in her foiling. Jezebel proved a useful tool, a figure who could be brought out of the gaps in the kings' history to be one of those marked figures whom the Israelite audience could boo, one against whom the 'true-believing' could be measured. She was there and available for fitting with key roles in other Ahab or Omri dynasty texts, which were also 'political and linguistic projects'. The episode of Naboth's vineyard in 1 Kings 21 is a good example of such a project. It begins with a typical storybook introduction, the 'it came to pass', Israel's equivalent to 'once-upon-a-time'. Once-upon-a-time Naboth the Jezreelite had a vineyard. As Alexander Rofé notes, the story itself in vv. 1-16 'is framed by this vineyard, providing an inclusio'.[26] The key point is that it was 'beside the palace of Ahab, king of Samaria', which is not so much a simple detail of geographical location as an ominous clue to what is soon to follow. Naboth's vineyard is

25. J.Z. Smith, 'What a Difference a Difference Makes', p. 46. This provides a good example of the strategy noted in Chapter 2, where this term is quoted.

26. Alexander Rofé, 'The Vineyard of Naboth: The Origin and Message of the Story', *VT* 38 (1988), pp. 89-104 (90).

just what the Israelite king, Ahab, wants for a vegetable garden, but Naboth refuses—despite the offer of better land or a good price—claiming the moral high ground, that this is land gifted by Yahweh as divine inheritance. The plot is now under way, and the reaction immediate. Ahab goes off 'angry and resentful', not taking this divinely legitimated opposition kindly. But read after ch. 20 this is not surprising; the text has already alerted me, as its reader, to this being the way of Ahab when confronted by divine challenge or reproach, for the episode immediately before the Naboth encounter ended precisely this way with Ahab setting out back to Samaria 'angry and resentful' (20.43). What at first glance might seem a simple narrative description of Ahab's reaction to Naboth's rejection of the deal, is much more finely nuanced. For ch. 20, that episode in Ahab's life in which an opposing king was allowed to go free, or, more to the point, remain alive, carried a sobering echo of Saul in 1 Samuel 15, alerting me to watch this Israelite king carefully, for if the analogy with Saul holds, the downfall and the end of this doubly 'angry and resentful' king may not be too far off. But the Ben-hadad incident was also a reversal of the Naboth affair in that, according to the text, as Israel's enemy, 'Ben Hadad deserves to be killed while Naboth does not'.[27] This is a king who clearly cannot distinguish right from wrong.

But Ahab not only went off, he sulked, lying on his bed and refusing to eat. The setting has moved from public dealing to private domesticity. I only await the entrance of the woman! 'Who can find a good wife?', asks the book of Proverbs. Answer here: Ahab, since such wives, according to Proverbs 31, can be depended upon to have initiative and good business acumen. But was that in the sense to be revealed here? Once again there is the significant reversal: if this is 'a bedroom conversation'[28] this is not the traditional or expected gender ordering, for here it is the king, Ahab, passively reclining on his bed, with Jezebel, the queen, taking the initiative, plotting and persuading. But what is it that she says to Ahab in v. 7? Significantly, later translators cannot agree: was she stating a fact, 'Now is the time to show yourself king over Israel' (JPSV), scoffingly asking a rhetorical question, 'Do you now govern Israel?' (NRSV), being plainly sarcastic, 'You make a fine king of Israel!' (JB), or making a comforting prediction 'Now you will exercise royal authority in Israel'[29]? While the text allows the choices, there is no doubt about her own statement, 'I, I will give you the vineyard of Naboth the Jezreelite', the repeated 'I' contrasting with the repeated 'you' addressed

---

27.   Larry L. Lyke, *King David with the Wise Woman of Tekoa: The Resonance of Tradition in Parabolic Narrative* (JSOTSup, 255; Sheffield: Sheffield Academic Press, 1997), p. 134.

28.   Rofé, 'The Vineyard of Naboth', p. 91.

29.   One of the options given by Richard D. Nelson, *First and Second Kings* (Interpretation; Louisville, KY: John Knox Press, 1987), p. 141.

to Ahab.[30] Who is acting as king? Surely Jezebel! There is resounding silence from Ahab. Did he realize the import of Jezebel's remark? I am not sure, again the text leaves that to the reader's imagination.[31]

The text here simply describes Jezebel as 'his wife'. But I have not forgotten this wife in her role as the Israelite, but still in effect Phoenician, queen. I know that she has been hosting four hundred prophets of Asherah at her table (18.19) and threatening the prophet Elijah to the extent that he has fled for his life (19.3). I have no doubt at all that this Jezebel will have a ploy for dealing with the reluctant seller; only the means by which she will do this remains the storyteller's surprise. It is, in fact, a death set up by correspondence. Deadly letters under the seal of Ahab are to be the means of deathly trickery in this telling. Letters are sent, and two worthless or worse individuals—I briefly wonder whether this is Jezebel's assessment or the narrator's—are primed with a false accusation of blasphemy[32] and treason. The details are carefully set out, for two is the least number of witnesses required for a death sentence according to Deut. 17.6 and 19.15. So, just the hint of the niceties of a trial and that disposes of Naboth. That the men, the elders and the nobles of the city, who put all this into action following their orders to the letter, knew that Jezebel was responsible for the orders is clear from the statement (v. 14) 'they sent to Jezebel, saying "Naboth has been stoned; he is dead"'.[33] The response is immediate. Jezebel is heard once again persuading her husband, this time to get up and take possession of the land, which the text implies now legally reverts to the crown.[34] Was Ahab aware at all of the intervening activity? Again the text gives no hint.

30. Jerome T. Walsh, *1 Kings* (Berit Olam; Collegeville, MN: Liturgical Press, 1996), p. 321, notes the speech also makes a contrast with Naboth; he will not give the land, but Jezebel will.

31. Janet Howe Gaines, *Music in the Old Bones: Jezebel through the Ages* (Carbondale and Edwardsville: Southern Illinois University Press, 1999), p. 60, interprets the silence as acquiescence.

32. The Hebrew uses the word *brk*, reversing its more common sense of 'bless' in the same way as in Job 2.9.

33. As Walsh, *1 Kings*, p. 327, notes, by drawing the elders and nobles into this act, that is, the elite, Jezebel 'thereby rends the very fabric of Israelite covenantal identity'. John Gray, *I and II Kings*, p. 440, comments that 'the fiction of communal justice' suggests that 'Ahab was personally influential', perhaps by virtue of his family's status in Jezreel. Walsh, *1 Kings*, p. 323, notes too the rather clumsy structure of v. 8, which serves to highlight its last word, *Naboth*, emphasizing that these are Naboth's 'own fellow citizens, bound to him in the web of covenantal obligations that constituted Israel as Yahweh's people'. Whether Walsh is right in reading the subject of the verb in vv. 13b-14 as only the scoundrels, as the grammar would indicate, rather than more broadly all those involved, is debatable.

34. There has been considerable discussion concerning the legalities of this land matter, but as Walsh, *1 Kings*, p. 326, comments on the issue of whether the law permitted

Naboth's death does not end the matter; there is a sequel, once the news reaches Elijah, whose reappearance might have been anticipated. This second episode, beginning once again in the vineyard and so paralleling vv. 2-3, is framed now by the ominous divine formula, 'the word of Yahweh came to Elijah the Tishbite' (vv. 17, 28). In customary divine voice, the prophet puts the accusing question to Ahab, 'have you killed, and also taken possession?', or more ironically, 'did you kill to get your will?'[35] A speech of ominous and devastating irony follows: Ahab wanted a plot of land on which to grow vegetables but it is he himself who is to be consumed. After the legitimating 'thus says Yahweh' comes the prophecy, 'in the place where dogs licked up the blood of Naboth, dogs will also lick up your blood' (21.19). God is seemingly applying the law of talion. But the prophet has not finished. Not only is Ahab to be consumed, but 'anyone belonging to Ahab, who dies in the city' (v. 24). Read canonically, the prophetic judgments of vv. 21 and 24 repeat those in 14.10-11 and 16.2-4, with all the added force that such repetitions bring. But sandwiched here between the two death-to-Ahab's-house prophecies in vv. 21 and 24, almost in parenthesis, are the words 'also concerning Jezebel, Yahweh said, "The dogs shall eat Jezebel within the bounds of Jezreel"'. Yet, as Phyllis Trible has noted, while Jezebel has been responsible for the death of one man, Elijah, in the name of Yahweh, has prophesied the death of Ahab's entire 'house',[36] a discrepancy that seems of little concern to the writers and editors of this text, although perhaps the editor thought this ending an overkill and so added 'there was no one like Ahab, who sold himself to do what was evil in the sight of Yahweh, urged on by his wife, Jezebel' (21.25). I note the marked irony in the use of the word 'sold', repeated from Elijah's words in v. 20: Ahab could not persuade Naboth to sell, but willingly sold himself, to do evil.

But, as I asked of Rahab's narrative, so now I need to ask here too whose interests are behind the shaping of this story. In the larger Ahab account, the story, as it is now told, would appear to serve as one of the justifications for the perceived rightful usurpation of the house of Ahab by the military leader Jehu, accomplished through a bloody *coup d'état*. The fact that Jezebel was responsible for the death of one Israelite surely pales almost into insignificance when read alongside the massacre of Ahab's family in 2 Kings 10. Death of Israelites was certainly not the issue. A quick glance sideways at other texts makes it clear that killers did not need to be cast as foreigners. The episode has read suspiciously like the David–Bathsheba tale, as many

this reversal, while we cannot be sure, 'presumably the original audience knew the answer'.

35. Walsh, *1 Kings*, p. 329.

36. Phyllis Trible, 'The Odd Couple: Elijah and Jezebel', in Christina Büchmann and Celina Spiegel (eds.), *Out of the Garden: Women Writers on the Bible* (New York: Fawcett Columbine, 1994), pp. 166-79 (175).

have noted, with Elijah as the latter day Nathan; his question, 'have you killed, and also taken possession?', could equally have been directed at David, although Naboth's death might have been higher on the list of evils, since he, of course, had been an Israelite and not a Hittite.[37] But the texts themselves seem to agree that what each has done was 'evil in the eyes of Yahweh' (2 Sam. 11.26; 1 Kgs 21.20), and in both the judgment on the fate of their house is similar (2 Sam. 12.10; 1 Kgs 21.21-24). What is the point of the parallel? That this was the way of kings? Was it meant to be read as a parallel?

A major difficulty in setting up biblical narratives as parallels is deciding which is drawing upon which. John Van Seters, for example, argues that it is the Court History of David which draws upon the Deuteronomistic History for a story of prophetic judgment and not vice versa.[38] The Naboth tale can, however, also be read as 'an Esther in reverse',[39] not only with its mirrored good/bad foreign queens, but also in its details of the fast, reversing the feasting, with Naboth sitting at the head of the assembly as unwitting as Haman, but in this case an innocent counterpart. But Esther, of course, as an Israelite queen in a Persian court, is honoured as the hero/ine who saves the Israelite day; that she is recorded as being responsible for the death of many appears to be of no concern for her reputation. The intertextual possibilities mount, with the suggestion of Susanna as yet another mirror version. As Rofé notes,

> Both stories relate how the wicked, moved by their passions and transgressing either portion of the Tenth Commandment ('You shall not covet your neighbour's house; you shall not covet your neighbour's wife...' Exod. xx 17), start an action against a defenceless innocent. In both cases, the latter is charged with a capital crime by two false witnesses, professedly conforming to the procedure of Mosaic law. The innocent, in both cases, is found guilty and condemned to death.[40]

37. Lyke, *King David with the Wise Woman of Tekoa*, p. 151, sets out the parallels: 'Just as Uriah is put at the front of the battle, Naboth is put at the head of the assembly. In both cases the murder is committed for the king by others, and in both cases the king takes possession of the object of his desire once his "rival" is taken care of. Finally, in both stories the punishment for the wrong-doing of the king devolves on his son.' The major difference would seem to be, as Gaines, *Music in the Old Bones*, p. 68, notes, that 'The Deuteronomist exonerates David because he remains loyal to monotheism'.

38. John Van Seters, 'Creative Imagination in the Hebrew Bible', *Studies in Religion/ Sciences Religieuses* 29 (2000), pp. 395-409.

39. So Robert P. Carroll, 'Textual Strategies and Ideology', in Philip R. Davies (ed.), *Second Temple Studies 1: Persian Period* (JSOTSup, 117; Sheffield: JSOT Academic Press, 1991), pp. 108-24 (121); Gaines, *Music in the Old Bones*, p. 62; and Helena Zlotnick, 'From Jezebel to Esther: Fashioning Images of Queenship in the Hebrew Bible', *Bib* 82 (2001), pp. 477-95.

40. Rofé, 'The Vineyard of Naboth', p. 104. The roles of Susanna and Naboth may have been reversed, but Rofé suggests the linkage points to 'an antagonism between

Was the evil simply the matter of the killing of Naboth? The note about 'going after idols' in v. 26 asks to be read in the context of Joshua to 2 Kings where this becomes but one incident in the much larger tale of Israel's evil of rejecting Yahweh and Yahweh's prescribed ways of living in the world. If I follow the view of those who would see these chapters as comprising the Deuteronomistic History and therefore the work of Deuteronomistic editors, then I need to be aware that here too I am reading a very carefully con-structed narrative. For in this understanding such scribes were significantly more than technical joiners in their gathering and seaming together of Israel's inherited traditions.[41] It is assumed that they had a purpose in this task, an intent to 'draw logical conclusions',[42] the evaluation of Ahab in 1 Kgs 16.30-33 being the result of just such a logical conclusion. My more pressing question is: 'What lay behind these conclusions?'[43] If, as the tradi-tional view of the Deuteronomistic History suggests, the work was an attempt to answer the problem of theodicy raised by the experience of exile, then the murder which Elijah describes as an 'evil in the sight of Yahweh' (1 Kgs 21.20) becomes part of that cumulative evil that led to Israel's disaster at the hands of the Babylonians. In this larger scenario for Naboth's vineyard read Israel, and Naboth's story is now recognized for what it is, a carefully crafted *mise en abyme*. This is Israel's story, writ small. The loss of Naboth's vineyard is the loss of Israel's land. Read this way, further ominous ironies are visible: the verb chosen to tell Ahab to go and take possession (*yrs*) after the mur-derous deed is done, is a verb from Israel's conquest traditions.[44] And if the word 'vineyard' is read, as so often in the Hebrew Bible, as a symbol for Israel itself, then 'an idolatrous king, that is, one who would lead Israel to other gods, would be guilty of stealing the vineyard of Yahweh from its proper owner'.[45]

different groups in post-exilic Judah, opposing each other because of their different origins and on social and religious issues'.

41.   Both Chapters 1 and 3 have noted the ongoing debate among scholars concern-ing the Deuteronomistic History.

42.   Nadav Na'aman, 'Prophetic Stories as Sources for the Histories of Jehoshaphat and the Omrides', *Bib* 78 (1997), pp. 153-73 (160).

43.   While Rainer Albertz, 'In Search of the Deuteronomists: A First Solution to a Historical Riddle', in T. Römer (ed.), *The Future of the Deuteronomistic History* (Leuven: Leuven University Press, 2000), pp. 1-17 (10), suggests that 'the Naboth theme was already connected with the story of the Jehu revolution, which was of crucial importance for the Deuteronomists', he concludes that 'the original social conflict[s]' was 'interpreted by them along theological lines as apostasy'.

44.   See, among others, Num. 14.24; 21.24, 32, 35; Deut. 1.21; 2.24; 3.12, 18; 4.5, 14, 22, 26; Josh. 21.43; Judg. 11.21, 22.

45.   Jerome T. Walsh, 'Methods and Meanings: Multiple Studies of 1 Kings 21', *JBL* 111 (1992), pp. 193-211 (201). See also Nelson, *First and Second Kings*, p. 14.

But where does Jezebel fit into this scenario? As I think back to her introduction in 1 Kgs 16.31, I realize that that was given to provide the interpretive clue. As the daughter of the Baal-named king of the Sidonians, Ethbaal,
she is the key to the disasters, now to be named as evils, that pursue Ahab
and his family. Why did Yahweh allow Babylon its conquest? Answer:
because Israel had followed other gods and not heeded Yahweh's word as
delivered through the prophets, such as Elijah. Why did Israel do this?
Answer: in this case, because of the evil influence of the foreign Baal- and
Asherah-worshipping queen Jezebel. It is all very neat. Elijah represents the
word of God, Jezebel the false word that leads astray.[46]

Various dates for the Deuteronomistic History have been offered together
with complex redactional histories,[47] but the fact that this story concerns
land rights, and the dire results of a cultural intermarriage makes the connection with the post-exilic setting proposed by Rofé both possible and
credible.[48] Read against the postexilic context of concern for a holy people
or 'holy seed' (Ezra 9.2), possessing the land granted by their God as a sacred
entitlement, Jezebel, the Sidonian, remains an equally key figure to the
agenda. For in such a proposed Persian era context the returnees from Babylon come back to meet a people of the land, ethnically related, but whom
history has divided from them. The issue at its simplest is: which of these
two groups has the right to the land? Answer: those who are true Israelites.
But now comes the more complex question: who are these? What are the
criteria? As in the exilic answer to the questions of theodicy, so here worship
praxis appears to be of prime importance. What has distinguished the group
of Israelite returnees has been their move towards monotheism, as opposed
to the 'abominations of the peoples of the lands', further described as like
those of the Canaanites, Hittites, Perizzites *et al.* (Ezra 9.1), a distinction
which must be heightened in any way possible. And so the wedge of a

46. So Walsh, 'Methods and Meanings', pp. 204-205, who sees Elijah and Jezebel 'in
functionally parallel roles: both advance the plot by mean of their words... Jezebel's word
is false from its inception... Elijah's word is true.' So too Trible, 'Exegesis for Storytellers',
pp. 3-19.

47. See Person, Jr, *The Deuteronomic School*, for a recent overview.

48. So too Trible, 'The Odd Couple', p. 169. Rofé, 'The Vineyard of Naboth',
pp. 97-101, provides a cluster of data to argue this case, including the use of the late
word ḥorim in vv. 8, 11, which, he maintains, 'conforms to the socio-political reality of
5th century Judah', to which Carroll, 'Textual Strategies and Ideology', p. 122, gives a
qualified response that 'Rofé's claim that "I Kings XXI appears to be an important source
for the history of Judah in the midst if the Persian period", may be correct, but I am sure
that it cannot just be read as straight historiography'. Rofé's suggestion (pp. 101-102),
however, is that there may have been an old story of Naboth which was retold in the
fifth or fourth century, 'shifting the guilt from King Ahab to Queen Jezebel and to the
ḥorim'.

rhetorical ethnicity, an ethnicity that in all probability belongs solely to the discourse, is exploited to the full.[49] Canaanites and others, who worship gods such as Baal and Asherah, must not only be avoided, they must be actively excluded, for, as Jezebel demonstrates, they are capable of leading the true Israel astray, even at the highest level of leadership, and of destroying a true Israel for the sake of its land. The addition of a murderous Jezebel has served to bring this narrative in line with the post-exilic, anti-foreign wives agenda of Ezra and Nehemiah,[50] an evil Jezebel having been fashioned out of the bones of a history and painted, as foreigner, as vividly evil as the text has her literally paint herself in the chapter of her death.

In each possible scenario, exilic or postexilic, Jezebel is functioning as a symbol of God-forbidden evil. But perhaps what is most striking is that the text appears to fracture under the weight of this agenda, for who is it who stands accused of the theft of Israelite land by killing? Is it Jezebel or is it the king? In vv. 17-19, in the initial confrontation by Elijah, it is Ahab alone who is called to account as the perpetrator of the crime. This continues down to v. 23, where the significant 'and also' introduction to 'concerning Jezebel' reads almost as an afterthought, with v. 25 functioning as the discrepancy resolution: if it was Ahab who was responsible, he acted that way because of Jezebel's dire influence. Yet, having made my way reading from v. 1, I have been led to believe that it was indeed Jezebel who had set this up. The text now, however, carries on to Ahab's ameliorating repentance, where once again there is no place for Jezebel. This time, however, the silence is not so much puzzling as ominous. In the eyes of the narrator her role in Ahab's evil has been pivotal, yet Ahab, and notably not Jezebel, has the space in which to repent; he refuses food, wears sackcloth, and so on (21.27), with the result that the punishing death is delayed for a generation. But the fractures are now widening: by the end of the chapter Naboth's vineyard is moving out of sight altogether, having apparently served its purpose. Curiously, the elders who passed the death sentence seem to have got off completely free, nor is any attention given to the fact that these leaders of the community singularly failed to question Jezebel's order, which the text has explicitly set out as transgressing a basic understanding of

49. Following Smith-Christopher, 'The Mixed Marriage Crisis in Ezra 9–10 and Nehemiah 13', p. 247: 'the possibility remains that these "mixed-marriages" were considered "mixed" *only* by Ezra and his supporters, and in the first case by the married persons themselves'. The named peoples are not so much ethnic labels of the time but 'old terms that almost surely have become stereotypically pejorative slurs' (p. 257). Tamara C. Eskenazi and Eleanore P. Judd, 'Marriage to a Stranger in Ezra 9–10', in Eskenazi and Richards (eds.), *Second Temple Studies 2*, pp. 266-85 (269-70), suggest difference in religious practice and belief as one of three possible distinguishing factors.

50. As suggested by Rofé, 'The Vineyard of Naboth', p. 102.

ancestral property. The explanation about the idols in v. 26, with its echo of the ominous information given in the introduction to Jezebel in ch. 16, now appears as the explicit key to the editorial agenda.

The fractures continue: details fail to add up. Elijah's prediction, 'Thus says Yahweh: In the place where dogs licked up the blood of Naboth, dogs will also lick up your blood' (21.19), is not accurate. Naboth dies in Jezreel (21.8-14); Ahab dies a warrior's death in battle in Ramoth-gilead (22.29),[51] although his body is brought back to Samaria where the dogs do lick his blood (22.37-38), with the further graphically nasty detail of the prostitutes washing themselves in this. The account in 2 Kgs 9.21-26 is admittedly a later scene, with a shift to Jehu, commander in the army of Jezebel's son Jehoram, throwing the body of his king, the said Jehoram, onto the plot of ground that had belonged to Naboth. But again it is Ahab alone who is mentioned as responsible for the murdering deed (v. 26), with the further unexpected and previously unrecorded detail that Naboth's sons were killed as well.[52] Then a further problem: this plot of ground, notably not described as a vineyard, is not next to the palace at all, but land a riding distance away. This adds to earlier geographical puzzlement: where is Ahab in 1 Kgs 21.18? In Samaria or in the vineyard which v. 1 stated was in Jezreel?[53] This is indeed a fractured and uneven text.

Detecting an original tale behind the work of later editors is always risky and open to considerable conjecture. And it is possible that the kernel of the story may have been a much more materially political tale protesting the exploiting greed of kings, where what was at stake, following Habel, was 'the conflicting principles of royal and peasant ideologies'. Elijah would fit equally well into such a scenario, 'enter[ing] the scene on behalf of the victim by espousing the ancestral household ideology'.[54] Jezebel then may have been

---

51. There is, of course, the famous discrepancy between the statement in 22.34-37 that Ahab dies in battle and the closing formula in v. 40 that he 'slept with his ancestors', usually understood as referring to a peaceful death. The solution has traditionally been that of differing sources. Na'aman, 'Prophetic Stories', who highlights the work of the Deuteronomist in integrating such source material, provides a case for the death in battle (22.29-37) being originally attached to the narrative of 2 Kgs 3.4-27.

52. Peter D. Miscall, 'Elijah, Ahab and Jehu: A Prophecy Fulfilled', *Prooftexts* 9 (1989), pp. 73-83 (79), suggests that this is a quite deliberate addition on the part of Jehu, to justify his subsequent killing of all Ahab's family.

53. This has occasioned much discussion. See B.D. Napier, 'The Omrides of Jezreel', *VT* 9 (1959), pp. 366-78; Nelson, *First and Second Kings*, p. 138; Walsh, *1 Kings*, p. 317; David Ussishkin, 'Jezreel, Samaria and Megiddo: Royal Centres of Omri and Ahab', in J.A. Emerton (ed.), *Congress Volume: Cambridge, 1995* (VTSup, 66; Leiden: E.J. Brill, 1997), pp. 351-64.

54. Habel, *The Land is Mine*, p. 31. Rofé, 'The Vineyard of Naboth', p. 91, has suggested that the contrast between Ahab and Naboth 'is not only that of rich versus poor,

no more than the devoted helpful wife! And while Ahab may have been unwisely exploitative, it is equally possible that in his own time Phoenicians may not have been regarded as evil-bringers at all, that the sharp differentiation between Israelite and Canaanite, if it existed at all, may not have been a major concern.[55] On the contrary, his marriage may have been the marker of 'a routine alliance of peace between two powers, in which the inferior power (Ahab) becomes son-in-law to the superior power (Ethbaal)',[56] and so have made good political sense for its time. Hayes and Miller, for example, write that Omri and Ahab were 'the most gifted and energetic rulers who ever occupied Israel's throne'.[57] And if one views this marriage from a Phoenician angle, then it can be seen as an acceptance of the Omri house by a significant neighbouring power.[58] If Jezebel's Phoenician background was a troublesome factor in Israel it may not have been because of her gods per se, but more simply because, according to recent epigraphic evidence, Phoenicians had 'an exalted notion of the king'. So, in the eyes of this Phoenician

but also that of traditional society against a kind of plutocracy'. Gale A. Yee, '"She is Not My Wife and I am Not Her Husband": A Materialist Analysis of Hosea 1–2', *BibInt* 9 (2000), pp. 345-83 (362), also suggests that Elijah's 'stringent critique…demonstrates the extent of the monarchy's exploitation of small holders'. Habel, *The Land is Mine*, p. 31, likewise sees 'a conflict between two ideologies' but curiously supposes that Jezebel 'reflects the royal ideology of Israel, which gives the monarch the right and power to appropriate lands as the wisdom of the monarch dictates' as against those who see a cross-cultural dynamic here: Jezebel came from a much more autocratic Sidonian monarchy, and either does not appreciate the different situation in Israel or deliberately flouts it. So Nahum Sarna, 'Naboth's Vineyard Revisited (1 Kings 21)', in *idem* (ed.), *Studies in Biblical Interpretation* (Philadelphia: The Jewish Publication Society of America, 2000), pp. 271-80 (271-72).

55.   As J. Alberto Soggin, *An Introduction to the History of Israel and Judah* (trans. John Bowden; Valley Forge, PA: Trinity Press International, 1993), p. 217, comments of the religious conflict of the final version, 'it is not easy to prove whether there really was such a conflict, or whether it is the product of later narrators'.

56.   Noll, *Canaan and Israel in Antiquity*, pp. 202-204, suggests this on the basis of the wealth and cultural dominance of Phoenicia spanning the Late Bronze Age through to Iron Ages I and II.

57.   John H. Hayes and J. Maxwell Miller, *Israelite and Judaean History* (Philadelphia: Westminster Press 1977), p. 399. They follow Alt's theory that there two capital cities, Samaria and Jezreel, one Canaanite and the other Israelite, and that it was the tension between the two that led to trouble (pp. 403-408). This, however, is not a majority view. See, for example, Ussishkin, 'Jezreel, Samaria and Megiddo', who proposes on archaeological grounds that Jezreel was not a royal capital, but was built and served as a military base.

58.   Zlotnick, 'From Jezebel to Esther', pp. 478-79, suggests that apart from Solomon, 'only Ahab achieved the kind of "international" status that made him a desirable match in the eyes of neighboring kings'.

queen having come to Israel with Phoenician expectations of a Phoenician king,[59] of course the king should have had his vegetable garden! The rub came when Naboth responded as an Israelite with an Israelite concept of theology, to which Jezebel responded with the wrong cultural assumptions.[60] But it was later Judah, Judah in exile or Yehud, or at least that grouping responsible for such writings as the Deuteronomistic History and Ezra–Nehemiah, which took this early narrative and used it to construct a sharp binary opposition of 'Them' and 'Us', based on a cluster of distinguishing features, such as ethnicity and worship practice, which together defined a chosen community, understood by Ezra as a community of 'holy seed'.

If this is so, what I have been watching in this ancient drama has been a tale of layered interests. Earlier features of what may have been an independent narrative now lie beneath a concern for a much later God-given identity. Regina Schwartz's identification of 'a principle of scarcity' offers a way of understanding the concept of exclusive chosenness that now appears to overlie the Jezebel–Ahab narrative. For through this 'principle of Oneness (one land, one people, one nation) and in monotheistic thinking (one Deity)' not only are one people chosen and therefore entitled to what is available, but such exclusive possession necessarily requires the silencing or the removal of those who would challenge this.[61] History appears to show movements to and from a welcoming of hybridity and difference and its resistance; at certain periods such cultural mixing is of little concern, at others it is vigorously resisted. Once again I hear this talk of possession and silencing with quite particular resonances. Applying a postcolonial lens I am able to detect connections between the strategies of the writers or editors of the Jezebel texts and those of my own postcolonial context. For the colonial era, as a whole, is also to be seen as one of 'managing heterogeneity, dealing with difference through imposition and restriction, regulation and repression'.[62] Although there is an added complexity in that 'the typical settler narrative' has a doubled goal, in that while 'it is concerned to act out the suppression or effacement of the indigene; it is also concerned to perform the concomitant indigenization of the settler' so that

---

59. See Brian Peckham, 'Phoenicia and the Religion of Israel: The Epigraphic Evidence', in Patrick D. Miller, Jr, Paul D. Hanson and S. Dean McBride (eds.), *Ancient Israelite Religion* (Philadelphia: Fortress Press, 1987), pp. 79-99 (81).

60. Also suggested by Camp, '1 and 2 Kings', p. 103.

61. Schwartz, *The Curse of Cain*, p. xi.

62. David Theo Goldberg, 'Heterogeneity and Hybridity: Colonial Legacy, Postcolonial Heresy', in Henry Schwartz and Sangeeta Ray (eds.), *A Companion to Postcolonial Studies* (Oxford: Basil Blackwell, 2000), pp. 72-86 (82), referring here to the work of John Comaroff in 'Reflections on the Colonial State, in South Africa and Elsewhere: Factions, Fragments, Facts, and Fictions', *Social Identities* 4 (1998), pp. 317-58.

> In speaking back against the Imperium, in the interests of its own identity
> politics, the settler site of enunciation will always tend to reappropriate the
> position of all those others with and against whom it has mediated that
> power.[63]

While for exilic or postexilic Israel that imperium was Babylon and Persia
respectively, for my own country it was Great Britain. In particular, those
entering Persian ruled Yehud were as concerned to be identified as the rightful Israel over against the 'people of the land' as they were to be a self-identified Israel within a Persian rule, just as the descendents of the much later
settlers in New Zealand were to regard themselves as rightfully New Zealanders, and not merely British sojourners. Different histories have, of course,
different circumstances and different time scales, and parallels will be valid
only to a point. But just as Phoenician and Israelite may have once lived
together without conflict and with certain intermarriage, so it was initially
with Maori and European settlers. Inevitably, however, given the power of
the colonialist advance, this did not last, and land wars and restrictive
legislation became the marks of the colonialist era in New Zealand. Ironically, in both cases, it could be described as a move away from the third
space of hybrid togetherness proposed in postcolonial analyses, particularly
by Homi Bhabha, to the sharp binary opposition of colonialisms. But the
task of restricting the flow of cultures is not easy, for, as Johnson and Lawson
point out, 'the boundaries of cultures are…porous' so that settler cultures are
inevitably 'sites of rehearsal, of (re)negotiation'.[64] The discourse of identity
may change and be changed, but traces and signs of fracture soon appear.
Later generations know this fracturing well. As I have already stated, my
own identity is as *Pakeha*, yet one of the Maori politicians in parliament is
descended from the same Scottish stock, and is thus a distant cousin. And
while our mutual Scottish forebears settled here in New Zealand as a self-
contained Gaelic speaking community, they had spent sufficient time in
Canada on the way here for a marriage with a Canadian indigenous woman,
my great-great-grandmother, so that my family identity as Scottish had fractured even before the arrival in New Zealand. But the memory of this was
soon silenced and only the genealogical searching of a cousin has recently
brought it once again to light. (Re)negotiation continues—just as land issues
that resonate with the Naboth narrative continue to be renegotiated. At the
time of writing, Wellington Maori had recently received a report from the
Waitangi Tribunal[65] recommending compensation for the land of which they

63. Anna Johnston and Alan Lawson, 'Settler Colonies', in Schwartz and Ray (eds.),
A Companion to Postcolonial Studies, pp. 360-76 (369-70).
64. Johnston and Lawson, 'Settler Colonies', pp. 369-70.
65. The Waitangi Tribunal was constituted in 1975 to inquire into and make recom-
mendations to the Crown on claims submitted to it by Maori. Such claims are based on

had been deprived, including the very land upon which much of Wellington, the capital city of New Zealand, now stands. In response, Dr Love, one of Maoridom's leaders in the area, stated 'The lifting of the curtain has revealed a history of calculated wrong-doing... The weapons of acquisition were the familiar ones of colonisation—the big guns, the musket, the sword, and the mightiest of all—the pen.'[66] Settlement negotiations will now follow. New Zealand's narrative continues, as reports indicate the legal fractures underlying present ownership.

Reading the penned role of Jezebel in the Naboth tale, and drawing on the analyses of postcolonial criticism, has led me to ask sharp questions not only of Jezebel as the silenced 'subaltern'[67] but of the very 'itinerary of silencing'.[68] For while in the text Jezebel does indeed speak, the words put in her mouth may well have been part of the mechanics of silencing an historical Jezebel. The fractures in the seaming together of the Ahab narrative clearly raise the possibility that she may have had nothing to do with Naboth or his vineyard. Yet, as the narrator's ventriloquist dummy, she now mouths a part by which, as Phoenician, she will be remembered by generations of biblical readers as the evil foreign murdering queen, not only involved in the theft of Israelite land, but finally responsible for the downfall of her Israelite husband's dynasty. If this is so, then I am reading the deliberate polemic of a religio-political movement within Israel or Judah or Yehud. If, as I have been attempting, I read it with my own political and contextual narratives in mind, how am I to respond ethically to such a divisive discourse?

For, as was the case with the Rahab narrative, the strategy itself is timeless. In an interesting postcolonial twist it can be seen in action in Albert Wendt's latest novel, *The Mango's Kiss*.[69] In this Samoan based story the main character Peleiupu, both in her quest for her missing brother Arona and her desire to build up a profitable and expanding business, becomes embroiled in a murky politics far removed from the life of their village in

the understanding that Maori are prejudicially affected by legislation, policies, acts or omissions of the Crown inconsistent with the principles of the 1840 Treaty of Waitangi, whereby the Chiefs ceded to the Queen all the rights and powers of Sovereignty (in the English version), Governorship or *Kawanatanga* (in the Maori version) of their lands, while being guaranteed the full exclusive and undisturbed possession of the Lands and Estates, Forests, Fisheries and other properties under their possession.

66. From a speech by Dr Ngatata Love reported in the *Sunday Star-Times* (18 May 2003), p. A7.

67. Gayatri Chakravorty Spivak, 'Can the Subaltern Speak?', in Cary Nelson and Lawrence Grossberg (eds.), *Marxism and the Interpretation of Culture* (Urbana and Chicago: University of Illinois Press, 1988), pp. 271-313.

68. Gayatri Chakravorty Spivak, *The Post-Colonial Critic: Interviews, Strategies, Dialogues* (ed. Sarah Harasym; New York: Routledge, 1990), p. 31.

69. Albert Wendt, *The Mango's Kiss* (Auckland: Vintage Books, 2003).

Samoa. The bent *palagi* (Polynesian equivalent of *pakeha*) industrialist Blundell says of Arona, whom he has had killed in New Zealand: 'He tried to fight me in my own patch… But…[u]nderneath that brain, that cunning criminal inclination and ability, he was still the honest pastor's son'.[70] The inference is clear, Arona, the son who left his family and his family's ways, became infected by the evil ways of the Western world, became 'quite monstrous' and 'without conscience',[71] and so met his death on the orders of Blundell, who Tavita, Pele's husband, describes as 'a white god who thinks he can stomp on us black ants'.[72] And yet Pele is finally infected too. Not only is she attracted and even tempted sexually by the *palagi* detective, but she in turn orders the killing of Blundell. The complexity of the conflicting cultural mores is nicely nuanced. Pele remembers 'the story of Ume and how he was killed by their ancestral frigate (i.e. frigate bird), in revenge for betraying his sister. She persuaded herself that, in a profound way, her revenge for Arona was that of the frigate'.[73] And indeed, with her sister and aunt, she takes the ashes of her brother and his wife and buries them in a hidden grove of pre-Christian spirituality. Pele is caught in the tension between ancient tradition and the seductions of the Western world. And so her husband, Tavita, who has been kept in the dark about the planned murder, accuses her, 'Pele, I've watched you being corrupted by wealth and power'.[74] The narrative is longer and much more complex than this would imply, but it builds to the climax, once again, of the killer woman. The difference here is that unlike Jezebel who remained steadfast to her Phoenician beliefs, Pele, while attempting to keep her own cultural ways in balance, is finally seduced by the power plays of a world that opposes that of traditional Samoa. But once again, the motif of death at the hand of a woman is used to convey the ideological agenda.

And so my fear that if I and readers similarly situated fail to ask the question of how we respond to a divisive biblical narrative carefully edited to set culture against culture and position the image of the killer woman in the forefront, then this may be not only a fractured but a potentially fracturing text.

If Jezebel had been a useful tool in the narratives explored in this chapter, she was still a force to be reckoned with at the close of 1 Kings. The description of her death in 2 Kings 9, however, brought sinister echoes of that Levitical threat of vomiting land. Attempting to understand what led the biblical writers to pen such a violent end requires another chapter.

70. Wendt, *The Mango's Kiss*, p. 437.
71. Wendt, *The Mango's Kiss*, p. 440.
72. Wendt, *The Mango's Kiss*, p. 438.
73. Wendt, *The Mango's Kiss*, p. 450.
74. Wendt, *The Mango's Kiss*, p. 459.

5

VIEWING THE DEATH OF JEZEBEL

Re-vision—the act of looking back, of seeing with fresh eyes, of entering an
old text from a new critical direction—is for women more than a chapter in
cultural history; it is an act of survival.[1]

The image stays in my mind, that final glimpse of Jezebel, standing at her
window, her eyes painted, her hair so carefully arranged, a woman fit for the
gaze of the world (2 Kgs 9.30), only to lie shattered a mere five verses later, a
scattered skull, feet and the palms of her hands all that will remain of her
(v. 35). As a biblical reader I have become used to deaths, from the murder
of Abel onwards. Throughout the chapters that I have been reading in the
book of Kings, detailing the turbulent times from Zimri through the Omrides
to Jehu, with all their power seeking and power destroying wars, there have
been dead bodies in plenty left strewn on the pages—but a death, an ending
like this still has the power to jolt. Even though I have attempted to follow
the narrator in the previous chapters, and understand something of his interests, the question still persists: why does she attract 'such visceral hostility'?[2]
What is it that I am seeing in this framing of Jezebel in ch. 9? If, as I concluded in the previous chapter, Jezebel was a useful cipher in the deliberate
polemic of a religio-political movement within Israel or Judah or Yehud,
does this entirely and even satisfactorily explain the violence of this description of her end? Why did Jezebel have to be destroyed so graphically? As
I search for ways of approach, for some further tools of understanding that
will make sense of what I am seeing in this text, I am mindful of Susan
Suleiman's observation that 'the cultural significance of the female body is
not only (not even first and foremost) that of a flesh-and-blood entity, but of
a symbolic construct'.[3] For it seems to me that it is not only a matter of

1. Adrienne Rich, 'When We Dead Awaken: Writing as Re-vision', in her *On Lies,
Secrets, and Silence: Selected Prose 1966–1978* (New York: W.W. Norton, 1979), pp. 33-49
(35).
2. Fewell and Gunn, *Gender, Power and Promise*, p. 166.
3. Susan Rubin Suleiman, 'Introduction', in *idem* (ed.), *The Female Body in Western
Culture* (Cambridge, MA: Harvard University Press, 1986), pp. 1-4 (2).

wrong gods, but that it also has something to do with the female body, and with what that female body signifies.

As I gaze at this last, and so unnervingly lasting, portrait of Jezebel, I note the details of those painted eyes and coiffeured hair, themselves framed in verbal acts set in train by Jehu, the erstwhile commander of Jehoram's army, but whose future as king of Israel has already been prophesied by Elijah (1 Kgs 19.16). This is Jezebel, the queen mother, *gebira*, of Israel, who has moved swiftly and cosmetically in response to the news of Jehu's arrival in Jezreel. I gaze at her, so clearly visible, so carefully 'made-up', as she looks out the window; the interpretive frame for understanding what I see is so much harder to discern. At first glance a woman waiting at a window could be a woman looking for her lover, and there are other ancient Near Eastern texts that provide possible parallels for such a suggestion.[4] Set within a Phoenician frame, this could be the goddess Astarte watching and waiting for the procession of her godly lover Eshmun, as they each play their part in the never-ending cycle of life and death.[5] But here, in ch. 9 of the Ahab cycle, this is Jehu, the killer of Jehoram, Jezebel's son. This is a warrior who, far from coming to meet his lady love waiting above at her window, is a Jehu fresh from battle, having indeed just shot not one king but two. Moreover, Jezebel's words—'Is it peace, Zimri, murderer of your master?'—dispel any thought of this being a lover. Simon Parker has suggested, citing an Ugaritic root to justify translating Zimri as 'strong one' or even 'protective one', that she may have been plotting not only to seduce Jehu, but to draw him into a political alliance sealed by their sexual union.[6] But this loses the sarcastic biting force of a Jehu addressed as a 'Zimri'. Her words come ringing out as a battle taunt, declaring she knows full well that this Jehu is already to be listed in the fateful tradition of murdering usurpers (1 Kgs 16.16). But could she be saying even more than this? If that earlier archetypal Zimri reigned only seven days (1 Kgs 16.15), could this be wishful hinting of a similar fate for Jehu? If so, history was not on Jezebel's side. But there is another sinister intertextual echo in the use of the name Zimri, for the book of Numbers in ch. 25 tells of another time preserved in Israel's memory, of an encounter with foreign women with foreign ways and foreign gods, and again most particularly with Baal (of Peor), which caused the death of 24,000 by plague. That threat was epitomized in the action of an earlier Zimri bringing his Midianite wife Cozbi into the very heart of Israel. And its resolution? The death of both by a single spear, an act hinting in itself to the closeness of

---

4. Ze'ev Weisman, *Political Satire in the Bible* (Atlanta: Scholars Press, 1998), p. 22, also notes the similarity to Jer. 4.29-31.

5. See Peckham, 'Phoenicia and the Religion of Israel', p. 84.

6. Simon B. Parker, 'Jezebel's Reception of Jehu', *Maarav* 1 (1978), pp. 67-78 (68-69).

this illicit love, to the glory and renown of Phineas, the dispatcher (Num. 25.10-13; Sir. 44.23-24). It would appear that Jezebel is saying more than she knows.

Why these details of her appearance? Is there a deliberate feminizing of the portrait of this potentially powerful queen mother standing at the window uttering battle taunts with her hair done and her eye shadow on? Perhaps a proleptic move by the writers to signal in advance that she would not be the winner in this confrontation, for in Israel, as in most cultures, warfare was for the most part the province of the virile male. This would then be an example of feminizing being used as a countering strategy for those considered inferior, particularly for the victims or losers in war.[7] Avtar Brah has pointed to the way in which this strategy also continues as a common racist stereotype.[8] If this is so here, is this a hint that those responsible for recording the fact that Jezebel as queen mother was holding power in Israel found this a problem? So, their solution: emphasize her feminine make-up. For what is happening in this text is the next stage in the military *coup d'état*, as the commanding soldier Jehu continues in the process of toppling the royal house, represented here by its powerful queen, Jezebel. Claudia Camp has suggested that Jezebel's appearance in all her queenly glory was a political ploy to rally the people behind her,[9] but viewed as the writer's rather than Jezebel's ploy I think its planned effect may have been similar to that of a German postcard from World War 1 days, described by Harold Washington, picturing 'a "French" female figure—with full decolletage, high heels...labelled "*la France*" (with) [f]acing her...a grinning German soldier with a huge cannon'.[10] Jehu may or may not be smiling in this Deuteronomistic equivalent but the writer shows him equally clearly setting his sights on her in his plan to be the winner.

Read together with the end of the chapter, there could be even more implied through this battle scene scenario. For these attracting details could be conveying the message that not only is this queen mother marked out to be the loser, but that such a powerful and assertive woman deserves what is coming to her. I am meant to be shocked by the dissonance of a woman with all her femininity displayed being apparently engaged in a military encounter and uttering battle taunts. The writer wants his readers to understand that while this is indeed a woman in all the feminine senses, this is one who has not acted her part as woman in Israel, and women who do not behave like

7.   See Harold C. Washington, 'Violence and the Construction of Gender in the Hebrew Bible: A New Historicist Approach', *BibInt* 5 (1997), pp. 324-63 (330-31).

8.   Avtar Brah, 'Re-framing Europe: Engendered Racisms, Ethnicities and Nationalisms in Contemporary Western Europe', *Feminist Review* 45 (1993), pp. 9-28 (12).

9.   Camp, '1 and 2 Kings', p. 104.

10.   Washington, 'Violence and the Construction of Gender', p. 332.

women—according to this narrator's gender construction—must fall from
their place. Crossing boundaries, including gender boundaries, has fateful,
even deathly, consequences; such people must be removed for the health and
wellbeing of the greater good. The writer could summon good scribal warrant, for a woman uttering battle taunts from the confines of her house is
easily seen as the deadly killer-woman, the one who invites but then leads
those who enter her house down to the shades (Prov. 9.18). And indeed that
earlier recorded Naboth tale implied just such a parallel.

I decide, however, to leave the choices of possible framings of the feminizing open as I move on to consider Jehu's counter question: 'Who is on my
side? Who?' (2 Kgs 9.32). Is this a countering taunt, even a dare? I note he
has no word for Jezebel at all. The tension in the text mounts as the two or
three attendants look down. A single-worded order rings out from below.
The taunting is over: a single-worded statement turns order to acted deed.
These eunuchs are decidedly not of the stuff of Jezebel, not even hesitating
in their choice to show allegiance to Jehu as they throw down the very one
they should have been protecting. This is chilling bodily betrayal with
deathly consequence. Yet questions of text arise following the downfall. Was
it the horses which trampled Jezebel's body underfoot or was it Jehu himself
(v. 33)? Did the Masoretic scribes get it right with their singular verb with
the translators being perhaps a little more squeamish in their change to the
plural?[11] The text itself does not linger on the victim's dying pain, its economy of detail leaving me, as the reader, the choice of activating or closing
down my imagination at this point. Then there is another cut by this verbal
camera to domesticity again: Jehu goes in to dinner. Is it the narrator or is it
Jehu himself who is so shockingly insensitive, with no sense of the proprie-
ties? A body lies outside, only to be remembered in the midst of the pleasures
of eating and drinking (v. 34). Then the details of that chilling discovery,
only the skull, feet and palms of the hands left there after that other eating,
by the ravenous dogs of Jezreel. However it is to be understood, there is the
skilled crafting of a double splicing, two eating scenes juxtaposed, with
minimal detail, each with just sufficient to allow the imagination full play.
All that is detailed is that Jehu went in and ate, but the order to bury 'that
cursed woman', seemingly delivered as an afterthought, moves the scene to
the eating taking place outside.

As I read the passage in the context of the larger literary work, one of the
most disturbing facets of the account is that this ending was already in place,

---

11. As Cogan and Tadmor, *II Kings*, p. 112, comment 'the MT singular with Jehu as
subject is the more striking reading and adds to the characterization of the protagonist'.
The Septuagint, Syriac and Targum readings, however, have the plural verb. It is interesting to note the variations in modern translations. The NRSV have the horses trampling
her while GNB expands the text to read 'Jehu drove his horses and chariot over her body'.

as it were, before Jezebel even arrived in the land. Over her brief, but highly charged, introduction there already hung the shadow of her death. For in that very same chapter another Jehu, a name in retrospect with sinister over-tones, had declared a similar divine prophetic word of dogs eating anyone dying in the city who were unfortunate enough to belong to the previous dynasty, the house of Baasha (1 Kgs 16.1-4), words spoken earlier by yet another divinely inspired prophet, Ahijah, against the house of Jereboam (1 Kgs 14.11).[12] The text has no record of Jeroboam or Baasha or any of their families being eaten by dogs or birds, but the words haunt the air as this deathly deferral now hangs over Jezebel. Elijah, the confrontational Yah-wistic prophet of this prophetic narrative, repeated these ominous words once again in the context of the Naboth incident, but in his update named both Jezebel and Ahab (1 Kgs 21.23), as does the unnamed young prophet who anoints Jehu at the beginning of this very chapter (ch. 9), only chang-ing Ahab to 'the whole house of Ahab' (v. 8). I, as the reader, am primed to await the outcome, asking in the tension of the deferral: 'Will the prophets' words be proved true? Will God do this? Can God do this?' Now in ch. 9 those free-floating, but death-predicting words fall to earth in a cluster. I recognize that blood splattering the wall as the urine of the doomed (1 Kgs 14.10; 16.11; 21.21; 2 Kgs 9.8)[13] and the image of consumed dung (1 Kgs 14.10) as the literal end of Jezebel.[14] While the crescendo that has built up and led to this ending has included a line of kings, the full power of the predicted death has fallen on Jezebel. Chillingly, the inference is that God has acted; with her death comes the reassurance that God's reality in Israel is not in doubt.

Clearly there are questions to be raised about the political dynamics of the world or worlds behind the text. If one accepts, with scholars such as Elisabeth Bronfen and Sarah Webster Goodwin, that a community's identity is intimately tied to those it chooses to kill,[15] then what is clear is that this

12. Those dying in the field were to be eaten by the birds of the air.

13. As noted by Peter Miscall, 'Notes and Readings: Elijah, Ahab and Jehu: A Prophecy Fulfilled', *Prooftexts* 9 (1989), pp. 73-83 (78), 'parallels underline the grotesque-ness of the scene'. He notes not only the echoes of the prophecies against 'All the males in Ahab's line', designated as those 'who piss against a wall', but also those of texts in Exodus and Leviticus concerned with 'regulations for splattering or sprinkling (*nazah*) blood on people and the altar'.

14. While the words for excrement vary, the image remains. In 14.10 the term is *galal*, while in ch. 9 the word is *domen*. What is particularly telling is the probable pun on Jezebel's name, for it seems most likely that this is a distortion of one of Baal's titles (*zabul*) turning it instead into a word for dung (*zebel*) attested in Arabic and Akkadian.

15. Elisabeth Bronfen and Sarah Webster Goodwin, 'Introduction', in *idem* (eds.), *Death and Representation* (Baltimore, MD: The Johns Hopkins University Press, 1993), pp. 3-25 (15-16).

woman who has been so clearly presented as 'Other' in crucial respects such
as ethnicity and religious belief, represents what Israel wants eliminated from
its midst, or, at the very least, what a section of later Israel wants written as
elimination. If rape can symbolize the fracturing of the body politic,[16] a
death that not only destroys but consumes most of the body must surely
denote the total destruction of its dynastic house.[17] Susan Suleiman's observation of the female body as a symbolic construct has a place here. But why
was such destruction necessary? The previous chapter followed Jezebel's story
in Kings from her introduction in 1 Kgs 16.31-33, where she appeared as the
Sidonian daughter of a Baal worshipper, a foreign queen who went on to
entertain Baal, if not Asherah, prophets (18.19), and who was responsible
for the death of a faithful Israelite, Naboth. This woman was clearly a danger, a woman to watch. Jehu's words, 'for she is a king's daughter', act as the
closure of an inclusion for Jezebel's story has been framed as that of a royal
Sidonian daughter in Israel. As I continue reading in this line I realize that I
am reading the tragedy of a textual Jezebel caught in the politics of the
religious and cultural 'Othering' processes of Israel, which, as I have suggested in the previous chapter, may well be the key to what happened in the
earlier Naboth episode. The later writers needed this figure of Jezebel as a
means of asserting their own sense of Israelite identity; she is to be the
measure of what they are not, by definitions that carry divine sanction. The
fact that this sacrificial 'Other' is the queen makes the message all the more
powerful. The text from the beginning has been saying: look at her deathly
influence upon the king, for as Gail Corrington Streete suggests, the text is
implying that 'Jezebel is lethal not only to the prophets of YHWH and to
Naboth but also to her husband and her son Joram, whose deaths are indirectly attributed to her machinations, her "sorceries"'.[18] The message of the
writer(s) is: look to yourselves, Israel. Israelites are Israelites and Phoenicians
are Phoenicians. Or even more explicitly, Baal and Asherah worshipers are
one people, Yahweh worshipers are quite another. Don't confuse the two.
Take great care that you are not falling into the sin of Ahab!

The full force of this 'Othering' worldview is sharply underlined in the
violence of this death and those devouring dogs. Susan Niditch has suggested that 'deep in the mythological framework of Israelite thought, war,

16.   See Amy-Jill Levine, '"Hemmed in on Every Side": Jews and Women in the Book
of Susanna', in Athalya Brenner (ed.), *A Feminist Companion to Esther, Judith and Susanna*
(The Feminist Companion to the Bible, 7; Sheffield: Sheffield Academic Press, 1995),
pp. 303-23 (309).

17.   As Cogan and Tadmor, *II Kings*, p. 120, note, it also brought to an end the half-
century alliance between Samaria and Phoenicia.

18.   Corrington Streete, *The Strange Woman: Power and Sex in the Bible*, p. 65.

death, sacrifice, the ban, and divine satisfaction are integrally associated'.[19] If the death of Jezebel has an analogy with the ban, which Niditch thinks may have been Jehu's motivation, then the expectation in killing her can be understood as a way to gain 'God's favor through expurgation of the abomination', for abomination is what Jezebel represents.[20] As Jehu says, the woman was cursed, therefore she had to be killed. It is this that allows the victor to eat so apparently carelessly; the burial was merely a sop to her royal origins. The feasting may even be seen as a victory banquet, celebrating the completeness of the victory, which is reinforced by the details of the body being almost entirely consumed. Read this way even the dogs appear to be carrying out God's consuming work, just as it is God's sword rather than God's self that will devour and drink according to oracles such as Jer. 46.10 and Isa. 34.5-6. This, then, is a death-as-God's-justice, to adapt a phrase from Susan Niditch,[21] where the figure of God is to be glimpsed lurking behind the grisly details of the text.

At this point I remind myself that I am viewing through an ancient Israelite lens, and that the issue is theirs and not mine. René Girard's suggestion that 'violence exists at the heart of the sacred' may provide a frame here, together with his emphasis on the generative role of violence, where peace and order rest on 'the unanimity-minus-one of the surrogate victim'.[22] In which case, is Jezebel to be framed as a surrogate victim? She is clearly without champions for her cause, even the eunuchs have refused to stand by her, and there is no indication that anyone weeps.[23] As Girard states, 'When scapegoating is unanimous, it becomes the almost indestructible "truth" of the scapegoaters'; it is this unanimous factor that provides much of the generative force. Applied to the Jezebel death, it can be read as the

---

19. Susan Niditch, *War in the Hebrew Bible* (Oxford: Oxford University Press, 1993), p. 40.

20. Niditch, *War in the Hebrew Bible*, p. 57.

21. Niditch, *War in the Hebrew Bible*, p. 74.

22. René Girard, *Violence and the Sacred* (trans. Patrick Gregory; Baltimore, MD: The Johns Hopkins University Press, 1977), pp. 258-59. Girard's theory includes the mechanism of mimetic desire and the concept of the 'monstrous double' both of which lead to 'the ritual sacrifice'. He himself, however, in the 'Discussion' paper in Robert G. Hamerton-Kelly (ed.), *Violent Origins* (Stanford, CA: Stanford University Press, 1987), pp. 106-45 (116-18) sets the Bible apart from other early texts as 'reinterpreting mythical themes from the standpoint of the rehabilitated victim' to the extent that the Bible has replaced 'the scapegoat structure of mythology with a scapegoat theme that reveals the lie of mythology'. Whether Girard would see a redemptive subversion of the scapegoat mechanism in the death of Jezebel, as one of the readers of this paper comments, is, of course, questionable.

23. See Burton Mack, 'Introduction: Religion and Ritual', in Hamerton-Kelly (ed.), *Violent Origins*, pp. 1-70 (8), for the summary of Girard's criteria.

Deuteronomistic writer transferring 'upon this vicarious victim…the fears, hostilities' and sense of 'sin' that fitted his tradition's programme.[24] Therefore all are to conclude that the fears and hostilities projected upon this one woman have been justified. If I read according to the supposed programme of the Deuteronomistic History, it falls into place as part of the great theodicy resolution to the angst of the exile, although the problem was one of which the historical Jezebel, of course, would have had no knowledge.[25] The Deuteronomists have provided the script whereby the mechanisms of sacred violence are seen in all their aw(e)ful action and Jezebel falls victim to the 'collective delusion'.[26] As with all universal theories there needs to be a little tweaking to gain a perfect fit. It can be questioned whether Jezebel as queen can be considered an 'irrelevant victim'.[27] While Girard's discussion of mimetic rivalry may provide further understanding, for certainly in such Deuteronomistic thinking there can be no rival for Yahweh in Israel, Regina Schwartz's theory that locates the origins of violence 'in identity formation' may provide a more fitting frame.[28] In either case, the very act of presenting Israel's queen as Other was not only her death knell, but her grisly death knell.

There remain other frameworks for understanding this deathly scene. García-Treto has read this text as a carnivalesque tale, raising the question of whether this is a deliberate tale of reversals, in the tradition of the carnival, which turns key characters into their 'others'.[29] Certainly that scene of Jezebel at the window might be seen to fit Bakhtin's identification of the 'the mock crowning and subsequent decrowning of the carnival king' as 'the primary carnivalistic act'.[30] The bodiless Jezebel at the end is certainly the 'nonbeing' or the 'inside out' of the coiffeured queen of the beginning, and the carnivalesque move to dwelling on the 'lower-body stratum' which Bakhtin identifies also fits well here. But that word 'mock' screams out from

24. René Girard, 'Introduction', in James G. Williams, *The Bible, Violence, and the Sacred: Liberation from the Myth of Sanctioned Violence* (San Francisco: HarperSanFrancisco, 1991), pp. vii-x (vii).

25. Chapter 3 noted the debate about the Deuteronomistic History. I am supposing, for the purpose of this chapter, that there was a consistent worldview through much of these texts, while accepting that earlier and later traditions have been edited together.

26. See Girard's essay, 'Generative Scapegoating', in Hamerton-Kelly (ed.), *Violent Origins*, pp. 73-105 (81) for this term.

27. Girard comments in the final 'Discussion', in Hamerton-Kelly (ed.), *Violent Origins*, pp. 245-56 (251), that 'violent displacement of violence on an objectively irrelevant victim is exactly what I mean by scapegoating: nothing less and nothing more'.

28. Schwartz, *The Curse of Cain*, p. 5.

29. Francisco García-Treto, 'The Fall of the House: A Carnivalesque Reading of 2 Kings 9 and 10', *JSOT* 46 (1990), pp. 47-65.

30. Mikhail Bakhtin, *Problems of Dostoevsky's Poetics* (ed. and trans. Caryl Emerson; Minneapolis: University of Minneapolis Press, 1984), p. 124.

the sentence. This was no 'mock' death, this was real. At the same time, a carnivalesque lens highlights aspects of the text that might not so easily come into focus otherwise. If Jezebel has associations with the goddess Asherah, as previous chapters have indicated, then it is possible that these too might be seen graphically degraded along with her, as in carnival, where 'all that is sacred and exalted is rethought on the level of the material bodily stratum'.[31] The chilling contrast of the feasting Jehu with the feasted-upon remains of Jezebel fits the visual representation of what Bakhtin describes as 'the old world that has been destroyed...offered together with the new world and...represented with it as the dying part of the dual body'.[32] But there is a vital element of carnival which is missing from this scenario, namely, that 'joyful relativity of everything', the 'ambivalence and laughter' in the car-nivalized image, which 'celebrates the shift itself, the very process of replace-ability, and not the precise item that is replaced'.[33] There may be elements of an upside-down carnival world, its reversals and grotesque realism, but this is not a world that recognizes relativity, this is a world parading in the security of its own rightness and there is certainly no laughter.

There is, however, yet another framing that would seem both to fit that initial figure at the window, and to explain the full threat of Jezebel's 'Other-ness'. For, painted as she is, Jezebel may surely also be seen in the tradition of 'woman at the window', a motif not only shared by such biblical figures as Sisera's mother, and David's wife, Michal, but also found on a series of ninth- and eighth-century ivory plaques, unearthed from four ancient Near Eastern sites, including Samaria. The significance or role of this window-bound woman continues to be debated.[34] Peter Ackroyd has suggested that she 'represent[s] the goddess as sacred prostitute'.[35] While there is also continuing debate about sacred prostitution,[36] painted women at the window have had, and, of course, continue to have, a long association with prostitu-tion. There would be a nice irony in Jezebel, the wife so devoted that she had a man killed for the field her husband wanted for his vegetables, being

---

31. Mikhail Bakhtin, *Rabelais and His World* (trans. Helene Iswolsky; Cambridge, MA: MIT Press, 1984), p. 370.

32. Bakhtin, *Rabelais and His World*, p. 410.

33. Bakhtin, *Problems of Dostoevsky's Poetics*, pp. 125, 164. García-Treto does admit in his concluding remarks that 'it is not easy to discern in it (i.e. the Jehu narrative of 2 Kgs 9 and 10) positive, life-giving elements'.

34. See the summary of views and discussion in Susan Ackerman, *Warrior, Dancer, Seductress, Queen: Women in Judges and Biblical Israel* (New York: Doubleday, 1998), pp. 155-62.

35. Peter R. Ackroyd, 'Goddesses, Women and Jezebel', in Averil Cameron and Amélie Kuhrt (eds.), *Images of Women in Antiquity* (Detroit: Wayne State University Press, rev. edn, 1993), pp. 245-59 (258).

36. See Corrington Streete, *The Strange Woman*, p. 44.

seen as a prostitute. But, as if foreseeing this difficulty, the text has already set in place the grounds for such a charge; the peace/murder opposition of v. 31 picks up an earlier interchange of Jehu and Joram in v. 22 where Jehu had roundly declared that any chances of peace had been blotted out by the enormity of Jezebel's prostitution and sorcery activities. Although the text has carefully provided signposts so that we, as readers, will recognize Jezebel as a 'bad' woman, this last charge seems quite superfluous. Or perhaps this was simply another cultural assumption; Israelite writers 'knew' that women have a natural inclination for promiscuity, so a bad woman would naturally include prostitution in her 'sinning'.[37] But Israel also had a long tradition of connecting worship of unapproved gods, or worship in unapproved ways, with whoring, using the latter as a well-tried metaphor.[38]

While debate continues about this ancient window representation of women, the fact that the ivory plaques were carved by Phoenician craftsmen provides an immediate link with Jezebel. The further fact that one of the ivory plaques dates from the days of the Omride dynasty and was found in a building that may have been the 'ivory palace' of Ahab and Jezebel certainly bolsters the suggestion that there is a connection to be found here. Eleanor Beach's funerary *marzeah* reading of these ivories adds to the possibilities of their interpretation,[39] in which case, Jehu's shattering of Jezebel as the removal of the last remaining obstacle to the throne may have been a deliberate insulting dismissal of the appropriate royal funerary rites with which the *marzeah* images were associated. But there is yet another possibility. One of the distinguishing features of these window-framed women is their carefully coiffeured hair, worked in the style that characterizes the Egyptian goddess Hathor, who elsewhere is associated with the goddess Asherah.[40] Is it coincidence that one of Jezebel's defining features is her hair-do? If so, the destruction of Jezebel may also have been represented as a shattering of the goddess Hathor/Asherah herself. Another frame with deep historical

37.   It is not only the Israelite prophets and sages who assume this, among whom the later sage Ben Sira is, of course, the prime example. Christine Brooke-Rose, 'Woman as a Semiotic Object', in Suleiman (ed.), *The Female Body in Western Culture*, pp. 305-16, notes that the structuralist scholar, Greimas, sets non-matrimonial relations under the 'nature' heading in his culture/nature opposition, understood as one of the universal deep structures of human social relationships.

38.   But as Camp, '1 and 2 Kings', p. 104, notes, 'What was initially a metaphor, however, came to be understood with increasing literalness. Thus Jezebel is often interpreted today not as the woman of political power that she was, but as a seductress.'

39.   Eleanor Ferris Beach, 'The Samaria Ivories, *Marzeah* and Biblical Texts', *Biblical Archaeologist* 56 (1992), pp. 130-39.

40.   See Hadley, *The Cult of Asherah*, pp. 9, 47, 161; Ackerman, *Warrior, Dancer, Seductress, Queen*, p. 178.

shadings may also allow this goddess connection in a rather different sense. Susan Ackerman has suggested that Asherah devotion may have been expected of Israelite and Judaean queens and queen mothers, on the grounds that the motif of divine sonship in Judaean royal ideology may have had a feminine equivalent, so that just as Yahweh was the adopted father of the king, who became his earthly representative, so the queen or queen mother became the earthly counterpart of Asherah.[41] This in effect became the source of her power. While the Deuteronomists, assuming that they were the writers or editors, are hardly likely to have shared such a belief they might well have delighted in a slippage that allowed the image of Asherah to appear in human guise. And the woman at the window motif, with which they would have been familiar, would conveniently convey this possibility.

If there was an element within Israel which in the writer's, or writers', eyes posed a threat to true Yahwistic practice,[42] then Jezebel seen as an image of Asherah would add to the call to eliminate the threat, for there is surely only one way to deal with the Jezebel/Asherah image; quickly, quickly 'cut' her down.[43] Viewed through this lens, the unmaking of Jezebel, once woman, but now overlaid with threatening goddess features, is seen once again as a key item in the programme of reconstructing and reforming Israel's religious identity. But there is now a double dimension in view, for the window dispatch is not only the tipping out of an earthly human queen but also the degrading and bringing down to earth of a queen who embodies the sacred. For a brief moment, before this embodiment is consumed in a parody of sacred feasting by the dogs, the dismembered head and hands carry a sinister echo of the fragmented god of the Philistines, destroyed by the power of the

41.   Susan Ackerman, 'The Queen Mother and the Cult in Ancient Israel', *JBL* 112 (1993), pp. 385-401 (400). See also her later work, *Warrior, Dancer, Seductress*, pp. 152-54. This would be all the more likely for queen mothers if Asherah herself was celebrated as queen mother among the gods in Ugarit, as Ackerman argues appears to be the case, judging from KTU 1.6.I.44-46, where Asherah is called upon to nominate one of her sons to succeed the 'dead' Baal (*Warrior, Dancer, Seductress*, pp. 139-40). See also Cyrus H. Gordon, 'Ugaritic *RBT/RABITU*', in Lyle Eslinger and Glen Taylor (eds.), *Ascribe to the Lord: Biblical and Other Studies in Memory of Peter C. Craigie* (JSOTSup, 67; Sheffield: JSOT Press, 1988), pp. 127-32. The biblical text that gives the clearest indication of this Asherah/queen mother link is, of course, 1 Kgs 15.2, 9-13.

42.   There is now a body of opinion that the Baal/Asherah concern is not so much about foreign practices but is an in-house Israelite debate. Ephraim Stern's article, 'Religion in Palestine in the Assyrian and Persian Periods', in Bob Becking and Marjo C.A. Korpel (eds.), *The Crisis of Israelite Religion* (Leiden: E.J. Brill, 1999), pp. 245-55, is one of the many recent discussions of this.

43.   That this is a Deuteronomistic programme rather than part of Jehu's agenda is suggested by the fact, if 2 Kgs 13.6 is correct, that Jehu left the asherah which Ahab had erected still standing.

Ark in 1 Samuel 5. Is this what happens to 'foreign' gods opposed to Yah-weh? The addition of the word 'flesh' adds a particular chilling significance to the prediction repeated in v. 36.

It seems clear that whoever was responsible for this text was determined to highlight the destruction and elimination of this image of female 'Otherness', and most probably for reasons of their own politico-religious agenda. There may, of course, have been more than one hand involved in shaping this telling and more than one agenda. But was there a motivating force more deeply hidden that added force or fervour to their determination? Are there aspects yet to be explored which might add a further significance to the visible details of this death? While admittedly there are pitfalls in applying later European theorizing of the unconscious to early Israel, the possibility of there being certain universal subliminal drives which leave traces in the conscious, observable in the text, does allow a further explora-tion of some of the more chilling aspects of the text. With such a possibility in mind I return and look again at that woman's body thrown through the window. Gazing at it now through the frame of psychoanalytical theory I wonder again at its symbolism, recognizing that 'house' itself may be func-tioning as 'a metonymical symbol of woman',[44] with the window represent-ing the birthing canal. But if this is a birthing, it is a birthing in reverse, leading not into life, but into death. Modern psychoanalytical theory has much to say about the subconscious desire to kill the mother figure, the one who is always M/Other, which may go some way in explaining other graphi-cally violent details that haunt the reader and refuse to leave the memory. Is it significant or coincidental that the last mention of Jezebel before the death passage talks of her as mother (v. 22)? If a Freudian reading might understand the mother as dying the wished-for death, compensating for that early infantile loss of the mother–child separation, then I may well be view-ing not only the queen mother fulfilling this on a national level, but the god-dess-as-mother fulfilling the same desire on another level.[45] The underlying

44.   J. Cheryl Exum, *Fragmented Women: Feminist (Sub)versions of Biblical Narratives* (JSOTSup, 163; Sheffield: JSOT Press, 1993), p. 47. Elisabeth Bronfen, *Over Her Dead Body: Death, Femininity and the Aesthetic* (Manchester: Manchester University Press, 1992), p. 65, drawing upon the work of Jurij Lotman, writes that 'The lack of boundaries between the concepts such as womb, tomb, home is traditionally linked to the analogy between earth and mother, and with it, that of death and birth, or death—conception and birth—resurrection'. In Maori tradition in Aotearoa New Zealand the tribal meeting house is understood to represent a body, with the door as the vagina, so that the dead are carried in through the window, as a person cannot re-enter a mother's womb.

45.   As Bronfen, *Over Her Dead Body*, p. 35, writes, drawing upon Freud and Irigaray, 'the maternal body serves as a figure doubly inscribed by the death drive—as trope for the unity lost with the beginning of life and also as trope for loss and division always already written into life'.

drive then adds its force to the political agenda. This fits with Julia Kristeva's suggestion that 'separating oneself from the mother, rejecting her, and "abjecting" her', which she conceives as the essential step in gaining self identity, 'constitutes an essential movement in the biblical text's struggles against the maternal cults of previous and current forms of paganism'.[46] But desire for the lost mother remains, and may be repeated in the desire for the woman lover.[47] Perhaps, then, there was an ambiguity in that first scene; perhaps, if these images belong together, Jezebel, the queen mother, was also marked and indeed painted as lover in that first glimpse in the window. Because she is M/Other to the man, there is an inherent anxiety about woman as lover, with the underlying and lurking fear that she will lead to further Otherness which may spiral down even as far as death. Such connections between the lover and death lead back to that framing of the strange outsider woman against whom the ancient Israelite sages took such care to warn their pupils.

This leads again to the matter of the death itself, that trampling of the horses, that spattered blood—that skull, feet and palms of the hands, the all that remains. A death that is disintegration and destruction of all visible signs of sexuality is surely disempowerment indeed of the fearfulness of the sexual object. 'Woman' without a 'body' is surely a contradiction in terms, especially in a patriarchal world where 'Female sexuality and women's powers of reproduction are the defining (cultural) characteristics of women'.[48] And yet that head, so graphically described at the beginning of the scene, with its made-up eyes and coiffeured hair, refuses the erasure of femininity. And even the feet and the palms of the hand remain as traces of the sexual, when read as the ancient euphemisms for penis and genitalia. In the psychoanalytic terms of Freud and Lacan, this is both the castrated body and the phallic head of the mother. Here the fantasy of the phallic mother is being played out in the political world of Israel for all to see, its lack so clearly visible, its dangers resolved by Jehu, the male of the phallic power, the male embodiment countering that lack of the opposing female. Jehu is hero indeed. And if the femaleness of Jezebel carried within it the femaleness of goddesses, then this is double death, double erasure. Jezebel/Asherah has thus been dispatched, her body eaten by the dogs so that 'no-one can say this is Jezebel' (v. 37).

46. Julia Kristeva, *New Maladies of the Soul* (trans. Ross Guberman; New York: Columbia University Press, 1995), p. 118, continuing, 'as well as using this negation to resume contact with her, to define oneself according to her, and to "rebuild" her'. Kristeva suggests that the mother figure is ambiguous, that she is an '*ab-ject*—a magnet of fascination and repulsion'.

47. Bronfen, *Over Her Dead Body*, p. 118.

48. Elizabeth Grosz, *Volatile Bodies: Toward a Corporeal Feminism* (Bloomington: Indiana University Press, 1994), pp. 13-14.

Yet there is an ambiguity even within the telling. The messengers report the existence of the head, feet and palms of the hand, which implies that 'There is still something of the subject bound up with them', which in turn adds to the feelings of disgust and repulsion that body bits evoke.[49] But Jehu's response in vv. 36-37 is in terms of the earlier prophecy that talks of those remains as dung. This, of course, intensifies the horror, for if human corpses have the power to disturb, lying between the living and non-living, and indeed a fragmented corpse even more so,[50] a corpse whose chewed remains have been incorporated into the stomachs of dogs to end as dung lying on the ground leaves an even more profound sense of disturbance and disquiet, as the disturbing horror of a life/death anomaly.[51] If, as in Kristeva's theory of abjection, death as the abject 'confronts us...with those fragile states where man strays on the territories of *animal*', Jezebel's deathly remains evacuated from an animal's feasting must surely confront us with abjection upon abjection.[52] It is, of course, yet another reversal of the natural order, for instead of the male penetrating the female, the female has entered the body of a dog, and been expelled as polluting dung. The contamination that has moved from Jezebel, the woman, to the dogs and which now lies on the ground is visible proof of the danger which Jehu has manfully overcome. If 'Excrement poses a threat to the center—to life, to the proper, the clean— not from within but from its outermost margin', then this threat calls for the one able to 'get rid of it quickly'.[53] This Jehu has done; Israel is safe again. Thanks be to Jehu! That is what the text would have us believe. But in its very attention to the danger that it wished to eradicate, it has made sure that this repression would fail.[54] While Jehu's words 'no-one can say this is Jezebel' (v. 37) close the chapter, not only does that muted head, feet and hands remain in view, but I, as the reader, may still gaze at Jezebel, the figure in the window, and detect the passage of the fall of the feminine divine. While in Lacanian terms the feminine is essentially symbolic of a lack,

49. Grosz, *Volatile Bodies*, p. 81.

50. So Bronfen, *Over Her Dead Body*, p. 54, 'narrative representations of death (whether visual or textual) serve to show that any "voyeur" is always also implicated in the field of vision and that the act of fragmenting and objectifying the body of another ricochets back by destabilising the spectator's position as well'.

51. Julia Kristeva, *Powers of Horror: An Essay on Abjection* (trans. Leon S. Roudiez; New York: Columbia University Press, 1982), p. 4.

52. Kristeva, *Powers of Horror*, p. 12.

53. Grosz, *Volatile Bodies*, p. 207, drawing upon Kristeva.

54. See Elisabeth Bronfen, 'From Omphalos to Phallus: Cultural Representations of Femininity and Death', *Women: A Cultural Review* 3 (1992), pp. 145-58 (146): 'representations are symptoms that visualise even as they conceal that which is too dangerous to articulate openly, but too fascinating to repress successfully... At the same time these representations let the repressed return, albeit in a disguised manner.'

understood as the lack of the phallus and all that that represents, in a twist of this understanding the queen mothers of Israel, and most notably, this Phoenician queen mother, whom the text itself has associated with Asherah, carry within the texts signs of the feminine divine, now lacking in the deity, and witness to Israel's desire to thrust that out of its midst. In their careful use of the traditional woman-in-the-window motif, the writers have unwittingly allowed the trace of the repressed a continuing presence.

Many of these frames for reading bear close resemblances to each other, and each allows a certain aspect to appear more clearly. In the end, no single frame can do justice to this many-layered portrait of the woman who now lingers as body parts, likened to excreta, this once powerful, once Phoenician, once goddess-associated woman. The final question, of course, is whether such careful viewing matters—after all, this is merely text, and ancient text at that. And if the passage is a painful and even unsettling one to read, then, as Richard Bowman and Richard Swanson have written, 'The violence of the Christian and Jewish Scriptures is neither new nor surprising'. But their next words set the challenge: 'What ought to be surprising are the strategies adopted by readers that enable them to ignore this violence… Our world is violent; our texts are complicit in that violence; our interpretations share in that complicity.'[55] Attempting to understand something both of the strategies employed and the underlying motivating fears links the biblical and contemporary worlds, for our contemporary contexts and our present world provide their own examples of violent 'Othering'. Jezebel, the woman, was an outsider in Israel's political manoeuvrings. As Elisabeth Bronfen writes in the context of her study of the visual and textual representation of the death of women in eighteenth- and nineteenth-century European culture, 'As the outsider per se, Woman can…stand for a complete negation of the ruling norm, for the element which disrupts the bonds of normal conventions… Over her dead body, cultural norms are reconfirmed or secured.'[56] This, I suggest, would accord well with the view of the writer or writers of the books of the Kings. As one item in their programme, that dead, dismembered body helped to secure the cultural view they wished to present as the desirable, and in their perception quite crucial, 'norm'. But my framing has also highlighted that other quite particular aspect of their work, their need for the death of the goddess who would oppose the power of the one (male) deity Yahweh, who gave identity to Israel. But if the story of Jezebel's death is the story of the attempted death of the M/Other), known in one

55. Richard G. Bowman and Richard W. Swanson, 'Samson and the Son of God or Dead Heroes and Dead Goats: Ethical Readings of Narrative Violence in Judges and Matthew', *Semeia* 77 (1997), pp. 59-73 (59-60).

56. Bronfen, *Over Her Dead Body*, p. 181.

guise as Asherah, the biblically hidden consort of Yahweh,[57] and in another as the Sidonian, the Canaanite (Gen. 10.15), whose early shared history Israel was at such pains to deny, it is paradoxically a tale told by a muted head, a remnant of the (his)story of the northern kingdom, so soon to be cut from its lower body, Judah—a tale in a long history of a people notably ambivalent about the stranger in their midst.[58]

Or has such framing overpowered the text? Perhaps, at the end of the day, Jezebel was just as the text has painted her, an overpowering murdering woman who caused both her husband and her husband's people to 'sin', and who therefore deserved her end. I imagine the writer or writers would be pleased if I accepted that verdict. No; it is too late. My interest in the framings of Jezebel, and the careful crafting of these interest-laden viewings denies me that easy option. The overlays that I have glimpsed have persuaded me that there are dynamics within this text whose consequences reach far beyond the world of the houses of Ahab and Jehu. For while on the textual level of my engagement with 2 Kings 9 I shall mourn the destruction of the woman Jezebel and welcome that sign of feminine deity that I have glimpsed standing at the window, resisting final erasure, I read it with an awareness that this is one of the many stories told over time and in many places to justify the rejection of the Other, and as such adds to their force. Kristeva finds in the 'problem of foreigners'

> an invitation…[t]o discover our disturbing otherness, for that indeed is what bursts in to confront that 'demon', that threat, that apprehension generated by the projective apparition of the other at the heart of what we persist in maintaining as a proper, solid 'us'.[59]

But what is the ethical responsibility of the reader, when faced with a text such as this, that denies and rejects such an invitation?[60] For while the different frames may have highlighted different outlines and shadings behind and within this chilling death scene, each of the images has carried with it profound messages to the reader which have served to compound my

---

57. But suggested by the inscriptions found at Kuntillet 'Ajrud and Khirbet el-Qom.

58. As I noted in Chapter 2, such ambivalence is particularly marked by the distinction made between the *zar* and the *ger*.

59. Julia Kristeva, *Strangers to Ourselves* (trans. Leon S. Roudiez; New York: Columbia University Press, 1991), p. 192. She concludes, p. 195, that 'A paradoxical community is emerging, made up of foreigners who are reconciled to themselves to the extent that they recognize themselves as foreigners'.

60. Norma Claire Moruzzi, 'National Abjects: Julia Kristeva on the Process of Political Self-Identification', in Kelly Oliver (ed.), *Ethics, Politics, and Difference in Julia Kristeva's Writing* (New York: Routledge, 1993), pp. 135-49 (136), notes, 'the strange absence of any consideration of racism and racial estrangement in Kristeva's theoretical work'.

discomfort. Gary Phillips and Danna Fewell have issued a call to read texts with an openness and responsibility to the Other, with the challenge that 'Our responsibility as critical readers is to uncode all of the text's mortal faces that plead for us to snatch them back from the Nothingness'.[61] Have I uncoded and uncovered the face of Jezebel? Among the images that I have seen through my shifting frames was there a face of a Jezebel waiting to be snatched back? I am not sure that I have seen all her faces even yet, but I have recognized framings that I would wish to remove, framings that have been applied to many others over the centuries, and harmfully. If a careful attention to detail and textual strategy is to be more than a scholarly exercise, if 'assuming responsibility for our critical studies' involves 'a moral obligation toward all those…who are affected by our critical biblical studies',[62] if, in Adrienne Rich's much-quoted words, 'We need to know the writing of the past, and know it differently than we have ever known it; not to pass on a tradition but to break its hold over us',[63] then yes, indeed, I am convinced that such careful viewing matters.

61. Gary A. Phillips and Danna Nolan Fewell, 'Ethics, Bible, Reading As If', *Semeia* 77 (1997), pp. 1-21 (7-8).

62. Daniel Patte, 'Critical Biblical Studies from a Semiotics Perspective', *Semeia* 81 (1998), pp. 3-26 (22).

63. Rich, 'When We Dead Awaken', p. 35.

6

FURTHER FRAMINGS

No text is an island.[1]

All of an idea's interactions are a part of its identity. The truth about the idea
thus cannot be comprehended by a single consciousness.[2]

If careful viewing matters, there is also the question of what one views. Texts
are never read in a readerly vacuum, but are constantly spiralling out into
conversation with other texts. The term 'intertextuality', introduced by Julia
Kristeva, but owing much to the work of Mikhail Bakhtin, is a recognition of
this.[3] Kristeva ascribes to Bakhtin the much-quoted insight that 'any text is
constructed as a mosaic of quotations; any text is the absorption and transformation of another'. As she explains further: 'the notion of *intertextuality*
replaces that of intersubjectivity... Bakhtin considers writing as a reading of
the anterior literary corpus and the text as an absorption of and reply to
another text'.[4] For, as Carol Newsom explains, 'an idea does not live in a
person's isolated individual consciousness but only insofar as it enters into
dialogical relations with other ideas and with the ideas of others'.[5] Of course
the very setting of texts within a canon already sets up an expectation that
these texts are not meant to be read in isolation, but read together can be
understood as texts in a dialogic relationship, with conversations naturally
flowing to and fro. The very phrase 'to and fro' implies that this is not a

1. Peter D. Miscall, 'Isaiah: New Heavens, New Earth, New Book', in Danna Nolan
Fewell (ed.), *Reading Between Texts: Intertextuality and the Hebrew Bible* (Literary Currents
in Biblical Interpretation; Louisville, KY: Westminster/John Knox Press, 1992), pp. 41-56
(45).
2. Carol A. Newsom, *The Book of Job: A Contest of Moral Imaginations* (Oxford:
Oxford University Press, 2003), p. 23.
3. See Julia Kristeva, 'Bakhtin, le mot, le dialogue at le roman', *Critique* 33 (1967),
pp. 438-65.
4. Quoted from the translation of Kristeva's 'Word, Dialogue and Novel' by Alice
Jardine, Thomas Gora and Léon S. Roudiez, in Toril Moi (ed.), *The Kristeva Reader*
(Oxford: Basil Blackwell, 1986), pp. 34-61 (37, 39).
5. Newsom, *The Book of Job*, p. 37.

time-bound matter of conscious tradition-critical reworkings of former motifs or themes or deliberate intratextual borrowings but is a recognition that ideas are always in flux. While later writers may quite consciously and deliberately rework earlier texts into their own to set a conversation in action and provoke their readers or audience to consider what is involved in such a parallel or contrast, or even dissonance, earlier images and expressions may almost surreptitiously find a place in later texts. Where these appear and are detected, we, as readers, may discover dimensions within the texts of which the authors were quite unaware, and enter into an intertextual conversation of which the author heard not a whisper.

The possibility of detecting traces of such conversations between certain later texts and those of the Rahab and Jezebel narratives encourages me to explore this further. Will I find echoes of these earlier texts? And, if so, will it be possible to make any decisions, at this distance in time, as to whether these were deliberately encoded, or whether these are echoes that have settled in the texts by chance, but to the enrichment of the reading? And might there be a combination of the two, some echoes seemingly intended to be decoded, others much more likely to be a matter of happenstance? And if such echoes now link several texts, what might be the cumulative effect of such a multi-dimensioned or polyphonic reading on me as the reader? This chapter is therefore an exploration to see whether there are any discoverable traces of Rahab and Jezebel in other texts, and, if so, what the effect of these might be.

It was an article by Jim Perkinson that alerted me to the traces of the earlier Canaanite in the account of Jesus' encounter with the Syrophoenician woman, an encounter told both in the Gospel of Mark (Mk 7.24-30) and the Gospel of Matthew (Mt. 15.21-28).[6] In the version told in Mark, Jesus goes off to the region of Tyre in search of peace and quiet only to be confronted by a Syrophoenician woman, begging healing for her daughter (Mk 7.24-26). A Syrophoenician met in Tyre is, of course, not only a Gentile but a person of the land. And while Tyre may not be Sidon, a Syrophoenician woman allows an immediate connection with those chapters in the book of Kings that I have been reading in connection with Jezebel. An echo is already sounding. If a key feature of those earlier texts was the matter of identity and difference, am I to read these versions of this encounter with the expectation that Jesus too is about to be drawn into this? In Matthew's telling, however, the echoes of other texts reach even further back in time, for Matthew describes her not as Syrophoenician but as Canaanite (Mt. 15.21-22), a word that, as Perkinson writes,

6. Jim Perkinson, 'A Canaanite Word in the Logos of Christ; or the Difference the Syro-Phoenician Woman Makes to Jesus', *Semeia* 75 (1996), pp. 61-85.

opens an old memory, a rent in Matthew's text... He writes the woman back into the beginning, the founding discourse of his entire tradition. Or more accurately, he writes the tradition forward into a crisis of his present... She re-presents primally unfinished business... The erasure of the Canaanite presence in Israelite history was part of the mode of constructing the national identity. But here, the erased begins to reappear like a palimpsest.[7]

So, in this chapter my intent is to prise this biblical rent open a little further.

Using Perkinson's metaphor, I want to pull this rent apart and set it as a frame through which I can peer and look more closely at the face of this Syrophoenician woman whose features may be carrying traces of other Canaanite women. It is the use of that word 'Canaanite' by writer of Matthew's Gospel that is sending me back to those texts which I have already been considering in the books of Joshua and Kings. As Luz and others have noted, the author of Matthew's Gospel is a writer of considerable skill, working carefully as a literary code-setter in his craft as he embeds clues for the perceptive reader audience.[8] It is the deliberately employed skill of doublespeak, as shown in the title (1.1) where his use of the term *genesis* with its double meaning of birth or genealogical origin signals a flashback to Gen. 2.4 and 5.1 as well as providing a clue to what follows, by virtually announcing that Matthew is 'writing the Bible anew' with a new 'book of the origins'.[9] What is not at all expected by the reader, coming by the route of the earlier texts of the Hebrew Bible, is that there, embedded in this new beginning, are four women, and probably all non-Israelite.[10] At least one of these is notably a Canaanite, although 'the C word' is not mentioned, the text simply stating that Salmon fathered Boaz by Rahab. The reference seems unambiguous and deliberate, although some, in fact, have wanted to argue that Matthew's Rahab is quite other than Joshua's.[11] Perhaps more to the point is the question of how Rahab could have mothered a son who lived

7. Perkinson, 'A Canaanite Word', pp. 64, 79.

8. Ulrich Luz, *The Theology of the Gospel of Matthew* (trans. J. Bradford Robinson; Cambridge: Cambridge University Press, 1995), p. 2; Jack Dean Kingsbury, *Matthew as Story* (Philadelphia: Fortress Press, 1986), p. 32; Elaine Wainwright, *Towards a Feminist Critical Reading of the Gospel According to Matthew* (Berlin: W. de Gruyter, 1991), p. 114.

9. Luz, *The Theology of the Gospel of Matthew*, p. 24.

10. Tamar in later tradition was considered an Aramaean (*Jub.* 41.1). Ruth is clearly a Moabite, Rahab a Canaanite, while Bathsheba is introduced as the wife of the Hittite Uriah.

11. So, for example, J. Quin, 'Is Rahab in Matthew 1.5 Rahab of Jericho?', *Bib* 62 (1982), pp. 225-28: 'The Racab of Mt. 1.5 ought not to be translated with Rahab, the name of the harlot of Jericho'. But see R.E. Brown's swift reply, 'Rachab in Matthew 1.5 Probably is Rahab of Jericho', *Bib* 63 (1982), pp. 79-80. Certainly there is a difference in spelling, Racab in the Gospel rather than the Raab of the Septuagint, Hebrews and James, but since Josephus used both Racabh and Raab, an argument from spelling alone is less than convincing.

so many decades later! The text, however, sees no problem. But the more interesting question is: what is such a Canaanite Other doing here in the first book of the New Testament?

Rahab, however, now has female company. Tamar, Ruth and the wife of Uriah are all present with her in the genealogy. There has been long and continuing discussion about the ties that link these four women. As the present reader of this text I can only join the long trail of those who have mused, questioned and speculated.[12] Were these four chosen and inserted because all were sinners, or because, on the contrary, they were models of faith and righteousness? But if the latter why not have the great matriarchs of the tradition, such as Sarah or Rachel? Or were the four chosen because they were women showing outstanding initiative when circumstances suddenly plunged them into difficult situations? For if their children were conceived somewhat irregularly this could be interpreted very positively as 'a divine irregularity' showing that 'God's salvific action sometimes chooses unexpected ways'.[13] The women, then, are not only exonerated of any possible 'sin', but, on the contrary, are to be held up high as models of faithfulness, praised for taking such initiatives. Although if their so-called problems are all part of God's plan, this perhaps raises more questions about God than it does about the women. On the other hand, if the women are to be held responsible for their 'extraordinary or irregular' situation, then, as Elaine Wainwright notes, this too easily falls in line with a gender politic that recognizes women 'only when they are problems'.[14] Or is it that in a gospel advocating mission to the Gentiles it is not only a matter of gender, but of ethnicity? These four have been chosen specifically because they are foreign women, in which case, Jesus, the Jewish Messiah, has an ancestry traced through Gentile women. That is a quite particular point. For, whatever the reason behind their inclusion, what is certainly significant, as has long been acknowledged, is that these four intrude into what is otherwise the

12. For example, see R.E. Brown, *The Birth of the Messiah: A Commentary on the Infancy Narratives in Matthew and Luke* (Garden City, NY: Doubleday, 1977); Janice Capel Anderson, 'Matthew: Gender and Reading', *Semeia* 28 (1983), pp. 3-27 (6-8); Amy-Jill Levine, 'Matthew', in Newsom and Ringe (eds.), *The Women's Bible Commentary*, pp. 252-62 (253-54); Stephenson Humphries-Brooks, 'The Canaanite Women in Matthew', in Amy-Jill Levine (with Marianne Blickenstaff) (ed.), *A Feminist Companion to Matthew* (The Feminist Companion to the New Testament and Early Christian Writings, 1; Sheffield: Sheffield Academic Press, 2001), pp. 138-56.

13. Ulrich Luz, *Matthew 1–7: A Commentary* (trans. Wilhelm C. Linss; Edinburgh: T. & T. Clark, 1989), p. 109. Others who support this thesis also highlight the working of the Holy Spirit, seeing a connection with the working of the Holy Spirit in 1.18.

14. Elaine M. Wainwright, 'The Gospel of Matthew', in Elisabeth Schüssler Fiorenza (ed.), *Searching the Scriptures*. II. *A Feminist Commentary* (New York: Crossroad, 1994), pp. 635-77 (642).

accustomed pattern of a linear male genealogy, the purpose of which was 'to ground a claim to power, status, rank, office, or inheritance in an earlier ancestor'.[15] These four intruding women have become part of the legitimating team. A further interesting detail is that if 'the earlier ancestor' is David, then Rahab's presence is doubly curious, for she has not appeared in Davidic company before.

Although I am primarily interested in the effect of such a literary intertextual dimension of the text, I briefly wonder whether the historical circumstances behind this Gospel might throw some light on why this echo found a place in Matthew's writing. As so often is the case with biblical texts, both the purpose and the place of origin of this Gospel remain open to debate. Antioch has long been held as a likely placing, but one recent suggestion has added a further move: the community had once been based in Palestine but had fled to Syria at the outbreak of war in 66–70 CE, as advised in Mt. 24.15-16.[16] This could provide one possible explanation for what appears to be an anti-Gentile attitude apparent in several of its texts (Mt. 5.47; 6.7, 31-32; 18.17).[17] For, not only might this have been a factor in Palestine after the country became a Roman province in 44 CE, but it could have been held even more strongly among an exilic group that was attempting to keep its Jewish, albeit Jewish-Christian, identity alive in the Gentile world of Syria.[18] Another more persuasive suggestion to account for these texts sees the Matthean community as much more varied, 'heteroglossal' rather than 'monoglossal'.[19] What has resulted is a gospel in which both sides of a debate about Gentile mission can be heard, with Matthew himself on the pro-Gentile side.[20] But he had a problem: how could he legitimate this mission

---

15.   Robert R. Wilson, 'Genealogy, Genealogies', in *ABD*, II, pp. 929-32 (931).

16.   Mark R.J. Bredin, 'Gentiles and the Davidic Tradition in Matthew', in Athalya Brenner (ed.), *A Feminist Companion to the Hebrew Bible in the New Testament* (The Feminist Companion to the Bible, 10; Sheffield: Sheffield Academic Press, 1996), pp. 95-111 (98). His proposal seeks to account both for Matthew's Gospel having 'a distinct ring of "Palestine" to it' while seeming 'to have its setting in Syria, probably Antioch'.

17.   Elaine M. Wainwright, *Shall We Look for Another? A Feminist Rereading of the Matthean Jesus* (Maryknoll, NY: Orbis Books, 1998), p. 44, raises the question of whether *ethne* in 6.31-32 and *ethnikos/ethnikoi* in the other passages are to be understood as referring to Gentiles per se or are simply used as derisive terms in a more general sense.

18.   But as Christians rejected by the synagogue communities, they would also have considerable anti-Jewish feelings, as evidenced in texts such as 4.12; 9.35; 10.17, and so on. See Graham N. Stanton, *A Gospel for a New People: Studies in Matthew* (Louisville, KY: Westminster/John Knox Press, 1992), pp. 156-57, on the tension caused by the parting of the ways.

19.   Wainwright, *Shall We Look for Another?*, p. 42.

20.   So Stanton, *A Gospel for a New People*, p. 330: 'For Matthew, Israel's rejection of her Messiah at the end of the life of Jesus leads to the acceptance of the Gentiles'.

when Jesus' own ministry had been restricted to Palestine?[21] Much easier if Jesus could be shown to have had Gentile ancestors himself. The answer: add these four women to the opening genealogy. Rahab the Canaanite who helped legitimize the Israelite conquest of her land would now help Christianize the Gentiles. It is a persuasive possibility.

What is clear, however, is that by including Rahab in this new book of origins Matthew is nudging me as the reader to return to the fading but not yet faded first layer of this palimpsest text, that first book of landed origins, Joshua.[22] I had already listened to the Canaanite Rahab declaring to the spies hidden under the flax, 'I know that Yahweh has given you the land, and that dread of you has fallen on us... For we have heard how Yahweh dried up the water of the Red Sea before you...and what you did to...Sihon and Og, whom you utterly destroyed' and been suspicious. And her remarkable affirmation, 'Yahweh, your God is the God of heaven above and earth below', had already convinced me that there was a credibility problem here. In Chapter 3 I discussed the possibility that, as the reader, I was hearing not the voice of Rahab but tuning in to another conversation, meeting the words of an ancient Israelite writing team, most probably Deuteronomistic. Reading through the lens of hermeneutical suspicion I came to the conclusion that the Canaanite features of Rahab's face had already been erased and overpainted in Israelite, and probably more particularly Deuteronomistic, colours, by being set in a clearly Israelite ideological frame. The possibility of catching even a glimpse of a Canaanite who, according to tradition, had remained resolutely Canaanite then sent me forward to Jezebel, recognizing that her story, coming as it did much later in the chronology of the Deuteronomists' History, in the books of the Kings, had already been framed by the Rahab tale placed at its beginning. Read together, these texts provided a striking contrast. For if Rahab was portrayed as a Canaanite who qualified for an 'in' place in Israel, there seemed little doubt that the writers of the History wanted Jezebel 'out'. But once again, as I have indicated, I could not help wondering whether this was really Jezebel. Did she do this? Could she have done this? Wasn't there a credibility problem here too in this tale of a foreign queen with such power and malignity? If the Rahab narrative provides the clue then it follows that her major crime was that she failed to walk in the path of Rahab, the Canaanite turned Israelite.

21.   Assuming that the encounter with the Syrophoenician woman took place this side of Tyre, or if not, that it was the exception. Bredin's point ('Gentiles and the Davidic Tradition in Matthew', p. 108 n. 2) that 'it does seem difficult to understand the later controversies in Acts if Jesus had explicitly taught about a later gentile mission' seems well made. Luz, *The Theology of the Gospel of Matthew*, p. 144, also suggests that in this respect Matthew 'turns Jesus' teachings upside down'.

22.   So too Wainwright, *Towards a Feminist Critical Reading*, p. 105, and Dube, *Postcolonial Feminist Interpretation of the Bible*, pp. 127-55, 157-95.

If the Rahab and Jezebel narratives were framed by Israelite interest, did that framing follow the Syrophoenician woman into the Christian Gospels? Jim Perkinson's metaphor of the overwritten manuscript to describe the re-appearance of the Canaanite in Matthew's gospel might suggest so. But the story as it is told is not Matthew's alone; it was first told in Mark's Gospel, in a brief encounter in six verses (Mk 7.24-30). There the woman was described not as Canaanite but as Gentile, of Syrophoenician origin, so marking her as an outsider by religious belief as well as by ethnic origin. Both of which details add, of course, to the fact that she is also a woman, and even more to the point in this encounter, the mother of an afflicted daughter. Do I ask whether this was a 'true' account? And what would I mean by 'true'? While the community tradition may well have kept and preserved the memory of such an incident,[23] it is the telling itself, the details gathered into its shaping and crafting of the memory to carry such a gospel 'truth', which is the interest of my exploration. I note the echoes of that Elijah narrative in 1 Kgs 17.8-24, discussed in Chapter 4, which was also set in Sidon. Geography itself is a key code; one has to watch where Jesus goes and ask questions of that too. Perkinson comments that

> His trek north into the rural district surrounding the urban centers of Tyre and Sidon constitutes a kind of self-exile. He exits 'the nation' proper... And he does so seeking anonymity. He is at least 'on retreat'.[24]

But in Tyre and Sidon?! Both were cities with a long textual history of Israelite condemnation (Isa. 23; Joel 3.4; Ezek. 26–28; Zech. 9.1-4); both were long viewed by Israel as being beyond the pale. This is a border-crossing of some significance. Or is it? If this is, in some sense, a palimpsest text, it is also not easy to get a clear view of the surface level, for an ambiguity blurs the details of the borders of this meeting in so many senses. Does Jesus cross over or merely go towards, and does the woman merely 'come out' as in 'out' into Jesus' path or 'out' from her region? The text is teasing in its ambiguity.[25]

---

23.   William Loader, 'Challenged at the Boundaries: A Conservative Jesus in Mark's Tradition', *JSNT* 63 (1996), pp. 45-61 (51), notes that 'the anecdote would cohere with the image of a quasi-Cynic Jesus, deliberately subversive of accepted boundaries', although his own view is that 'crossing such boundaries was the exception rather than the rule for Jesus' and that 'if the anecdote has claim to any link with the historical Jesus, then the explanation which sees in it a reluctant yet definite positive response to a Gentile is likely to be more accurate'. Loader's point is that this is just the attitude that 'might have been expected from a conservative Jew confronted with such a violation of purity law' (p. 60).

24.   Perkinson, 'A Canaanitic Word in the Logos of Christ', p. 66.

25.   Wainwright, *Shall We Look for Another?*, p. 87, noting this ambiguity, describes the woman as 'a *skandalon*, a boundary-walker'.

In any case, the mention of both Tyre and Sidon has been kept in the version told in Matthew's Gospel. As Gail O'Day points out, this is surely 'more than happenstance'. The two episodes immediately preceding this encounter have been concerned with purity requirements, so that read in sequence this move can be read as a journey from 'the land and the people who are "clean", to enter a land that is unclean'.[26] The erased in the palimpsest scroll is already showing through. I am beginning to read this as much more than a simple retreat. And indeed if I view this travelling Jesus through a postcolonial lens the geographic coding carries a more disturbing message to the reader; this is a traveller with imperializing intent, and in Jesus' case, that intent is divinely legitimated.[27]

But briefly to the story itself. In itself it is a story of cryptic dialogue. If Rahab and Jezebel were kept within their houses, to be glimpsed through their windows, then, in one sense, this woman is markedly different; she is meeting Jesus publicly out in the open. My suspicion of the interests of the writing team behind the previous narratives makes me want to query the writer of Matthew. For, as I have noted, it is Matthew, in contrast to Mark, who has chosen to describe the woman as Canaanite. It is Matthew who now has her meet Jesus outside, presumably so that Jesus cannot be seen breaking the barriers between Jew and Gentile by appearing to share a table with her,[28] whereas in Mark this meeting took place inside the house. But, like Rahab and Jezebel, this is a woman not only seen but heard. She erupts into the gospel scene with her shout, 'Have mercy on me, Lord, Son of David; my daughter is tormented by a demon' (Mt. 15.22). Out in the open, in the public arena, this is already a confrontation with the accepted mores that would keep women in private space rather than public. This is a woman refusing to keep to the margins of society, a woman who is intent on moving directly to the centre. And yet she is shockingly an 'ex-centric', as the detail of her daughter being 'severely'[29] tormented by demons indicates, adding a further dimension to this picture of gender and ethnic outsidedness. This is

26. Gail R. O'Day, 'Surprised by Faith: Jesus and the Canaanite Woman', in Levine (ed.), *A Feminist Companion to Matthew*, pp. 114-25 (115).

27. Following Dube, *Postcolonial Feminist Interpretation of the Bible*, p. 146, who suggests that the 'form and ideology' of this scene is 'founded on the type-scene of land possession', and concludes (pp. 154-55) that it 'embraces imperialistic values and strategies'.

28. David C. Sim, 'Christianity and Ethnicity in the Gospel of Matthew', in Brett (ed.), *Ethnicity and the Bible*, pp. 171-95 (192).

29. Dube, *Postcolonial Feminist Interpretation of the Bible*, p. 148, suggests that Matthew's addition of the intensifying adverb, which heightens representation of the woman and her daughter as evil and dangerous, 'paves the way for the ideology of those who are in desperate need of divine redeemers and justifies travel and entrance into foreign nations'.

an even more dangerous encounter in a world where demons represented the powers that disturb the created order. In one move she is challenging not only the hegemony of both the Jewish and the male world, but the very safety of those at its centre. As I stop and consider the scene I would like to know how this woman, this outsider, had heard about Jesus. Had the news travelled through the women's networks? Had she been privy to some of the gossiping of the gospel even in Sidon and Tyre? The text, however, has no interest in such details.

The woman calls upon Jesus as 'Lord, Son of David' (v. 22), an Israelite title, but from the mouth of a Canaanite! This must surely be a glimpse of Matthew's pen, for again in contrast to Mark, it is Matthew alone who records her addressing Jesus with this title.[30] If I drop my suspicion of Matthew, can I hear this as the woman merely being polite, addressing Jesus formally as *kyrios*, and indeed being doubly polite in adding the full terms of his lineage? But no: a Canaanite using the address 'Son of David' with its connotations of the ancient ethnic and religious divisions stretches my credulity too far. I sense Matthew quite deliberately choosing to set these words in the woman's mouth, for can I really believe that a writer who has already set the encounter within the frame of the conflict traditions of early Israel, Canaanite vs. Israelite, and within a gendered tale of imploring out-sider woman and powerful Jewish healer, has no interest in these differ-ences?[31] Or could it be that Matthew, the gospel writer, is simply using this title to signal to those who have travelled through this gospel that they should remember the episode of 9.27-31, and so be prepared for another healing about to occur through the power of this man, Jesus?[32] I decide to keep these possibilities in mind and move to consider Jesus' response. Matthew not only includes Jesus' resistance, recorded in Mark, he intensifies it; not only are the disciples trying to get rid of the woman, but

30. Commentators note the similarity with the language of Israel's lament traditions. O'Day, 'Surprised by Faith', p. 119, who describes the passage as 'a narrative embodiment of a lament psalm', takes this further with her suggestion that it is this tradition which lies behind the woman's boldness in standing before Jesus.

31. Kwok Pui-lan, *Discovering the Bible in the Non-Biblical World* (Maryknoll, NY: Orbis Books, 1995) pp. 74, 82, notes the 'dense web of significations' in this narrative, that is, 'Jewish homeland/foreign lands, inside/outside the house, Jews/Gentiles, cleanli-ness/uncleanliness, children/dogs, woman/disciples, and faithful/unfaithful'. Following Theissen, she also notes the woman's knowledge of Greek, 'suggesting that she is edu-cated and from the upper class'.

32. Wainwright, *Shall We Look for Another*, p. 90, following Dennis C. Duling, 'Matthew's Plurisignificant "Son of David" in Social Science Perspective: Kinship, Kingship, Magic, and Miracle', *Biblical Theology Bulletin* 22 (1992), pp. 99-116 (112), rightly sees this title as multivalent, and so allowing varying possibilities among its cluster of meaning.

the messianic voice remains mute. It is a moment, in the first written attempts to articulate the *logos* of the Christ, of a surprising '*a-logos*'—'a refusal to speak'.[33]

Why this reluctance of Jesus? He had already healed the Roman centurion's servant in ch. 8. Had he forgotten or is there a gender hesitation here? If Perkinson is right in suggesting his silence 'can be read as an attempt at silenc*ing*', then perhaps it is specifically the 'uppity-ness' of the woman that is driving this attempt of Jesus.[34] The word 'attempt' is well-chosen, for as both the intervention of the disciples and their charge that she 'keeps shouting' (v. 23) indicate, she is not easily put off. But his silence also heightens the sense of the power of Jesus. As in the typical folktale genre, the hurdles to be overcome by the seeker are there, at least in part, as pointers to the value of what is sought. The next hurdle, of course, is verbal. But how does one interpret what Jesus says when he does speak? How significant are the differences with Mark's version? For Matthew now talks openly of 'the lost house of Israel', a hard saying which draws stronger boundaries between insiders and outsiders. And does Jesus say this to the disciples or to the woman? Once again the text is not clear; as Martin Scott comments, 'the reader is left in no small degree of confusion at this point'.[35] There is the question, of course, of whether Jesus ever said this at all, or whether once again this is an instance of Matthew's crafting, wanting to strengthen the Jesus saying in order to get the point across to the reader.

And the woman's response? She comes and kneels before him. Kwok Pui-lan suggests that in doing this she 'humbles herself and evokes the image of a devoted dog'.[36] But this 'dog' language is to anticipate; once again, as the story is told, the reader is caught in the tension. What will Jesus do? Will he be diverted from his task? He now responds with the dog speech, also reported by Mark, but in both Gospels it is not only dog but 'little dog' (*kunarion*). On a purely narrative level, I could agree with the suggestion

> that any intelligent Hellenistic woman, addressed in such terms by a barbarian, would have immediately reacted by slapping the man's face. And, as in English, so in other languages, to call a woman 'a little bitch' is no less abusive than to call her 'a bitch' without qualification.[37]

33. Perkinson, 'A Canaanite Word', p. 64.

34. See Sharon H. Ringe, 'A Gentile Woman's Story', in Letty Russell (ed.), *Feminist Interpretation of the Bible* (Oxford: Basil Blackwell, 1985), pp. 65-72, for the description of the woman as 'uppity'.

35. J. Martin C. Scott, 'Matthew 15.21-28: A Test-Case for Jesus' Manners', *JSNT* 63 (1996), pp. 21-44 (39).

36. Pui-lan, *Discovering the Bible*, p. 77. Dube, *Postcolonial Feminist Interpretation of the Bible*, p. 149, sees this as an example 'of depicting…foreign people as those who beseech and need subjugation'.

37. T.A. Burkill, 'Historical Development of the Story of the Syro-Phoenician Woman', *NovT* 9 (1967), pp. 161-77 (173).

Or is the point of the diminutive that Jesus is not only refusing adult Gentiles but Gentile progeny—'little Gentiles' who grow up into big ones?[38]
Once again, in contrast to Mark, Matthew has made this more uncom-
promising in that there is no longer the hint of the children being only fed
first. Martin Scott asks,

> Can the harshness and sharpness of Jesus' rebuke simply be dismissed as a
> literary device, justified by the need to deal with problems in a community
> some 40 years after the death of their founder? Surely a writer with the crea-
> tive ability of Matthew could have found a more sympathetic way to introduce
> the theme of the inclusion of Gentiles in the Christian community.[39]

But more sympathetic or more effective? This is now the third rebuff;
Matthew is telling this tale with a threefold opposition of Jesus. No-one is to
be in any doubt that mission to the Gentiles is an issue, and that the
recognition of the legitimacy of the woman's request was hard won, although
some have suggested that Jesus is merely testing the woman! Yet the woman
persists and even uses the same word 'puppies' in her counter move. But, as
Perkinson notes, in her very repeating of the gentler form, 'puppies', and
picturing them scrabbling for crumbs under the masters' table, 'she shifts the
implication from predatory scavenging outside the house', with its disturbing
intertextual echo of those dogs scavenging among Jezebel's remains, 'to an
internal domestic scene of begging for scraps'.[40] Her reply that if the crumbs
fall, the dogs will eat them up is a nice piece of household logic! But is she
accepting her place among the dogs, or is there an irony intended here? Or is
it, as Perkinson further suggests, that 'she creates a kind of "solidarity in
littleness" (linking "puppies" with "crumbs" and "little kids")'?[41] But there
are further changes; the spilt crumbs are now not from the children's but the
masters' table. Matthew has made this both more hierarchical and more
offensive. Yet, on the surface level, the woman seemingly 'accepts the disgraceful epithet of "dogs" for her people—for herself and her daughter—and
asks only to be treated as the dogs are treated, by being given the crumbs'.[42]

38. See David Rhoads, 'Jesus and the Syro-Phoenician Woman in Mark: A Narrative-Critical Study', *JAAR* 62 (1994), pp. 343-76, for a discussion of the use of diminu-
tives in Mark. Matthew has kept only those for the crumbs and dogs.

39. Scott, 'Matthew 15.21-28: A Test-Case for Jesus' Manners', p. 29.

40. Perkinson, 'A Canaanite Word', p. 75, with reference to Rhoad's article, 'Jesus
and the Syro-Phoenician Woman in Mark', p. 357.

41. Perkinson, 'A Canaanite Word', pp. 75-76.

42. F.W. Beare, *The Gospel according to Matthew* (Oxford: Basil Blackwell, 1981),
p. 340, quoted by Scott, 'Matthew 15.21-28', p. 40. On yet another level there is the
motif of surviving by eating the remnants, which is firmly rooted in Hebrew tradition (cf.
Judg. 1.7a; Lev. 19.9-10; Deut. 24.19; Ruth 2), as noted by P. Pokorny, 'From a Puppy to a
Child: Problems of Contemporary Biblical Exegesis Demonstrated from Mark 7.24-30/
Matt 15.21-28', *NTS* 41 (1995), pp. 321-37 (328).

Then the climax of the story. But here too Matthew has been at work, for the ending also differs from the way Mark told it. There Jesus simply said, 'For this saying you may go on your way; the demon has left your daughter', and the reader was told she went home where her daughter was found to be well again. Matthew makes much more of this: Jesus cries out 'Woman, great is your faith! Let it be done for you as you wish' and the healing is instant. This woman believed—that is the point. Matthew is making sure that those who read his Gospel recognize the woman as a model of faith to be followed. Significantly, only one other in the Synoptic tradition is praised in these terms, and that one is also a non-Jew, the Roman centurion of Mt. 8.5-13 and Lk. 7.1-10. Read together, it would seem that the Gospel writer is wanting to convey the message: the outsider has come in and the insiders, such as the disciples, have fallen behind! Matthew's pro-Gentile mission stance is clear: no longer is it a matter of crumby remnants, now the messianic abundance is to be spread before all comers, irrespectively.[43] But having come to this point by way of the previous narratives I want to ask: Is the point being made that it is faith in the Jewish Jesus' God that has achieved this? Is this a *rediviva* Rahab now programmed as a symbol of belief in the Matthean Gospel agenda? In terms of Jesus himself, can one also say that the woman has provided the way for Jesus to be the Christ who responds to the poor and the outcast and the rejected, and, even more particularly in this chapter, the Christ who heals and feeds, that she has indeed nudged Jesus to be the Christ?[44] As Perkinson asks: 'Whose word has wrought deliverance? Indeed, who has spoken to whom?'[45]

Musa Dube reads the Canaanite woman with two faces: the first is the face of the outsider woman who accepts her place among the dogs, and indeed is accepted by Jesus on the basis of that acceptance, contrasting with the second face of the worshiper who has recognized the lordship and divinity of Jesus.[46] There is, however, an interesting, and perhaps highly significant feature in the face of Jesus. For I, as reader, have already been told that Rahab is Jesus' ancestor, and if Canaanites are strictly Other to Israel, the intriguing question arises as to whether there is a trace of Otherness, of Canaanite-ness, in the face of Jesus the Jew.[47] I keep this in mind as I go

43. So Elisabeth Schüssler Fiorenza, *In Memory of Her: A Feminist Theological Reconstruction of Christian Origins* (New York: Crossroad, 1983), p. 138, 'The gracious goodness of the God of Jesus is abundant enough to satisfy not only the "children" of Israel but also the woman-child who as a female and as a gentile, is doubly polluted'. See too Anderson, 'Matthew: Gender and Reading', p. 14.

44. So Ringe, 'A Gentile Woman's Story', p. 68; O'Day, 'Surprised by Faith', p. 125.

45. Perkinson, 'A Canaanite Word', p. 65.

46. Dube, *Postcolonial Feminist Interpretation of the Bible*, p. 151,

47. For an interesting discussion of the possibility of Canaanite traces appearing in the faces of Israel, see Danna Nolan Fewell, 'Imagination, Method, and Murder:

back and watch his interaction again with the woman from Sidon, but the
retort about it not being fair to take the children's food and throw it to the
dogs brings an uneasy memory of that o/Other Sidonian, Jezebel. As I listen
to the woman replying, 'Yes, Lord, yet even the dogs eat the crumbs that fall
from their masters' table', and Jesus accepting her faith, I watch the interchange, detecting in this meeting of Canaanite woman and Jewish man a
recognition that is double facing; the Canaanite recognizes the healing
power of this Davidic Jesus, and the Davidic Jesus allows the faithful
Canaanite, as 'woman', not dog, a place at the table, which now expands to
accept the ethnically different.[48] I begin to sigh with relief. At last, this time,
Canaanites get to eat the meal. At last, Israelite dogs eating Jezebel's remains
are consigned to a past and fading memory. The Canaanite has spoken in
her own voice; to use Gayatri Chakravorty Spivak's much-quoted term, I
have heard the voice of the 'subaltern'.[49] Sharon Ringe some years ago
characterized Matthew's Canaanite as 'an uppity woman' but this woman in
her stand for Canaanite identity is showing more than 'uppityness'.[50] Leticia
Guardiola-Sáenz suggests that it may even be possible to hear her challenge
as not so much a request of a favour as a demand for restitution,[51] which
sounds immediately familiar to me reading from my own context where
Pakeha settlement and land deals have bequeathed a legacy of treaty claims
for restitution.

If I now view the scene through the lens of postcolonialism, remembering
that it is, in Sugirtharajah's words, 'a reading posture' rather than a method,
but one providing 'an active confrontation with the dominant system of
thought, its lopsidedness and inadequacies',[52] my suspicions find fresh explanations. While I note all the more clearly how Jesus 'places the obstacle of

Un/Framing the Face of Post-Exilic Israel', in Beal and Gunn (eds.), *Reading Bibles,
Writing Bodies*, pp. 132-52.

   48.   Wainwright, *Shall We Look for Another?*, p. 91, reads this pericope as a 'threshold
dialogue' with both characters 'crossing over' into new space and understanding.

   49.   So Perkinson, 'A Canaanite Word', p. 64.

   50.   Ringe, 'A Gentile Woman's Story', p. 65. Ringe does not, however, leave the
matter as one of 'uppityness', but talks of the woman's gifts of sharp insight and courage
(p. 72). Ringe returned to the story in its Markan version in 'A Gentile Woman's Story,
Revisited: Rereading Mark 7.24-31', in Amy-Jill Levine (ed.), *A Feminist Companion to
Mark* (The Feminist Companion to the New Testament and Early Christian Writings, 2;
Sheffield: Sheffield Academic Press, 2001), pp. 79-100, where she engages more sharply
with the political issues and finds the portrayals both of the woman and of Jesus 'more
ambiguous' (p. 99).

   51.   Leticia A. Guardiola-Sáenz, 'Borderless Women and Borderless Texts: A Cultural
Reading of Matthew 15.21-28', *Semeia* 78 (1997), pp. 69-81 (76).

   52.   R.S. Sugirtharajah, 'A Postcolonial Exploration of Collusion and Construction in
Biblical Interpretation', in *idem* (ed.), *The Postcolonial Bible* (Bible and Postcolonialism, 1;
Sheffield: Sheffield Academic Press, 1998), pp. 91-116 (93).

ethnicity across the path of a plea for help',[53] I can read his equally remark-able turn-around as an example of what Spivak calls 'unlearning one's privi-lege'. Yet, Landry and MacLean's definition of this as 'doing one's homework in the interests of unlearning one's privilege [which] marks the beginning of an ethical relation to the Other'[54] returns the focus to Jesus, and prepares the way for the woman to slip out of sight. The Canaanite woman has done her conscientizing work. And I wonder, perhaps whimsically, whether this has been most significantly in allowing Jesus to recognize that Canaanite trace in his own face.

But I have a few lingering doubts. While I would like to agree with those who hear a Canaanite voice speaking 'for a brief moment...in [Jesus'] place',[55] or even speaking as 'the christic one',[56] that retort of the woman in v. 27 leaves me wondering. It may be that there is an irony in her response, that her re-use of the term 'dogs' is a ploy which postcolonial theory would describe as 'a way of resisting and yet acknowledging the power of the domi-nant...allow[ing] a text to work within the constraints of the dominant while placing those constraints *as constraints* in the foreground and thus undermining their power',[57] and thus allowing the gospel message entry. I am not sure. Take away the suggestion of irony, and I can hear her accepting her place among the dogs, a woman colonized in the mind. Expanding Jesus' words so that both she and the 'children' receive the bread does not necessarily bring her out from underneath the table. And is it only crumbs and not a full meal?[58]

Pokorny sums up the encounter: 'This is the good news of this story: the puppy became a child'.[59] But I want to double check. I am wondering whether this is still a Canaanite child and whether she is out from under the table. I want to look again at whether recognition on both sides has allowed respect for both Israelite and Canaanite identity. My suspicion of Matthew remains as I note his immediate framing of this episode within the disciples' lack of understanding (15.10-20; 15.32–16.12).[60] Coming to this text by way

53. Wainwright, *Shall We Look for Another?*, p. 92.

54. Donna Landry and Graham MacLean, *The Spivak Reader: Selected Works of Gayatri Chakravorty Spivak* (New York and London: Routledge, 1996), p. 5.

55. Perkinson, 'A Canaanite Word', p. 80.

56. Wainwright, *Shall We Look for Another?*, p. 80.

57. Linda Hutcheon, 'Circling the Downspout of Empire', in Ian Adam and Helen Tiffin (eds.), *Past the Last Post: Theorizing Post-Colonialism and Post-Modernism* (Calgary: University of Calgary Press, 1990), pp. 167-89 (177).

58. Agreeing here with Wainwright's feminist rereading (*Shall We Look for Another?*, p. 92), that her 'great faith' implies 'recognition of and submission to kyriarchal power that provides her with the crumbs that fall from the masters' tables'.

59. Pokorny, 'From a Puppy to a Child', p. 337.

60. See the chiastic structure identified by Anderson, 'Matthew: Gender and Read-ing', p. 14. O'Day, 'Surprised by Faith', p. 117, notes that the pericope breaks down into

of Rahab and Jezebel makes me suspect that once again the Canaanite woman has been used as a foil, a cog in the ideological agenda. For I suspect that Gail O'Day has a case for suggesting that Matthew is presenting this woman not only as faithful, in recognizing the power of God embodied in Jesus, but that in highlighting her preparedness to challenge this embodied power, as so many in Israel's tradition have challenged God before her, he is going even further, that he is, in fact, setting her out, in contrast to the disciples, to be considered as 'more authentically Jewish'.[61]

And I stumble at that undisputed term 'dogs'. Jesus may have addressed the Canaanite as 'woman' but the word 'dog' remains unerased. I cannot help wondering whether Matthew has kept the word in the Gospel, and indeed built the gist of the dialogue upon it, not only to emphasize the change in Jesus' attitude, but because this was the way in which he, too, regarded the Canaanite. If the mouths of Israelite dogs are under control, Matthew has clearly not reined in the mouth of Jesus; the violence has not passed, but has moved from physical to verbal. So I am not entirely sure that this is the saving end to 'primally unfinished business'. But what is clear is that the matter is under negotiation again. As Regina Schwartz reminds us, 'On the question of the Other, the foreigner, the (biblical) narratives are decidedly inconsistent... Who is an insider and who is an outsider is perpetually negotiated...'[62] There is no closure here.

My initial wonderment was how the Bible regarded 'Other' women, and whether certain texts stand as frames for others. In these chapters I have watched three women in particular making their way through an ancient 'Othering' world, with compliance and survival, integrity and death, challenge and grudging reward. Jezebel's story read between the narratives of Rahab and Matthew's Canaanite woman, is the sobering tale of the cost of remaining resolutely 'Other'; it is a quite literal tale of the attempted death and burial of a culture. The connections with certain histories of the last centuries are chilling. My suspicious reading, informed by a feminist, ideological and postcolonial awareness, has revealed a Rahab speaking in the colonizers' language, an excreted Jezebel and a later Canaanite whose ambiguous stance was written in and then swiftly written over, leaving Jesus to be hailed in the name of the God of Israel (v. 31). The term 'framed' has

three units, the middle one, vv. 23b-24, recounting the interaction of the disciples with Jesus, in which the woman is 'the goad' prompting their conversation.

61. O'Day, 'Surprised by Faith', p. 124. O'Day argues this also on the basis of the woman being a 'full heiress of Israel's tradition of lament'. Pokorny, 'From a Puppy to a Child', p. 329, notes the intertextual connection between the woman's vision and the Israelite biblical tradition of the provision of the pickings for the *ger* as in Lev. 19.9-10 and Deut. 24.19.

62. Schwartz, *The Curse of Cain*, p. 197.

been all too apt, for not only Jezebel, seen standing in the window from which she would be cast out to her death, but for all three, who in differing ways, are all too easily read as framed by their writers, in the common legal sense.

But can I leave the matter there? Musa Dube insists on the necessity and urgency of recognizing that read in today's world, the Bible is now 'a post-colonial book, laden with the postcolonial burdens and challenges'.[63] Her own challenge, particularly to Western readers and critics, to take these seriously is sharp.

63.   Dube, *Postcolonial Feminist Interpretation of the Bible*, p. 20.

7

EXPANDING THE COLLAGE

> We all, from our various vantage points in society, and the kind of things we
> know about, perform distinct interpretive acts. And we have our various
> interpretive codes or methods with which we interpret.[1]

This is the challenge: to own our own vantage points and recognize that the
things we know about do have something to do with the way in which we
read—even biblical texts. This I am finding to be the challenge: to acknowledge on the one hand that I am performing distinct interpretive acts simply
by being the person that I am, and on the other to do this with a self-aware-
ness and a critical integrity. Musa Dube's statement, quoted at the conclusion of the last chapter, pointed to the Bible being now 'a postcolonial book,
laden with the postcolonial burdens and challenges'. I have been attempting
to take this into account in many of these readings—from my side of the
postcolonial divide. But I have been attempting to do this from within the
confines of the biblical world of study. The postcolonial scholar R.S.
Sugirtharajah, writing from his Indian context, has, however, raised another
aspect, suggesting that 'in a postcolonial, post-missionary era' there should
be a move to 'a wider intertextuality which will link biblical texts with
Asian scriptural texts'.[2] As I read this, I realized that just as I am *Pakeha* in
Aotearoa New Zealand, so the Bible itself is a 'resident alien', and that to
privilege this collection of writings as sacred scriptures moves, or has in
effect moved, the sacred traditions of Maori, the *tangata whenua* ('people of
the land'), to the margins. As in India, written text has been pitted against
oral tradition, and Sugirtharajah's comments reflect a similar history when
he writes that 'By privileging written texts as the valued medium for sacred
communication, missionary translations devalued the orality and rhetoric of
hearing'.[3] Sugirtharajah writes as an Indian.

---

1. Fredric R. Jameson, 'A Conversation with Fredric Jameson', *Semeia* 59 (1992),
pp. 227-37 (233).
2. Sugirtharajah, 'Textual Cleansing', p. 12.
3. Sugirtharajah, 'Textual Cleansing', p. 12.

Linking biblical traditions with those of the *tangata whenua* in the country in which I live cannot be done by *Pakeha*, that would be yet another instance of colonizing. Musa Dube, however, has taken this postcolonial sense of intertextuality a step further in a way that offers those of us who belong to the dominant cultures a way of opening the dialogue, of bringing other texts into 'a wider intertextuality conversation'. In her strong challenge to biblical scholars she has suggested that as scholars we have a choice as to how we approach texts that bear the colours of colonizing powers: we may overlook or bracket out their inherent imperialism and so collude in their strategies, we may 'reject and decolonize' such texts, or, as a third way, we may act as negotiators 'between colonizer and colonized by reading multiple texts and spinning hybrid interpretations'.[4] Dube is not limiting these multiple texts to those of scriptural traditions, but is suggesting taking this intertexual reading a step further, advocating

> Reading sacred and secular texts, ancient and contemporary texts, and imperializing and decolonizing texts, side by side, to highlight: (a) The ways in which they propound imperializing or decolonizing ideology; (b) their use of gender in the discourse of subordination and domination...[5]

In this chapter I am attempting to set up such a conversation. To do this I have decided to return to the story of Sarai. At the end of Chapter 1 I noted my earlier recognition that Sarai was a 'pawn of biblical storytellers' and flagged 'the challenge...to make my own considered choices of how she is to enter and speak to the concerns of my own world and context'. Having come to this chapter by way of Rahab, Jezebel and the Syrophoenician woman of Mark and Matthew's Gospels, I have an even keener interest in journeyings, in the entries people make into lands that are not theirs. I am conscious of Fernando Segovia's statement that 'at the core of the imperial/colonial phenomenon...lies the reality and experience of...unsettlement, travel, resettlement',[6] and note that one of the questions Dube requires to be asked in reading 'against imperial...forms of oppression' is: 'Does this text encourage travel to distant and inhabited lands and how does it justify itself ?'[7]

Sarai is there on the boundary in Israel's earliest literary or canonical memory of such an entry into 'a distant and inhabited' land. How the narrative beginning of Genesis relates to what actually happened is not my concern here. Israel's historical entry to the land remains a mystery, although it

---

4. Dube, *Postcolonial Feminist Interpretation of the Bible*, p. 157.
5. Dube, *Postcolonial Feminist Interpretation*, pp. 199-200. This is only a selection from her much longer list.
6. Fernando F. Segovia, *Interpreting Beyond Borders* (The Bible and Postcolonialism, 3; Sheffield: Sheffield Academic Press, 2000), p. 14.
7. Dube, *Postcolonial Feminist Interpretation of the Bible*, p. 201.

appears in many guises, told and retold as bible odysseys, scrutinized, ana-
lyzed and re-appropriated by readers, as model succeeds model, paradigm
after paradigm. For biblical readers, Israel's past, like that of so many peoples,
'is now not a land to return to in a simple politics of memory. It has become
a synchronic warehouse of cultural scenarios.'[8] Tales of biblical ancestors
entering the land, slipping peaceably through the countryside, either creeping with stealth or erupting with sword, are there for the taking, to become
part of other peoples' cultural memory. They mesh with other journeys,
other peoples' voyagings, other ethnic entries. What people do with these
received biblical traditions is one of the concerns that underlie this book. So
my interest settles once again on the Sarai who entered a land which was
not hers to become part of Israel's call narrative as it is told in Genesis 12.
But now, as I listen to this account once again, I have an ear attuned to
echoes of other journeyings from my own history, for as I have already indicated I am myself a descendent of travellers who journeyed long and hard to
reach Aotearoa New Zealand, in my case leaving the Highlands of Scotland
for Nova Scotia, before moving on yet again. Norman Habel's translation of
ger as 'immigrant' (Gen. 17.8), and his description of Gen. 11.31–12.9 as a
'migration narrative', help to key in these connections.[9] So I am now
following this story with the keen interests of a reader located in a much
later (post)colonial context. Parallels immediately come to mind. For, canonically positioned as Israel's, or Israel's ancestors', first arrival in the land, this
is where the Bible would have us believe it all begins for Israel; there is no
space for any earlier history in Canaan, just as in my postcolonial world

> settlers' ideologies involved in nation-building have a historical starting
> point, which occurs at the moment of colonial conquest and the beginning of
> settlement…the period prior to conquest and settlement is often constructed
> as pre-historical.[10]

8.   Arjun Appadurai, 'Disjuncture and Difference in the Global Cultural Economy',
Public Culture 2 (1990), p. 4, quoted by Françoise Lionnet, *Postcolonial Representations:
Women, Literature, Identity* (Ithaca, NY: Cornell University Press, 1995), p. 16.

9.   Habel, *The Land is Mine*, pp. 116-19.

10.   Stasiulis and Yuval-Davis, 'Introduction: Beyond Dichotomies', p. 21. My colleague Dr Margaret Eaton reminds me that this frequently coincides with the move from
oral to written tradition. The use of the word 'ideologies' is apt here for the earliest
written material was, for the most part, set down by writers with a mission in mind. As
James Belich, *The New Zealand Wars and the Victorian Interpretation of Racial Conflict*
(Auckland: Auckland University Press, 1986), p. 327, notes, 'Much of the early literature
on New Zealand was in fact part of two great advertising campaigns: the effort to obtain
support for missionary activity and to cast its achievements in the best possible light, and
the effort to attract settlers to a young and distant colony in competition with better-
known fields of immigration such as North America where land was cheaper and the
voyage out shorter'.

This is how we learnt our own history when I went to school; it began with the arrival of the first Europeans, the period before that was of minimal concern.

Such an ideological parallel raises a suspicion that Sarai's (and Abram's) narrative may be lurking in 'the warehouse' of my country's 'cultural scenarios'. Edward Said has talked of 'a simultaneous awareness both of the metropolitan history that is narrated and of those other histories against which (and beyond which) the dominating discourse acts'.[11] His term for exploring this is that of a 'contrapuntal reading', not dissimilar to the intertextuality advocated by Sugirtharajah and Dube. If I am to attempt such an intertextual counterpoint I need to set this biblical text in dialogue with a narrative from the colonial history. And if I am to take my own context into account, the contrapuntal reading needs to include a voice or voices from Aotearoa New Zealand's colonial history. What further supports such a connection, of course, is that in countries, such as mine, which have a settlement history in which missionaries and churches have played a significant role, biblical texts, both consciously and subconsciously, have been a part of the cultural scenario. Just as the Bible had 'a constitutive role...in the construction of Western culture',[12] so it entered this country with those first steps off the boats that landed on our shores. And entered to make its mark, for 'written Maori was literally a biblical language, learned from the Bible'.[13]

As I was considering the ways in which past traditions, biblical and others, become part of the ongoing self-identity of a people, I happened to go to a visiting art exhibition where one of the central works was a large painting by an Australian artist Amanti Tillers, entitled 'Diaspora'. While it was one coherent work it gained its effect through being composed as a series of connecting panels, at the centre of which, as its focus, was the large and dynamic figure of a woman.[14] But what most caught my eye was that the panels comprised a visual intertextuality, for there, on panel after panel, were copies of familiar and influential works, setting the diasporic theme within its cultural context. So, works by a European Mondrian and a New Zealand McCahon, from opposite ends of the world, both had a place, representing their part in the life of a diasporic Australia. So it was with this in mind that I set out to attempt to place Sarai and her narrative in a collage, not of paintings, but of voices recorded in print which speak out of a

---

11.   Edward W. Said, *Culture and Imperialism* (London: Chatto & Windus, 1993), p. 59.

12.   Roland Boer, 'Remembering Babylon: Postcolonialism and Australian Biblical Studies', in Sugirtharajah (ed.), *The Postcolonial Bible*, pp. 24-48 (46).

13.   Belich, *Making Peoples*, p. 221.

14.   I have not managed to find the whereabouts of this painting since and now wonder whether the figure was indeed that of a woman as I assumed on first sight—this was, however, certainly my impression.

past that is part of the cultural scenario of *Pakeha* history in Aotearoa New Zealand.

In many ways academic biblical studies has long followed a collage methodology, interspersing the voices of other scholars in the field throughout each new study. But this extension advocated by the postcolonial scholars is a response to the call to read the Bible, as any other cultural text, 'not just for the history it reflects, but also for the history it has made' and continues to make.[15] The difficulty lies in assessing the influence of the biblical traditions. In my print collage I am setting spaces for the voices of some of the early European settler women who travelled across the world to enter the land of Aotearoa, fully aware that placing these colonial texts beside the Sarai narrative may simply be a reading of journeying and settling experiences which have no more in common than the parallel journeying experience. But, as I have noted, the Bible played a significant role in the lives of many of those who journeyed here, particularly those associated with the missionary movement. So, in setting these narratives together my wonder is whether the Bible's influence may be heard as a subtext, and whether whispers of Sarai and Abram might be heard either below or behind the settler women's words. At the very least, it will open up a brief conversation between text and context.

If Sarai's story begins with the call, admittedly to Abram, rather than to herself, there is also a sense of call in the letter to her cousin written by Charlotte Brown on the 8 April 1829, as she was about to leave London with her husband to work as Church Missionary Society (CMS) missionaries.

> If our Heavenly Father (as I trust He has) has indeed pointed my way He will support under every trial.[16]

And there is a sense of land promise underlying Maria Richmond's journal letter to friends, written from New Plymouth, 11 November 1853:

> The wonderfulness of the change, the ease and certainty with which one traverses such wastes of water...the feeling of coming home, as it were, to a country wanting you, asking for people to enjoy and use it, with a climate to suit you, a beauty to satisfy and delight, and with such capabilities and possibilities for the future.[17]

---

15. Guardiola-Sáenz, 'Borderless Women and Borderless Texts', p. 71.

16. Frances Porter and Charlotte MacDonald (eds.), *'My Hand Will Write What My Heart Dictates': The Unsettled Lives of Women in Nineteenth-Century New Zealand as Revealed to Sisters, Family and Friends* (Auckland: Auckland University Press with Bridget Williams Books, 1996), p. 60.

17. Porter and MacDonald, *'My Hand Will Write'*, p. 90.

Certainly there is no sense of this being other people's land, in contrast to Charlotte, who had added,

> It is true that we shall be exposed to the fury of an uncivilized people, but He in whose hands are all our ways can subdue the most savage natures and protect us as easily in New Zealand as in England.

While there is no expression of such apprehension in Genesis 12, there was a certain ambiguity in the biblical narrative in that both in 11.31 and 12.5 the land to which Abram was called was named 'the land of Canaan', and, as mentioned in Chapter 1, the *'elon* of Moreh (v. 6) perhaps hinted at a place of Canaanite worship, perhaps even of Asherah with her strong tree connections. There is a fundamental irony here, shared with the postcolonial reality, which Gelder and Jacobs explore in reference to Australia, in that for people whose history is one of entry to others' land:

> one's place is always already another's place and the issue of possession is never complete, never entirely settled…one is always (dis)possessed, in the sense that neither possession nor dispossession is a fully realizable category.[18]

According to Gelder and Jacobs, 'What is "ours" is also potentially, or even always already, "theirs"'.[19] As Mark Brett notes, this is the Genesis irony that the 'land promise is delivered in the very territory which is to be possessed by Abram's seed, at a site that was probably sacred to the original owners of the land'.[20] These categories of 'ours' and 'theirs' again raise those knotty questions of political division, of 'whose' land, mentioned earlier. For if, as scholars are now suggesting, and I have been mentioning throughout this book, Israelites and Canaanites were originally not distinct, but one people ethnically, then an Abram and Sarai marked as outsiders, with a deity quite distinct from those of the Canaanites, would hint of their being characters in a highly political, if not polemical, text, seeking to mark out quite deliberate and particular divisions. Details such as the altar to Yahweh are then not so much a sign of naïvety as of a polemical palimpsest, with the signs of a would-be erased memory of shared identity showing through. On this understanding that *'elon* of Moreh may well be the trace of an erased Asherah, to whom Abram, and perhaps even more particularly Sarai, would not have been strangers at all. The divine name, so carefully inscribed within the overlaying text that is responsible for the Call, and that dislocating move to a distant land with its promises of a future, which the present narrator is

18. Ken Gelder and Jane M. Jacobs, *Uncanny Australia: Sacredness and Identity in a Postcolonial Nation* (Melbourne: Melbourne University Press, 1998), p. 138.
19. Gelder and Jacobs, *Uncanny Australia*, p. 23.
20. Mark G. Brett, *Genesis: Procreation and the Politics of Identity* (London and New York: Routledge, 2000), p. 51.

at pains to present as the divinely legitimated past, is now the marker of a deliberate dissonance, the marker of a would-be ethnic and cultural divide. In my collage of readings I am also leaving spaces for those other texts that I have been exploring already in the previous chapters. And so I note that with this agenda the text is looking disturbingly similar to those of Rahab and Jezebel.

If Abram was building an altar on Canaanite land, there is no hint of tension in the way in which the narrative presents this, and, in fact, on the contrary, it seems to conjure up a picture that asks to be read alongside another intertextual panel, the Garden of Eden scene, for here too all seems idyllic, with the universal God walking among the trees and no major separations between peoples having yet occurred. It is only when read alongside Rahab's story, and other texts that followed as Israel ordered its scriptural tradition, which make it clear that these Israelite ancestors *were* 'other' than the indigenous peoples of the land, that there seems a certain naïvety in this assumed right to be there, in the company of those 'others' in v. 6 whose land they have just entered and are looking to appropriate. Listening for the cross-cultural echo, I wonder whether this is a similar naïvety to that expressed by Sarah Stephens writing to her sister, on the 23 January 1842:

> As we landed we saw two of the natives squatting with their blankets, their faces much tattooed. They looked so pleasant and held out their hands to shake ours which several of us did... What has been said of them, as far as I can judge, is not one bit more than they deserve. They are a fine race of people and there is a great deal of intelligence in their countenances.[21]

Was that a positive comment? There is at least a whiff of patronizing cultural superiority in her granting them 'a great deal of intelligence'. But certainly, once in the land, there is no expression of fear or sense of danger, such as Charlotte had anticipated. So too Sarai, in the silence behind Abram, apparently moved through the land in equal safety; no fears are expressed until the departure into Egypt.

Before I pick up this puzzling disjunction, I want to add another reading, yet another panel to this imagined collage of voices. Recognizing that readers read gaps as well as text, I want to move out from the scholarly conversations for a while to listen to those whose art is creative imagining, which may or may not have either scholars or the faithful in mind. So I wish to add Sara Maitland's and Jenny Diski's readings of Sarai to my panels, for these writers, too, are journeying with her:

> Once she prayed with the same zeal and faith as he does still. Then she learned that this God of his was not hers. Everything she knew of now belonged to Abraham: the sheep, the servants, the tents, herself. And his God, too. That it

---

21.   Porter and MacDonald, '*My Hand Will Write*', p. 33.

is not so somewhere else, far away, in the scented courts of her childhood, is little or no comfort to her. She left them proudly, she cannot return. Abraham's God does not listen to a word she says to Him.[22]

Perhaps she knew all along that there could be no return, that life was lived in only one direction and memory merely tormented the discontented with its capacity to look backwards, but, as in a dream where the dreamer suspects they might be dreaming but refuses to vacate the dreamscape, Sarai allowed memory to whisper to her of the past and chose to believe it said future. Though she thought she was humouring her deluded husband by going along on his trek to nowhere as ordered by no one, she was in truth no more in touch with reality than Abram... They came to a land called Canaan. It was no different from other places they had travelled through, a mixed land of desert and wells, lush enough in parts to sustain herds, with settlements here and there but with nothing of the urban sophistication of Ur or even of Harran... It seemed to Sarai to be just another place they were passing through on their journey of promised but never-to-be-reached destination.[23]

These two glimpses of a Sarai of the gaps stand at a distance, with barely a glance at the ancient scribes. Is this the biblical Abram's Sarai at all? But as I read Sara Maitland and Jenny Diski reading Sarai, I find myself nodding; I now recognize this woman of tormented memory and teasing dreams whom I have had such difficulty drawing out from the shadows of the biblical text. She is a woman that I can understand. She may still be keeping her place in the biblical scenario, but her face may not be so recognizable to biblical readers accustomed in their own minds to a Sarai supposedly agreeing wholeheartedly with her husband; a construct equally drawn from the gaps. But place this Sarai on the intertextual panel, and there is again a conversation to be found with the women in that early colonial world of Aotearoa New Zealand. For while Maria Richmond and Sarah Stephens may have felt optimistic and positive about life in the 'new' land, Fanny Dillon's letter to her sister Lilly, written from Waimea on 12 October 1843, sees it differently:

The government at Auckland is both imbecile and weak; they treat Rauparaha like an independent sovereign instead of one of the Queen's subjects and we are told not to resist him. The Maories [sic] are very cunning and very treacherous and never to be depended on either for good or bad.[24]

Such alarming fearful distrust stands closer in my collage to the panel representing the Egyptian episode that begins at v. 10. Here there is a narrative disjunction, a further storyline dislocation; for no sooner has Abram made his proprietorial tour around the land of the Canaanites, than the land itself disgorges him and sends him off to Egypt, where

22. Sara Maitland, *A Book of Spells* (London: Michael Joseph, 1987), pp. 113-14.
23. Jenny Diski, *Only Human: A Comedy* (London: Virago Press, 2000), pp. 126, 130.
24. Porter and MacDonald, 'My Hand Will Write', p. 109.

he said to his wife Sarai, 'I know well that you are a woman beautiful in appearance; and when the Egyptians see you, they will say, "This is his wife"; then they will kill me, but they will let you live. Say you are my sister, so that it may go well with me because of you'. (vv. 11-13)

If I had difficulty bringing Sarai into view in the first half of the chapter and needed to resort to the hermeneutics of imagination, that is now no longer the case. If vv. 6-9 allowed glimpses of a distant memory of a time without tension or conflict, this second narrative episode moves the reader to a world where all is suddenly thrown into separation. Sarai may have been hidden in those earlier verses, with only the gap-filling fictioning imaginers bringing her to voice, but the reader was given no reason to fear for her safety. Now with the flight to Egypt comes fear. There needs to be space here for a voice from those critical analysts whose theoretical templates combine gender with race and ethnicity. For current gender/race studies are pointing to the way in which 'in nationalist and racialist narratives...women often play important symbolic roles...carrying in their bodies the collective love and honour of "the nation"'.[25] It is, of course, not only the honour of Israel that Sarai is carrying in her body, it is also the hopes for the seed of the divine promise which will allow Israel to come into being. The biblical tension is now sharp. Is both the honour and the promise in jeopardy? Gender/ race findings again provide a fit, noting that the issues of 'protection/violation for women' are 'key themes' in national narratives. This is the dramatic tension for the bearer of the honour. Is there to be protection for her, or is she to suffer violation? Is such a fate even to be whispered by readers of this sacred ancestor narrative? What is disturbing in the Genesis narrative, if it can be assumed that up to this point she has journeyed under the protection of Abram, is that Sarai now apparently moves from that protection to violation, for once in Egypt, Abram's sole care is for his own protection. But there is yet another disturbing finding: while there is clearly a distinction to be made between the experiences of women who are protected and those who are violated, both moves can be recognized as each being 'exploitative in that each silence women'.[26] Sarai is still moving in the silence behind Abram. But there is yet another postcolonial template that may be laid over this text, for the tale of an outsider woman handed over to another man presumably for sexual possession resonates again with colonialist discourse. As Ellen Armour writes in the context of United States black/white polarity:

Only (in)visibly white women enter the domestic circle where they move from daughter to wife to mother (all positions marked by the phallus)... Her

25. Helma Lutz, Ann Phoenix and Nira Yuval-Davis, 'Introduction: Nationalism, Racism and Gender—European Crossfires', in *idem* (eds.), *Crossfires: Nationalism, Racism and Gender in Europe* (London: Pluto Press, 1995), pp. 1-25 (9).

26. Lutz, Phoenix and Yuval-Davis, 'Introduction', p. 10.

> desire is his desire, in many ways... The question or possibility of her *jouis-sance* has no place within the phallocratic economy.[27]

This is in contrast to African American women who 'are constituted as nothing but desire, nothing but sexuality'. Here colour is seen as the significant boundary marker, but 'otherness' in all its forms tends to divide women in these terms. Is this what Abram knows? That once they enter Egypt, Sarai will be seen as a woman of 'Otherness' and therefore presumed not only as desirable but as desiring? And he concurs! In view of the now well recognized connection between violated woman and violated land, this is a disturbing addition to an origin narrative.

And so to the final outcome of the story of ch. 12, which is the subsequent return to the land. Here, in the dividing of the land the narrator sees no discrepancy between Abram's statement to Lot, 'Is not the whole land before you?' (13.9), and his own comment that 'at that time the Canaanites and the Perizzites lived in the land' (v. 7). This returns me once again to my own colonial history, to the voices of New Zealand historians such as James Belich who writes,

> A situation of parity with, or inferiority to, peoples like the Maori simply did not accord with British expectations. The British were not satisfied with part of the land, part of the economy, or part of the government.[28]

Although apparently now uninvolved, Sarai has nonetheless played her part in the move towards this land-taking.

These panels of interpretative possibilities have added layers of vulnerability for Sarai. She is no longer to be seen simply as Sarai, the agreeing and faithful wife of an ancient once-upon-a-time Abram, if she ever was that. While as an immigrant woman her entry story resonates with those of later biblically literate settler women and raises sharp questions of colonialist appropriation, in the move to Egypt she remains an archetypal Sarai, but an archetypal woman in a gendered and ethnically polarized world of women's alienation, where both protection and the risk of violation see her silenced. If the analytical terms may be anachronistic, the dynamics show a disturbing fit.

But there is another aspect to Sarai. The collage is not complete. For 'Sarai was barren; she had no child' (Gen. 11.30). So the Bible introduces her, with a barrenness which hangs over and settles around those whose lives intersect with hers in the early chapters of Genesis, settling particularly on Abraham and Hagar, the slave girl, who enters the narrative in ch. 16, that 'Other' who, reversing the travel of ch. 12, comes up from Egypt to serve the

---

27. Ellen T. Armour, *Deconstruction, Feminist Theology, and the Problem of Difference: Subverting the Race/Gender Divide* (Chicago: Chicago University Press, 1999), pp. 176-77.
28. Belich, *The New Zealand Wars*, p. 304.

one who previously served the Pharaoh. As I move into this second narrative, I decide to read the text closely before setting up conversation partners or applying a postcolonial template.

There may have been an ambiguity in Sarai's serving in ch. 12, but this time there is no question and it is Sarai herself, the barren one, who plans a sexual serving for Hagar. But is it for Hagar, or for herself, or for Israel? Is it for Abram? Certainly it involves a now silent/silenced Abram, who seemingly acquiesces in this bodily, sexual, entry. As it is told, the subaltern Hagar has no voice, merely a look after the deed (v. 4), but a look that changes the tenor of the tale, turning Sarai's talk to one of suffered wrong and hurt. As Heard notes, 'the almost exact correspondence between Sarai's words in 16.5 and the narrator's words in 16.4 invites readers to see the situation described in 16.4 through Sarai's eyes'. Did Sarai imagine this? Was it 'a projection of Sarai's own lowered self-esteem onto Hagar'? The textual ambiguity of the genitive (subjective or objective) which Heard highlights in v. 5 may well indicate the careful and deliberate subtlety of the writer, for 'indeed the ambiguity is poignant: perceiving herself as a victim of wrongdoing, Sarai in turn inflicts wrongdoing on Hagar'.[29] And so the power shuttles between husband and wife but lands on Sarai, who deals with it harshly to Hagar's cost.[30]

There follows that cluster of motifs so significant in Israel's story, of wilderness trek, divine annunciation, divine notice of affliction, with the enigmatic naming of God, for who is the seeing one here, Hagar or God? Is this a case of the deliberately ambiguous suffix? I note Danna Nolan Fewell's reference to Levinas' point that 'encountering the face of the Other is ethically obligating'.[31] But what might that mean for Hagar? And whose is the son that is born? The final chiasm of this chapter sets Abram's naming of 'his' son as the crux, with Hagar, the birthing M/Other, little more than a grammatical subject, to the benefit of the two males, Abram and Ishmael. The last word is Ishmael—the gift of God's hearing, but one who is promised by God to get in everyone's face. Is this the promised heir for Israel? The sharp cut of the covenant slices these chapters into sections, just as it slices Ishmael's flesh in ch. 17, until finally the message of the promised heir reaches Sarai, now to be named Sarah. And she laughs, but a laughter paired with fear. Reading in sequence, with the Sodom and Gomorrah/Lot episodes

29.   Heard, *Dynamics of Diselection*, pp. 66-67.

30.   Danna Nolan Fewell, 'Changing the Subject: Retelling the Story of Hagar the Egyptian', in Athalya Brenner (ed.), *Genesis* (The Feminist Companion to the Bible, Second Series, 1; Sheffield: Sheffield Academic Press, 1998), pp. 182-94 (188), points to the fact that neither Abraham nor Sarah refers to Hagar by name, that she is only named by God and the narrator.

31.   Fewell, 'Changing the Subject', p. 185.

followed by the second sister/wife tale, the motifs of sin, punishment and intercession, breaches of the hospitality code, invitations to rape, divine destruction, protection/violation tumble into view in quick succession. What a world for this promised child of laughter to enter! The motifs of birth and cutting now come together as the laughing one is cut into covenant relationship at eight days old. Sarah makes the connection with God, it is God who has made 'laughter' come, who has made the unbelievable happen—a child of their old age. But there is an ominous ambiguity in her words 'everyone who hears will laugh', for is it laughter with or laughter at (Gen. 21.6)?[32] Brett catches this well in his translation 'Laughter has Elohim made for me; whoever hears will laugh at me'.[33] There is a disturbing slippery-ness in this text. For what is Ishmael doing three verses later? Masquerading as an Isaac or simply laughing? Laughter in this narrative has become heavy with the weight of divine promise, too weighty in the eyes of Sarah, whose talk is now of separation and division; the son of the slave woman is not to share inheritance with the child of the miraculous laughter. Sarah names neither mother nor son; they are no more than unwanted objects, to be cast out. Sarah neglects to mention the fathering; she has but one son, but Abraham has two. The fate Sarah demands for t/his son causes Abraham deep distress. One might ask where God is to be found in this, but it is God who recognizes Abraham's distress, and acknowledges his double sonship. There is to be a double line of descendents, separated by the naming of Isaac's offspring for Abraham. Immediate consolation for Abraham, but immediate distress for Hagar, now returned to the wilderness—for the second time. Is this a replay of ch. 16? Redaction criticism has long raised the question of whether this second wilderness experience could be a textual replay with variations.[34] But where her earlier flight was on her own initiative, now she is sent out by the very father of the child promised then. Where there was a spring of water, the skinful given by Abraham soon runs dry and death looms for the boy. There is no laughter here, only weeping. But the parallels have not been exhausted. Promising a nation from Hagar's son, the God of seeing now opens Hagar's eyes to see water; finally a divine rescue for these

32. Heard, *Dynamics of Diselection*, p. 85, notes that 'in its only other biblical occurrence (Ezek 23.32), *sehoq* clearly takes the sense "object of ridicule". If Sarah has this sense in mind in v. 6a, she may be anticipating that her bearing of a child will turn her into a laughingstock… If so, the simple sight of Ishmael laughing may be enough to arouse her anger… She may project her own feelings of embarrassment onto Ishmael, and imagine that he is laughing *at her*.'

33. Brett, *Genesis: Procreation*, p. 60.

34. So T.D. Alexander, 'Are the Wife/Sister Incidents of Genesis Literary Compositional Variants?', *VT* 42 (1992), pp. 145-53. See Sean E. McEvenue for an example of redaction criticism attributing different source material behind each account, in 'A Comparison of Narrative Styles in the Hagar Stories', *Semeia* 3 (1975), pp. 64-80.

two. And so the narrative ends with a wilderness life for Ishmael, with God and with two Egyptian women.

A short story—perhaps one tale with variations, perhaps a tale of disturbing repetition, but whatever else this is, it is at heart a story of embodied sexuality. But recognition of this leads to that other recognition, of the emotion, of the hurt and suffering involved, only a little of which is expressed in the text, most lying hidden beneath the textual surface. I, as all readers must, find myself attempting to fill in those gaps, left by the storyteller. Pamela Reis has imagined Abram saying in 16.6, 'What ever you do to her is fine with me, for I have no feelings for her whatsoever', in an attempt to reassure Sarai 'that she is still the sole wife, that she, alone, is loved'.[35] The novelist Jenny Diski supposes that

> Sarai discovered that playing God at his own game gave her all God's disadvantages. She could manipulate the world, but she could not participate in it. The world swelled with the life that she had willed into being, and mocked her for being unable to indulge in her achievement with any of her senses but that of sight... Sarai could do no more about her behaviour to Hagar than Hagar could do about her innately youthful triumph over her mistress. They were both prisoners of human conflict, of wishes perversely come true.[36]

I would like to suppose and imagine a little further into the depths of this tale, for what lies at the base of this human conflict? If this is a story about sexual conflict, then it is also a story of sexual passion and sexual using, but of the emotions involved in the bodily sexual encounters so little is mentioned. I return to the collage: there needs to be a place for an intertextual dialogue partner to highlight the sexual dynamics which lie at the base of this story but which the text leaves for the most part lying just beneath the surface of the text, glimpsed perhaps only in the look of ch. 16 and Sarah's mention of 'pleasure' in 18.12. Luce Irigaray's *Elemental Passions* with its offer of 'some fragments from a woman's voyage as she goes in search of her identity in love' within the silences of the Genesis script allows me an exploration of the emotional sub-text of this section of Israel's story.[37] I imagine how this could be the voice of Hagar:

> And I was speaking, but you did not hear. I was speaking from further than your furthest bounds. Beyond the place you were penetrating to reveal the secret of resistance to your tongue... From a captive and forgotten childhood lying beneath any of your potential gestures of mastery or appropriation... And it was not that I was withholding myself from you, but that you did not know where to find me. You searched and searched for me, in you. Wanting

35. Pamela Tamarkin Reis, 'Hagar Requited', *JSOT* 87 (2000), pp. 75-109 (87).

36. Diski, *Only Human*, pp. 180-81.

37. Luce Irigaray, *Elemental Passions* (trans. Joanne Collie and Judith Still; London: Athlone Press, 1992), p. 4.

me still to be virgin material for the building of your world to come. But how could it ever be reached if, in that quest, once again you wanted yourself as you already are?... Nothing from outside the place where you already are reaches you...[38]

You cling to me as to your ancient home, and you open up between you and me, me and you, that gap—death.[39]

And this the voice of Abram to Hagar:

My child of night, you have known nothing but a cold, dark womb, how can I console you? Even your tears are black... They are drowned in ink... Except, from time to time, a momentary flash from childhood. Still arising from a bottomless anguish. Refusing to be consoled. Avidly nurturing grief, a prey to solitude. Hands stretching out in all directions, clutching at empty air... But how can I become cold and dark enough to give you birth once more?... Reflective enough to remind you of your most ancient spectacles. So that you see reflected in me once more the hardness of your childhood emotions.[40]

Perhaps inevitably, sexual passion becomes entwined with the political; what may be metaphorical in Irigaray will be heard with sobering recognition of the more literal in Genesis:

You only encourage proximity when it is framed by property... Always you assign a place to me... You frame. Encircle. Bury. Entomb?... [T]he frame you bear with you, in front of you, is always empty. It marks, takes, marks as it takes: its fill... Could it be that what you have is just the frame, not the property? Not a bond with the earth but merely this fence that you set up, implant wherever you can? You mark out boundaries, draw lines, surround, enclose. Excising, cutting out. What is your fear? That you might lose your property. What remains is an empty frame. You cling to it, dead.[41]

Perhaps for both Hagar and Sarai the following are the defining words that lock them within their destinies, addressed not so much to Abram as to the world in which they live: 'You close me up in house and family. Final, fixed walls.'[42] And this the world from which Hagar flees:

Alone, I rediscover my mobility. Movement is my habitat... Whoever imposes a roof over my head, wears me out. Let me go where I have not yet arrived.[43]

But the story is also the story of the limitations of her flight; she, the outsider, the 'other', is destined to remain within Israel's narrative. Again Irigaray's words do double duty:

38. Irigaray, *Elemental Passions*, pp. 9-10.
39. Irigaray, *Elemental Passions*, p. 11.
40. Irigaray, *Elemental Passions*, p. 23.
41. Irigaray, *Elemental Passions*, pp. 24-25.
42. Irigaray, *Elemental Passions*, p. 25.
43. Irigaray, *Elemental Passions*, p. 25.

What you intend for me is the place which is appropriate for the need you have of me. What you reveal to me is the place where you have positioned me, so that I remain available for your needs. Even if you should evict me, I have to stay there so that you can continue to be settled in your universe. And this world takes place neither simply inside you or outside you. It passes from inside to outside, from outside to inside your being. In which should be based the very possibility of dwelling… Already inside and outside, I am continuously divided between the two spheres of your space, and you never meet me as a whole. You never meet me…where am I? Nowhere. Disappeared forever in your presence.[44]

Again, words that are describing the emotional turmoil of bodily encounter in Irigaray are read with an added layer of meaning in the desperation of a sexual act enjoined for the sake of an heir to the covenant community that would be Israel:

I gave you something to play for, let you have some play. Entranced at being your reserve. In sum, a surplus? So that you could pursue your path… The privilege of an omnipotent God. Feeding the cycle of your returns and repetitions from a breast that never runs dry. I had not begun to exist save in my pretension to be a needed womb and mother for you… You filled me with your emptiness. You filled me up with your lacks… I would bring you my most precious gift: my hollows. You were the one who became a gaping hole, I became full.[45]

There was also the pleasure of Sarah's miraculous conception:

Jouissance in the copula engenders form-body…bringing us into the world once more… Is fire not joy? Is burning with you not grace? The very lightest, dancing.[46]

While Irigaray was not intending her words to be applied to such a three-way encounter, nor to be read through any lens but the emotional and sexual, what she has written can be heard speaking on many levels; heard as the voice of difference, these words speak again for Hagar, the biblical 'other', destined for the wilderness, the borderland:

The whole is not the same for me as it is for you. For me, it can never be one. Can never be completed, always in-finite. When you talk about Infinity, it seems to me that you are speaking of a closed totality… The absolute of self-identity—in which you were, will be, could be.[47]

Irigaray's words fit well, for this is essentially a bodied story, of people using people sexually for gain, of the joy of a child born of sexual pleasure—sexual

44. Irigaray, *Elemental Passions*, pp. 47-48.
45. Irigaray, *Elemental Passions*, p. 61.
46. Irigaray, *Elemental Passions*, pp. 79-80.
47. Irigaray, *Elemental Passions*, pp. 89.

jouissance—albeit of a miraculous old age. It is not only postcolonial scholars who are exploring the possibility of dialogic conversations between texts quite removed from each other, and introducing an 'intertextuality', which as 'a reading strategy works by deliberately bringing disparate texts together, to see how one looks through the lens of another'.[48] Here the intertextual reading has been a reminder that this is a story of sexual, bodied humans in a human tale.

At the same time the Genesis text is very much a human tale told from 'somewhere' and a somewhere with its own colours and its own embedded messages encoded through the telling. If, as appears likely, Genesis came together as material gathered in the Persian era, then this tale also demands to be read keeping in mind those foreign wives driven out by their husbands in obedience to the requirements of the powers of the day according to Ezra chs. 9 and 10. My collage needs to reserve space for this. For, as Heard illustrates, this tale of family conflict, where both ethnic difference and inheritance are issues, fits neatly into such a scenario:

> As the paradigmatic product of a cross-ethnic intermarriage, Ishmael functions basically as object lesson for the 'proper' Yehudian response to intermarriage… Abraham's dismissal of Hagar and Ishmael stands as both a paradigm for action and a reassurance for the men called upon to undertake similar drastic actions. God demands that the voice of Sarai (or that of Nehemiah) be obeyed. No matter what one's attachment to one's half-Egyptian son, no matter whether he was circumcised at eight days (or thirteen years), God insists that the children of intermarriages, and their mothers, be dismissed from Abraham's household and from Yehud.[49]

Hagar as an Egyptian would have a quite particular significance in a world where the Egypto-Greek threat to Persian control of its lands was high on the list of concerns. How to discourage any tendencies towards pro-Egyptian attitudes and keep the people loyal to the Persian-authorized rule in Yehud?[50] Hagar, the Egyptian, would have been a useful tool, able to emphasize that no foreign wives and mixed-raced children were acceptable, and that those of Egyptian origin in particular were to be driven out. Such historical questioning is now no longer about possible Nuzi parallels and datings for the wandering of Israel's ancestors, but has an eye firmly fixed upon the scribe or

48.   David Jobling, Tina Pippin and Ronald Schleifer, 'Part III. The Conscience of the Bible: Introduction', in *idem* (eds.), *The Postmodern Bible Reader* (Oxford: Basil Blackwell, 2001), pp. 249-64 (254), with particular reference to the work of Mikhail Bakhtin and Julia Kristeva.

49.   Heard, *Dynamics of Diselection*, p. 176.

50.   See Brett, *Genesis: Procreation*, who draws in turn on the work of Kenneth Hoglund in *Achaemenid Imperial Administration in Syria-Palestine and the Missions of Ezra and Nehemiah* (Atlanta: Scholars Press, 1992).

scribes responsible for the form of the narrative as it appears on the scroll, who far from being historicists concerned with preserving past traditions for their own sake were 'directly engaged with the issues of their *own* day'.[51] The tools of historical criticism, traditionally understood, have been exchanged for those of the New Historicism, where the emphasis is on the reciprocal relationship of text and context, noting how traditions of the past are used to serve the interests of the present.[52] The whence of the origins of the ancestor tradition has slipped out of view; situated now in Persian Yehud, Sarah and Hagar are both shaped by and shapers of the world of the scroll-writer(s).[53]

At this point I wish to return to the postcolonial lens, for such fear of 'mixing' is all too familiar to readers from colonial or postcolonial contexts, being present from the earliest days of European so-called 'settlement'. Set Sarah and Hagar's tale alongside some of the accounts of those early cross-cultural encounters recorded in the diaries and writings of the missionaries and settlers, and the connections are disturbing. The Colensos provide just one such well documented example from my own context of New Zealand. This CMS missionary pair, Elizabeth and William, were partners in what was, in effect, a missionary marriage of convenience encouraged by Bishop Selwyn,[54] but five years later, in 1848, William entered into an affair with the housegirl, Ripeka. Although, unlike Sarai, Elizabeth had had no hand in this, and indeed was unaware for some time of what was happening, echoes of Genesis begin to be heard after the birth of the child Ripeka bore to William. Not surprisingly, the ramifications were significant for all involved; Ripeka was married (off) to another of the house servants, Hamuera,[55] as Elizabeth did her best to turn Ripeka's feelings away from William, who subsequently wrote in his autobiography, 'There followed a terrible time for

51.   Brett, *Genesis: Procreation*, p. 137.

52.   In Stephen Greenblatt's words in *Marvellous Possessions: The Wonder of the New World* (Oxford: Clarendon Press, 1991), p. 6, 'representations are not only products but producers, capable of decisively altering the very forces that brought them into being'.

53.   See Claire Colebrook, *New Literary Histories: New Historicism and Contemporary Criticism* (Manchester: Manchester University Press, 1997), p. 28, 'New historicism… moves towards the idea of the text as practice: the critic focuses on the material effects and circumstances produced by the text and in which the text is produced'.

54.   William noted in his autobiography that when they married 'we two had no love for each other', although he believed 'that mutual affection would surely follow'. Notably, 'all that I wanted was a suitable partner, particularly in mission work' (Porter and MacDonald, 'My Hand Will Write', p. 296).

55.   There is some debate about the date of this. It may have been the same year, 1848, although William records it as 1850. See William Colenso, 'Autobiography—Typescript 88-103-1/01', in *Further Papers* (ed. A.G. Bagnall; Alexander Turnbull Library, n.d.), Appendix 2, quoted by Cathy Ross, 'More than Wives?' (draft of unpublished PhD dissertation, Auckland University, 2003), n.p. (quoted with permission).

us all…' Elizabeth's letter to William some time later provides an echo of that much discussed 'look' directed at Sarai by Hagar:

> I recollect that Rebecca had said something to the same effect ['that I was not fit to be any mans' wife'] to the girls in the house which they told me of, and that she had it from you.[56]

Like Abram, William loved his son, but, in marked contrast, refused to allow him to leave with his mother in her comings and goings over the next two years. Here the differences with the Genesis story are notable, for in this case it was Ripeka who made the decision to leave, and William who acted to keep his son in his own household.[57] As for Elizabeth, if she was being truthful in the letter she wrote to William in 1852,

> Little Wi I love sincerely as though he were my own… I look upon him now as my own—given into my charge to bring up for God, and as long as life lasts I shall never forsake him. I trust I have been able to forgive all who have done me wrong from my heart…[58]

This, however, did not prove to be the case. Although a year later she writes from Wairoa that William is not to come for Wi or send for him, for she 'cannot part with him', once she reached Auckland and met the refusal of her own missionary father even to have Wi in his house matters changed. She now writes to William (May 1854):

> I solemnly assure you it was nothing but the fear of you that induced me to retain the child. You <u>forced</u> upon me in utter disregard of my natural feelings…<u>I was your slave and dare not refuse,</u> and therefore I prayed continually and most <u>earnestly</u> for grace to be kind towards him. And afterwards, through having no other object near me to love (my own being gone) I began to love the child with such love as pity and compassion for a helpless infant are sure to engender in a compassionate mind.[59]

While William Colenso loved his son and wished him brought up with his children by Elizabeth, the colonial missionary world had other views. It is difficult to separate the issues of the extra-marital sexual 'affair' and that of the mixed race child. The archdeacon, George Kissling wrote to his colleague of 'the most afflictive and disgraceful shock which our Mission has

56.   William Colenso, 'Letters from his Wife, Elizabeth 88-103-1/22' (Alexander Turnbull Library, 1843–99), Wairoa, 24 September 1853, quoted by Cathy Ross 'More than Wives?', n.p.

57.   As they left for the last time by canoe Ripeka and Hamuera attempted to take Wi with them. In his autobiography William recorded what happened, 'I rushed from the study, jumped on board, and demanded from R. my child; she gave you into my hands and I bore you off into the house; madly followed by the Maoris of the canoe'.

58.   Porter and MacDonald, 'My Hand Will Write', p. 298. Wi is the abbreviation for the child's name, Wiremu.

59.   Porter and MacDonald, 'My Hand Will Write', pp. 301-302.

sustained'[60] and Elizabeth herself records a Mr Grace, a CMS missionary
from Taupo, advising her against taking Wi to Auckland on the grounds that
'It would be such an injury to the <u>Cause</u> for Wi to be publicly seen'.[61] This
would seem to hint of an ideological attitude very similar to that of Ezra–
Nehemiah appearing once again. The end result for Wi, was, as Porter and
MacDonald express it, that he was 'decisively dumped as being a blot on the
missionary escutcheon'. Their suggestion is that Elizabeth's about-turn in
regard to Wi is yet another instance of the 'sense of duty to "the Cause"',[62]
and, indeed, Elizabeth writes to William in those terms in the letter quoted
above dated May 1854, accusing him of 'the irreparable injury you have done
to the Cause'. The 'injury' could be either the 'adultery' or its result or both.
Once in Auckland, Elizabeth seems to have wanted to deny the European
paternity of this child altogether, writing several times to William, both that
'Wi grows more and more like Hamuera', and that 'everyone who knew
Hamuera says he is *his* child. He grows more and more like him'—a suggestion which William regarded as 'strange, bitter and spiteful'.[63] His devotion
to Wi seems to have been unambiguous, most marked perhaps by his
defiance of Bishop Selwyn's order that Wi to be returned to his mother,
although Cathy Ross suggests another possible interpretation of this, in that
'although William was happy enough to "cohabit" with a Maori woman, he
did not want his child brought up by Maori'.[64] Her term 'cohabit' hints, at
the very least, at the flow of boundaries, the overflow, the refusal of contain-
ment; the result, of course, is embodied in the child Wi. The connections
between the loved but ultimately excluded Ishmael and Wi are challenging;
both stand as embodied 'moments of panic', that historical moment which
Homi Bhabha describes as resulting from 'a contingent, borderline experience [that] opens up *in-between* colonizer and colonized'.[65] Threatening to
the prescribed sense of decency and order, these panic-inducing children
must be dismissed and sent out of sight.

If Sarah and Hagar have appeared set in binary opposition over against
each other, so too have Elizabeth and Ripeka. Yet gender and postcolonial
analysis come together in highlighting the limitations of binary categories
when reading the lives of women of dominant cultures; so often they are
inside and outside, at the centre and on the periphery at the same time. Both

60. Porter and MacDonald, '*My Hand Will Write*', p. 297.
61. Porter and MacDonald, '*My Hand Will Write*', p. 298. In the same letter, Elizabeth writes, 'Do not make yourself uneasy about Wi. I shall not alter my conduct towards
him, let people say what they will.'
62. Porter and MacDonald, '*My Hand Will Write*', pp. 299-300.
63. Porter and MacDonald, '*My Hand Will Write*', p. 300.
64. Ross, 'More than Wives?'.
65. Homi K. Bhabha, *The Location of Culture* (London and New York: Routledge,
1994), pp. 206-207, uses this term in his discussion of 'the margin of hybridity'.

Sarah and Elizabeth were wives of the culture later assumed as dominant, and viewed through its lens this was in all probability the cause both of their problems and their actions. Sarah's barrenness was not acceptable in the world of chosen covenant partners required to replicate themselves over generations; Elizabeth's guardianship of her husband's mixed child Wiremu was not acceptable in the white European missionary world of her time.[66] No wonder Sarah reacted as she did to Hagar's pregnancy, and Elizabeth was so ambivalent about Wiremu. But both Ripeka and Hagar disappear from view, finally so peripheral that they are lost from sight; little is known of Ripeka's later life, Colenso seeing her again only once, ten years later. Hagar is already moving out of focus at the end of ch. 21; the reader's gaze is now firmly fixed upon Ishmael, with Hagar, his mother, mentioned only as negotiating his wife.[67] Setting Hagar and Ishmael beside Ripeka and Wi, and Sarai and Abram with William and Elizabeth, albeit with all their differences, provides a sobering, if not frightening, repetition of a theme, as alive in nineteenth-century New Zealand as in sixth-century Yehud.

But this, of course, assumes that all is as it appears on the surface of the Yehud-based biblical text. Just as the reader may need to ask questions of the interests lurking behind the text, so sometimes the reader may ask whether the biblical text is speaking in more than one voice even on the surface. So, here there is a question of whether the biblical text is condoning or critiquing its seeming anti-Egyptian stand. For the God who is 'seen' or 'seeing' in Genesis 16 seems double-faced; turning to Hagar, this God announces a divine annunciation and indicates compassionate hearing of her affliction, but turning towards Sarai sends her servant back to the harsh and bitter mistress.[68] So too in the second retelling, God expresses consolation for Abraham with divine promise of a nation of descendents, but there follows

---

66. See the view expressed only a few years earlier: 'It may be deemed a cold and mercenary calculation; but we must say, that instead of attempting an amalgamation of the two races—Europeans and Zealanders—as is recommended by some persons, the wiser course would be, to let the native race gradually retire before the settlers, and ultimately become extinct'; see Robert J.C. Young, *Colonial Desire: Hybridity in Theory, Culture and Race* (London and New York: Routledge, 1995), p. 9, quoting Anonymous, 'The New System of Colonization—Australia and New Zealand', *The Phrenological Journal and Magazine of Modern Science* 11 NS 1 (1838), pp. 247-60 (258).

67. I am indebted to Professor Cheryl Exum for drawing my attention to this parallel between Hagar and Ripeka. In December 1885 William writes in a letter to his son, now called Willie, that 1861 was the first time he had seen Rebecca since she had left the household in 1852, and that it was also the last time he ever saw her. See A.G. Bagnall and G.C. Petersen, *William Colenso, Printer, Missionary, Botanist, Explorer, Politician: His Life and Journeys* (Wellington, NZ: A.H. & A.W. Reed, 1948), p. 429.

68. In the text the order is reversed, and Brett, *Genesis: Procreation*, p. 59, may well be right in reading this as stating the *status quo* of the dominant ideology first, before the undermining promise to Hagar.

the pitiless expulsion of Ishmael with Hagar into the deathly rigours of the
wilderness. Yet, as Mark Brett suggests, 'the name of her son indicates divine
concern with all such suffering',[69] so the message heard is that one may drive
out such m/Others but one may not drive them out beyond the concern of
Israel's God. Ishmael is equally the son of Abraham, and God remains with
Hagar and Ishmael.[70] Ishmael, moreover, is not going to kowtow to anyone;
he emerges as a fiercely independent character. There are slippages in this
text and they are crafty.[71] The sub-text runs counter to what appears to be
the flow of the official storyline. In a world where there is an Egypto-Greek
threat to Persian control of its lands, readers can watch the Egyptian Hagar
sent—not once, but twice—into the wilderness. We get the message: no
Egyptian wives! But we also read the counter message; 'divine blessing flows
extravagantly over the covenant's borders to include Ishmaelites, Ammon-
ites and Moabites'.[72] While Yehud was small and under Persian dominion
and so understandably producing texts with a strong pro-Persian voice, pro-
Egypt and pro-Greece factions, as well as local resistance to outside influence
and ordering, would not be unexpected. Reading a sub-text in this way is to
read a coded resistance, in which, in effect, the ancient scribes or scribe were
employing that decolonizing strategy which effectively 'undermines the
operation of colonial power by inscribing and disclosing the trace of the
other so that it reveals itself as double-voiced'.[73] Did later readers miss the
message?

   In this strategy the role of the wilderness space is a crucial element.
Scholars have long recognized its significance in providing parallels with
the God/Moses and God/Israel stories,[74] so that these Genesis chapters may

   69.   Brett, *Genesis: Procreation*, p. 61, marking this with the 'if' of Hagar being taken
as 'exemplary' of the dispossessed.
   70.   As Brett, *Genesis: Procreation*, p. 71, notes, 'it is striking that the promise of a
"great nation" was precisely the first of the series of promises, given to Abram, that
climaxed in the language of covenant. In passing on this promise to Hagar and Ishmael,
Elohim devolves it to descendents of Abraham who were ostensibly separated from the
privileged covenant lineage in 17.19-22.'
   71.   See Brett, *Genesis: Procreation*, p. 137: 'The stories concerned with Hagar...are
indicative of the editors' theology, in that they subtly subvert any version of genealogical
exclusivism or moral superiority. This perspective on Israel's beginnings is conveyed
artfully but indirectly, in view of the fact that the editors were contesting the ideology of
the Persian-sponsored governors.'
   72.   Brett, *Genesis: Procreation*, p. 84. Note Fewell's point, 'Changing the Subject', p.
194, that the ending of this story might answer the questions asked in the time of Ezra
and Nehemiah: 'Where will these women and children go? How will they live?' with the
'opiate' response: 'Don't worry. God will take care of them.'
   73.   Young, *Colonial Desire*, p. 23.
   74.   A classic text is David Daube's *The Exodus Pattern in the Bible* (London: Faber
& Faber, 1963), pp. 23-38. See also Claus Westermann, *Genesis 12–36: A Continental*

be read as one initial episode or phrase in the larger 'rhythm of a divinely appointed destiny in Israelite history'.[75] It is not easy, however, to categorize or interpret its appearance in the biblical accounts. Dozeman, for example, has suggested that it has two quite different roles even in the Genesis drama, one following Victor Turner's rites of passage readings, where it functions as the place of the hero's initiation and transformation, and the other as 'the drift or borderland between civilization and chaos'.[76] But what is unexpected and arresting here in a gender-alert reading is that it is Hagar who sets this rhythm in motion, being the first person approached by God in the wilderness, according to the final ordering of the canonical text.[77] The fact that she is Egyptian becomes all the more significant when read with Exodus in mind: what is God doing coming to the rescue of an Egyptian?[78] A world where an Egyptian Hagar experiences a theophany and divine annunciation in the wilderness is surely a dissonance in the Israelite-focused world of Abram and Sarai, and if Hagar is a Moses in male drag this puts a different spin on things again. The political strategies within this text appear more complex at each reading.

The wilderness itself returns me to the colonial/postcolonial dialogue, with its current talk of borderlands and spaces of resistance. Borderlands, margins, and spaces of both transformation and mediating tension currently figure in works attempting to counteract the binary oppositions that have driven much of contemporary critical thinking. As I have been noting throughout this work, the role of such oppositions has a long history, for the

Commentary (trans. John J. Scullion; Minneapolis: Fortress Press, 1995), p. 344; Phyllis Trible, *Texts of Terror* (Philadelphia: Fortress Press, 1984); Thomas B. Dozeman, 'The Wilderness and Salvation History in the Hagar Story', *JBL* 117 (1998), pp. 23-43; Brett, *Genesis: Procreation*.

75. Robert Alter, *The Art of Biblical Narrative* (New York: Basic Books, 1981), p. 60.

76. Dozeman, 'The Wilderness and Salvation History', pp. 32-33, the latter 'as a location outside of civilization, where entire nations can live at risk with God'.

77. Dozeman, 'The Wilderness and Salvation History', p. 24, notes 'the absence of the wilderness in all other stories in Genesis' apart from three peripheral references. He asks whether 'Hagar's repeated journey there is intended to embed her story in a larger history in which parallels are created between the lives of Hagar and Moses, and also between the Ishmaelites and Israelites'. As he notes, the wilderness of Paran is both the dwelling place of Ishmael, and the entry point for the Israelites after they Sinai in Num. 10. His form-critical thesis (pp. 34-35) is that the Hagar story was reinterpreted by Priestly writers who shifted the point of comparison away from Hagar and Moses 'to the similar wilderness experiences of Ishmaelites and Israelites' and 'structured the additions within their preferred framework of promise and fulfillment'. In this the later genealogy of Ishmael (Gen. 25.12-18) has a significant part.

78. Dozeman, 'The Wilderness and Salvation History', p. 29, quotes Tsevat's statement that 'Sarai does to a child of Egypt...what the Egyptians would later do to Sarai's children'.

margin, the place of exclusion, the place of the 'Other', has long been regarded as the necessary marker of difference and identity, employed both by Ezra and Nehemiah and the later colonial world. As I read the diary entries of Elizabeth Colenso I had a strong sense of the missionary stations, however isolated they were, being the centres of their world in the eyes of the Europeans; of the homelands of Ripeka from which she came and went much less is said. They were the places to which the missionaries came to 'mission', so that there is a narrative tension between what is present in the narrative and what is left out, what is regarded as in some sense unrepresent-able. There is, of course, an inherent irony in the role of wilderness—an irony that it has any role at all, being as it is a place of the dispatched and excluded, and, as such, functioning much as the non-space of the ghetto or the closet. The further irony, however, is that while remaining within the text as the margin to which she is dispatched, it remains as the place of Hagar's experience of theophany and promise, and is therefore, in the much quoted words of bell hooks, most significantly 'the site of radical possibility, a space of resistance...(which) offers one the possibility of radical perspective from which to see and create, to imagine alternatives, new worlds'.[79] Some scholars are currently drawing upon the language of spatial construct theory and using the term 'Thirdspace' to express such a space of possibility, the understanding being that Thirdspace indicates a dynamic 'thirding-as-Other-ing' move to break down binary oppositions and so allow a third alterna-tive to appear.[80] This fits well with Dozeman's suggestion of a 'borderland between civilization and chaos', for while Hagar's wilderness is markedly not the space of Sarai and Abraham, it is also not Egypt. As the space between it is a space such as bell hooks describes as 'a site of creativity and power, that inclusive space where we recover ourselves, where we move in solidarity to erase the category colonizer/colonized' and which 'offers one the possibility of radical perspective from which to see and create, to imagine alternatives, new worlds'.[81] And so ch. 21 ends with Hagar, the Egyptian subaltern, to use Spivak's term, and her son Ishmael, functioning as the narrative representa-tives of that transformative and destabilizing space with its message of divine

79.   bell hooks, *Yearning: Race, Gender, and Cultural Politics* (Boston, MA: South End Press, 1990), pp. 149-50.

80.   So, for example, Edward W. Soja, *Thirdspace: Journeys to Los Angeles and Other Real-and-Imagined Places* (Oxford: Basil Blackwell, 1996), p. 5. See also *idem*, 'Thirdspace: Expanding the Scope of the Geographical Imagination', in Doreen Massey, John Allen and Philip Sarre (eds.), *Human Geography Today* (Cambridge: Polity Press, 1999), pp. 260-78 (269): 'This Othering does not derive simply and sequentially from the original binary opposition and/or contradiction, but seeks instead to disorder, deconstruct and tentatively reconstitute in a different form the entire dialectical sequence and logic'.

81.   hooks, *Yearning*, pp. 152, 149-50. It functions much as the *mestiza* borderlands in the often-quoted writings of Gloria Anzaldúa.

blessing that borders cannot stop. Sarah, while remaining in the dominant narrative, has already been returned to a textual silence.

Where has this collage chapter with its literary, historical and postcolonial panels taken me? At its simplest I have seen Sarah and Hagar from many more angles. A further emphasis of the New Historicist approach is the continuing performance of texts, the way in which they 'both produce and reveal mechanisms of power' in each new context of performance.[82] So it has been in this reading of the textual Sarah and Hagar. Setting the Genesis account in the context of a colonialist narrative performance has served as a reminder for those of us living in colonial/postcolonial contexts that that these chapters cannot be dismissed as merely an ancient text. But to recognize this speaking of texts over a span of time is also to recognize that our own historical texts are also not locked into a past, and the dialogue of both texts heard together has been a reminder that our present is equally built on the inequalities of an 'othering' history which must be acknowledged before the transformative readings of the wilderness can be celebrated.[83]

The postcolonial lens also links a discussion of colonizing space and the sexual intertwinings of the three Genesis players, explored in the parallel reading with Irigaray, for it recognizes the way in which the sexuality of the human body has been, and continues to be, used as a foregrounding site of political and ideological issues. If it is true that 'Body and body politic, body and social body, body and city, body and citizen-body, are intimately linked productions',[84] it is all the more true of colonial discourse, where to quote Homi Bhabha,

> The construction of the colonial subject in discourse, and the exercise of colonial power through discourse, demands an articulation of forms of difference—racial and sexual. Such an articulation becomes crucial if it is held that the body is always simultaneously (if conflictually) inscribed in both the economy of pleasure and desire and the economy of discourse, domination and power.[85]

My thesis here is that both Hagar and Ripeka are notably inscribed in both. In the reading following Brett, however, what was striking about the biblical account was the way in which the telling became a double-voiced production, allowing a colonialist reading of excluded space in a binary-conceived

---

82. Colebrook, *New Literary Histories*, pp. 27-28.

83. It should be noted that missionary attitudes in Aotearoa New Zealand varied and were as complex as any other human endeavour. While I was writing this section the bones of Bishop Pompellier, New Zealand's first Roman Catholic bishop, were being brought back for reburial with 'his' people, and his respect for Maori was being remembered and celebrated at each stopping place.

84. Barbara Hooper in an unpublished manuscript quoted by Soja, 'Thirdspace: Expanding the Scope', p. 273.

85. Bhabha, *The Location of Culture*, p. 67.

world, and at the same time destabilizing that reading with its underside 'thirding' reading of inclusive possibility.

The multi-voiced readings with parallel texts took the exploration of double-voice in quite other directions, to highlight the 'various vantage points' from which my reading comes, and the kind of things I either knew about, or was attempting to know about. In the end, this was, I hope, 'a distinct interpretive act'. The Sarah, Hagar and Abraham narrative was the beginning point. For, as Trinh T. Minh-ha has commented,

> A story is *not* just a story. Once the forces have been aroused and set into motion, they can't simply be stopped at someone's request. Once told, the story is bound to circulate; humanized, it may have a temporary end, but its effects linger on and its end is never truly an end.[86]

I, of course, have taken its effects in my own direction and according to my own interests. But I would suggest that interpretive explorations likewise never come to an end and conversations about texts will spiral out and spill over into new contexts. If the spatial theorists are right, Minh-ha's words 'set in motion' also have to be taken seriously, for

> the exploration of Thirdspace must be additionally guided by some form of potentially emancipatory *praxis*, the translation of knowledge into action in a conscious—and consciously spatial—effort to improve the world in some significant way.[87]

I think the scribes of Genesis would have said 'Amen'.

86. Trinh T. Minh-ha, *Woman, Native, Other: Writing Postcoloniality and Feminism* (Bloomington: Indiana University Press, 1989), p. 133.
87. Soja, *Thirdspace: Journeys to Los Angeles*, p. 22.

8

DECOLONIZING WITH THE GODDESS:
FOLLOWING JOHN OF PATMOS AND WITI IHIMAERA

> The traveler needs to know how to find the crack between the earth, ordinary reality, and the sky on the horizon, the alternate reality.[1]

'And I saw the holy city, the new Jerusalem, coming down out of heaven from God' (Rev. 21.2). And descending as a bride from heaven! I sense I am in a dream world with the familiar and the new jostling against each other. Ordinary reality and alternate reality are merging here without a crack and I, the reader, am quite unsure of my footing. My eye lingers too over Babylon and the Woman Clothed with the Sun. Is it a crisis-driven urgency or an adrenalin shot of imagination that has driven the writer to choose the shock tactics of this genre? What is it that drives his desire to create such a work that 'reshapes familiar perceptions of this world and refurbishes the dulled imagination'[2] by conjuring up such mythic images in a textually visual world of fantasy? Catherine Keller has asked whether this is a book of cosmic-historical revolution or paranoid patriarchy, or whether, in its 'double-edged speech', it is both of these.[3] So, as I gaze at the female figures each veiled in her apocalyptic fancy, I am prepared to hear a double-edged speech once again.

My interest lies primarily in detecting the writer's strategies, in watching the way in which he applies these character tools, for the final effect has proved eminently re-usable century after century. So I wonder whether it might be possible to move behind the veiling, to catch a glimpse both of the

1. Bruce J. Malina and John J. Pilch, *Social-Science Commentary on the Book of Revelation* (Minneapolis: Fortress Press, 2000), p. 6, following Felicitas Goodman, *Where the Spirits Ride the Wind: Trance Journeys and Other Ecstatic Experience* (Bloomington: Indiana University Press, 1990).

2. James L. Resseguie, *Revelation Unsealed: A Narrative Critical Approach to John's Apocalypse* (Leiden: E.J. Brill, 1998), p. 193. See also Elisabeth Schüssler Fiorenza, *The Book of Revelation: Justice and Judgment* (Philadelphia: Fortress Press, 1985), p. 22.

3. Catherine Keller, *Apocalypse Now and Then: A Feminist Guide to the End of the World* (Boston: Beacon Press, 1996), p. 41.

figures themselves un-veiled, and of the seer at work fitting them out for their tasks in this imaginative work. Keller's mention of the cosmic-historical revolution, however, reminds me that the Apocalypse was initially as earthed in a specific historical reality as any other biblical work. It is the work of one called John, written on the island of Patmos, although just when is not so sure. While 'there is no unambiguous internal evidence for the date of the composition',[4] most scholars place the seer and his writing either near the end of the reign of Nero (68–69 CE) or late in the reign of Domitian (90–96 CE). In either placing this John is a writer penning his work under the power of imperial Rome. But was it the tensions and injustices of life under that imperium that provided the catalyst for the Apocalypse? The reference to the seer's being on Patmos as a result of his Christian testimony (1.9) might presuppose some personal trauma, perhaps related to views thought dangerous by Rome or its representatives. If so, then I might read the work as an expression of the pain and the hopes of a community under some threat, although there is a general consensus that there is little evidence for any widespread persecution of Christians during the reign of Domitian, despite his negative reputation.[5] This, of course, does not necessarily deny the possibility of localized conflict. While, at the very least, a sense of loss of control over their lives and destiny would be understandable, it is equally possible that the book reflects not so much a political as a faith-centred concern. As Adela Yarbro Collins has argued, the motivating factor may have been the tension, the 'cognitive dissonance...between John's vision of the kingdom of God' and 'the social situation as he perceived it'.[6] As Leonard Thompson puts it, 'the seer opposed any Christian assimilation' to a Roman worldview because he 'quite correctly conceived of his all embracing world as incompatible with all embracing vision implicated in public Roman life'.[7]

---

4. Adela Yarbro Collins, *Cosmology and Eschatology in Jewish and Christian Apocalypticism* (Leiden: E.J. Brill, 1996), p. 204.

5. So, for example, Leonard Thompson, 'A Sociological Analysis of Tribulation in the Apocalypse of John', *Semeia* 36 (1986), pp. 147-74 (162): 'different Christian groups had different opinions on the nature and extent of assimilation compatible with the faith, but there is no indication that a social, political climate of persecution and oppression determined Christian opinion'.

6. Adela Yarbro Collins, *Crisis and Catharsis: The Power of the Apocalypse* (Philadelphia: Westminster Press, 1984), pp. 141, 106. Richard Bauckham, 'Economic Critique of Rome in Revelation 18', in Loveday Alexander (ed.), *Images of Empire* (JSOTSup, 122: Sheffield: JSOT Press, 1991), pp. 47-90, highlights the economic critique.

7. Thompson, 'A Sociological Analysis of Tribulation', p. 166. 'Tribulation as a hyperbolic theme in John's literary world functions not as reflection on tensions between faiths and sociopolitical realities but as an expression of the conflict which he perceived between the two "worlds"'. At the same time, Thompson acknowledges that elements contributing to the reality of tribulation in the seer's world included 'social-political

This in itself could explain the *thlipsis* John was experiencing. But there is the further question of whether this all-embracing worldview, this sense of cognitive dissonance, was shared by the whole Christian community in the area. Was the work, in fact, addressing an inner-Christian conflict, centring on the issues of assimilation and acculturation, as many are currently suggesting?[8] The various scenarios are of course not incompatible. What is clear is that the seer's call is for Christ's followers to be faithful witnesses, even if that should mean death (2.10). Whether or not they are a factional Christian grouping, this imaginative dreaming is speaking for a minority people attempting to preserve their own integrity under an imperial Rome. It is a political writing from the underside, a rhetoric of the 'hidden transcript',[9] that allows a community of Christians to hear themselves addressed as 'insiders'. Interestingly, while the specifics of its historical background continue to be debated, the work's carefully coded underside scripting has continued to provide 'subaltern' communities with a language that they too can employ as a 'countercultural code for dissent' in their own political 'hidden transcripts'.[10] Locating the female figures in a hidden transcript still in use makes my question of what they are doing there all the more urgent.

With the term 'subaltern' I am already using the language of postcolonial theory.[11] And indeed Tina Pippin and others are suggesting that when the

relations in the cities of Asia, and the affirmation of Christian separatism from the Roman world' (p. 170).

8. There is clearly the matter of the Nicolaitans (2.6, 15). See David E. Aune, *Revelation 17–22* (WBC, 52C; Nashville: Thomas Nelson, 1998), p. 918, noting the thesis of M. Rissi; Wilfrid J. Harrington, OP, *Revelation* (Sacra Pagina Series, 16; Collegeville, MN: Liturgical Press, 1993), pp. 11-12, and so on. See also John M.G. Barclay, *Jews in the Mediterranean Diaspora: From Alexander to Trajan (323 BCE–117 CE)* (Edinburgh: T. & T. Clark, 1996), for the use of these terms. Barbara R. Rossing, *The Choice Between Two Cities: Whore, Bride, and Empire in the Apocalypse* (HTS, 48; Harrisburg, PA: Trinity Press International, 1999), p. 129, is among those reading ch. 18 aimed at Christian merchants profiting from Rome's wealth and commerce.

9. To use James Scott's much-quoted term for a written discourse that takes place 'offstage, beyond the direct observation by powerholders'; see James C. Scott, *Domination and the Arts of Resistance: Hidden Transcripts* (New Haven: Yale University Press, 1990), also quoted by Keller, *Apocalypse Now and Then*, p. 9, who suggests (p. 1), that Revelation 'counts in Bible-based cultures as the master script of the hidden transcript'.

10. Keller, *Apocalypse Now and Then*, pp. 17, 38-39, referring to the liberation readings of the work by Allan Boesak and Pablo Richard in South Africa and Latin America respectively. Tina Pippin, *Death and Desire: The Rhetoric of Gender in the Apocalypse of John* (Literary Currents in Biblical Interpretation; Louisville, KY: Westminster/John Knox Press, 1992), pp. 54-55, also notes and quotes from Allan A. Boesak, *Comfort and Protest: The Apocalypse from a South Africa Perspective* (Philadelphia: Westminster Press, 1987).

11. See Gayatri Chakravorty Spivak, 'Can the Subaltern Speak?', in Cary Nelson and Lawrence Grossberg (eds.), *Marxism and the Interpretation of Culture* (Urbana: University of Illinois Press, 1988), pp. 271-313.

Apocalypse is read through the lens of the colonized and those currently challenging oppressing forces it 'becomes a decolonizing text'.[12] But if so, and assuming that its female figures are tools for that purpose, how does one recognize a decolonizing strategy? My suspicion is that colonizers and colonizers' descendents have become so accustomed to reading in line with colonizing strategies that we have difficulty in recognizing the countering moves. We need to follow those like Musa Dube who know the first all too well and have a keen recognition of the second. There are, of course, many ways of writing colonizing and decolonizing scripts, but Musa Dube suggests that 'a central part' of the resistance employed by the colonized 'involves the reaffirmation of their various religious traditions' which have been 'denigrated' by the ruling powers.[13] So, the challenge is to read the Apocalypse facing backwards, as it were, and see whether it is possible to detect signs of such a reaffirming and refurbishing strategy. But if this is a work justifiably described as a 'jarring ride through dreams and nightmares',[14] will it even be possible to talk of reaffirming?

As early as the second chapter a name signals that the Deuteronomists' Jezebel is gaining a vicarious second life, not so much entertaining or killing prophets as taking that office for herself (2.20).[15] But if a Jezebel, the charge necessarily includes deception and sexual seduction and deathly punishment for her children if not for herself (2.23), the threat chillingly delivered as 'the words of the Son of God, who has eyes like a flame of fire' (2.18). It is the nightmare rather than the reaffirmation that is beginning. A tool fashioned out of one living woman is being dusted down and used against another. The strategy of a political polemic is clear, even if the particular circumstances are less so, and I am immediately uncomfortable.

But I am still on the human side of the crack. As I move further into the work there is a notable shift in the contours of the dreaming. By ch. 12 I have moved a long way from the earth-bound encouragement of Israel-turning Rahabs, and the warnings against human Yahweh-rejecting Jezebels, a long way too from an accosted Jesus wandering the countryside. For with the second woman the vision is cosmic and eschatological. I now find myself

---

12. Pippin, *Death and Desire*, p. 55. Boesak, *Comfort and Protest*, p. 38, called it 'underground literature'. Dube, *Postcolonial Feminist Interpretation*, pp. 102-103, describes 'decolonizing literary strategies' as 'at once a secret and a public code... Their double-faced character...on the one hand...seeks to raise the awareness of the colonized; on the other hand, it also seeks to counteract the colonizer's claims and to subvert the colonizer's imperializing methods.' She therefore describes this as a 'subverting genre'.

13. Dube, *Postcolonial Feminist Interpretation*, p. 33. In her context it is 'Western Christian practitioners and texts' that have denigrated the indigenous traditions.

14. Steven J. Friesen, *Imperial Cults and the Apocalypse of John: Reading Revelation in the Ruins* (Oxford: Oxford University Press, 2001), p. 213.

15. As Friesen, *Imperial Cults*, p. 187, notes, 'John does not deny "Jezebel" her prophetic status' as he does not add the phrase 'but she is not', as in 2.2, 9 and 3.9.

gazing at a figure markedly different from those I have met before: a woman 'clothed with the sun, with the moon under her feet, and on her head a crown of twelve stars…crying out in birthpangs in the agony of giving birth' (12.1-2). I sense that I have travelled in time to a far distant era, that I have been taken back to the world of ancient Mesopotamian and Canaanite sun moon and star goddesses, the worlds of Ningal, Inanna, Ishtar, Nikkal and Shapsu and others.[16] I hesitate in wonderment; I may be reading the work that lies at the very end of the Christian biblical canon, but here in the middle of the book of Revelation is certainly what appears to be a cosmic goddess![17] Can this really be a reaffirmation, a revival of an 'archaic image' breaking in? For if so, it would be, in the words of Catherine Keller 'to dance a few steps of the unacceptable'.[18] And yet those twelve stars. If these are twelve for the twelve tribes of Israel, then might this be Israel's own ancient queen of heaven, whoever she might have been, perhaps an Asherah *rediviva*?[19] If so, then this is indeed an appearance of the 'unacceptable', a most unexpected example of Musa Dube's 'reaffirmation', and of a long-'denigrated' religious tradition, the key word here being 'long', for ancient

16. For Inanna and Ningal, see Diane Wolkstein and Samuel Noah Kramer, *Inanna Queen of Heaven and Earth: Her Stories and Hymns from Sumer* (New York: Harper & Row, 1983); for Ishtar, see Othmar Keel and Christoph Uehlinger, *Gods, Goddesses, and Images of God in Ancient Israel* (Minneapolis: Fortress Press, 1998), pp. 292-95; for Nikkal, the Mesopotamian moon-goddess (CTA 1.24) and the Ugaritic sun goddess Shapsu with the stars generally grouped after her (CTA 1.6 VI and 1.161), see Mark S. Smith, *The Origins of Biblical Monotheism: Israel's Polytheistic Background and the Ugaritic Texts* (Oxford: Oxford University Texts, 2001), pp. 61-64, 71, 124-25, 231 n. 73.

17. The structure of this work continues to be debated, but Edith McEwan Humphrey's case for the centrality of this chapter is well argued in *The Ladies and the Cities: Transformation and Apocalyptic Identity in Joseph and Aseneth, 4 Ezra, the Apocalypse and the Shepherd of Hermes* (JSPSup, 17; Sheffield: Sheffield Academic Press, 1995), p. 100. Adela Yarbro Collins, *The Combat Myth in the Book of Revelation* (HDR, 9; Missoula, MT: Scholars Press, 1976), pp. 231-32, who sees this as a 'pivotal' chapter suggests it is the 'paradigm of the Book of Revelation' in that 'the pattern of the combat myth is reflected in quite full form within this single chapter'.

18. Keller, *Apocalypse Now and Then*, p. 65.

19. Margaret Barker, *The Revelation of Jesus Christ* (Edinburgh: T. & T. Clark, 2000), pp. 200-11 (Chapter 13), suggests Asherah, although whether the range of feminine images gathered here all fall under the umbrella of Asherah might be questioned—and, as Keel and Uehlinger, *Gods, Goddesses and Images of God*, p. 338, point out, 'identifying the "Queen of Heaven" is especially problematic since, on the one hand, the epithet is very general and allows her to be compared to the Assyrian *sarrat same* (for Ishtar…), to the Egyptian *nb.tp. t* "Mistress of the Heavens" (for Hathor, Anat, Astarte, *Qudshu*, Ishtar), and also to the Aramean *mlkt smyn* of Hermopolis (Anat?)'. They concede (p. 339) that as the divine consort involved in the bestowing of blessings as at Kuntillet 'Ajrud and Khirbet el-Qom, Asherah as the Queen of Heaven 'has some plausibility'. As discussed later, it is more than likely that the writer has combined elements of different myths here.

female gods had a very long history of denigration from insider/outsider oppositions centuries before Rome appeared in the ancient Near East. I wonder, and read on. If I am indeed meeting with goddesses then at first glance I might expect the dragon to have a place here, playing its part in a 'goddess with serpents' motif. But all too soon it becomes apparent that it is not on the side of the Woman; this is the *Chaoskampf* adversary,[20] to be revealed as none other than the Satan thrown out of heaven with his angels. Figures are merging with one another as I watch, their referents jostling against each other in a clash of sounding echoes. And while Asherah may have been a mother god the woman's torturous birthpangs sound remarkably human, suffering the pain predicted in Genesis 3![21] And after the birth of the son, she appears as a second Hagar fleeing into the wilderness, where God prepares a place for her, but for her alone, as the son who is to rule the nations is snatched from the dragon and transferred up to heaven.

Earlier goddesses as well as Hagar have travelled this way, such as Nin-isinna and Inanna, the Sumerian weeping goddesses, lamenting the loss of their sons to the netherworld.[22] The ascent of the Son, however, flies in marked contrast to their sons' descent. But, human or divine, what is she doing here in this chapter? Having given birth and having had the child snatched away, in vv. 13-16 she is busy escaping from the satanic dragon. I briefly wonder whether this might be the *nahash* of Genesis 3 in devilish drag.[23] But escape she does, thanks to the wings of the great eagle. If there is an affirmation of Israel's ancient traditions to be heard here, then, as Adela Yarbro Collins points out, it is Exodus that offers the most fitting key, for

20. Yarbro Collins, *The Combat Myth*, p. 57, notes that the combat or *Chaoskampf* myth is found in 'nearly every major ethnic tradition' of the time.

21. Susan R. Garrett, 'Revelation', in Newsom and Ringe (eds.), *The Women's Bible Commentary*, pp. 377-82 (379), follows the theory that the woman is indeed human in that 'she represents the people of Israel, which gave birth to the Messiah *and* to the church', so that 'John's use of goddess imagery serves to portray Israel in the most exalted terms possible'. So too Yarbro Collins, *The Combat Myth*, pp. 134-35. Resseguie, *Revelation Unsealed*, pp. 144-45, also identifies her as 'the mother of the salvation community, while the child represents the salvation community in its inviolable state, ruling with God in heaven'. Biblical antecedents of a woman in the anguish of birth pains include the daughter of Zion in Jer. 4.31 and Mic. 4.10.

22. Samuel Noah Kramer, 'The Weeping Goddess: Sumerian Prototypes of the *Mater Dolorosa*', *Biblical Archaeologist* 46 (1983), pp. 69-80. Inanna describes herself as Queen of Heaven.

23. As Harrington, *Revelation*, p. 130, notes, the identification of the serpent with the devil had already been made in the book of *Wisdom* (2.24). Richard Bauckham, *The Climax of Prophecy: Studies on the Book of Revelation* (Edinburgh: T. & T. Clark, 1993), pp. 193-94, suggests that the origin of 12.9's image of the devil as the dragon lies in an identification of Leviathan with the serpent of Gen. 3, but he argues strongly for hearing Isa. 27.1 here: 'the defeat of the Dragon may be expected once he is recognized as the dragon of Isaiah 27.1'.

'Like Israel at the time of the exodus she is carried to safety by eagles' wings. Like Israel she is nourished in the desert by God…assuring the hearers that they will not be overwhelmed by the threat that Rome poses to them.'[24] But there are echoes too of the eagle of Moses' song in Deut. 32.11-12 and Isaiah's salvation hymn in Isa. 40.31. Once in the wilderness she is left, without her newborn child, or her other vulnerable children, albeit 'nourished for a time and times and half a time' (12.14).[25] But does she even reach its safety? The very mention of nourishing is swiftly swept away as the dragon appears on the attack again.[26] Alert now to any goddess traces I wonder whether 'Earth' is to be understood as another mother god as she comes to the rescue, swallowing the dragon's spewed out river in a gendered variation on the ancient *Chaoskampf* theme.[27] Resseguie reads the woman of this chapter as 'an image of life in the midst of travail',[28] but if so, the travail is not abated, for the dragon goes off like a spoilt child to spend its anger upon the woman's children who are keeping to the ways prescribed as good. I leave this chapter still unsure about this figure, clothed as much in ambivalence as in her cosmic finery.

If there were echoes of Asherah and others behind the woman clothed with the sun, there might seem to be echoes of Inanna or Anat, those warlike feisty goddesses of 'wanton love',[29] in ch. 14, where the great cry goes

24. Yarbro Collins, *Crisis and Catharsis*, p. 149.

25. Many point to the temporary nature of her time there. Yarbro Collins, *The Combat Myth*, p. 29, argues that 'the open-endedness of the rescue of the woman' is a deliberate literary move to heighten the tension, relieved by 'the ultimate rescue or salvation of 21.1–22.5'. Reading the desert or wilderness as a New Exodus motif, this then moves to the New Conquest. There is disagreement, however, over whether the women of chs. 12 and 21 are one and the same. McEwan Humphreys, *The Ladies and the Cities*, p. 118, for example, concludes that the pursued woman, identified as 'the community of witnesses' is finally 'displayed gloriously' as one, having come down from heaven…fit to be married as bride to the *Kronzeuge*, the Lamb of God'. Rossing, *The Choice Between Two Cities*, p. 12, and others disagree.

26. Much of the ambiguity is assumed to be the result of redactional workings. Verse 14, which is virtually a doublet of v. 6, seems notably out of place. See David E. Aune, *Revelation 6–16* (WBC, 52B; Nashville: Thomas Nelson, 1998), p. 664, and other commentaries.

27. Friesen, *Imperial Cults*, p. 186, argues that those who see only four important female figures in the work are overlooking the role of Earth (Ge) in 12.16 who 'is a well-known figure from Greek mythology; she is also mentioned in Scripture'. He cites Num. 16.32-34 and Exod. 15.12 as examples, following Aune, *Revelation 6–16*, p. 707. See also Pippin, *Death and Desire*, p. 79.

28. Resseguie, *Revelation Unsealed*, p. 145, further described as 'a life reliant upon God's protection and provision, but at the same time subject to the distresses and persecutions of the dragon (Satan)'.

29. For Inanna, see Tikva Frymer-Kensky, *In the Wake of the Goddesses: Women, Culture, and the Biblical Transformation of Pagan Myth* (New York: Free Press, 1992),

out: 'fallen, fallen is Babylon the Great!' But Isaiah (21.9) has provided the script and Jeremiah (51.7) the charge that she 'made all the nations drink of the wine of the wrath of her fornication' (14.8). But this is merely the prelude; Babylon appears in all her awe-full glory three chapters later, her identity emblazoned on her forehead, 'Babylon the Great, Mother of Whores'. As I gaze at her seated on many waters (17.1-3), representing 'peoples and multitudes and nations and languages' (v. 15), the picture conjures up more ancient memories, of those great maternal monster gods of the waters, memories of Tiamat and Rahab.[30] But if so, the description of her so splendidly 'clothed in purple and scarlet, and adorned with gold and jewels and pearls' (v. 4) would have a courtesan god. But, taken together with her statement that she is a queen (18.7), this rich and costly clothing reminds me once again of Jezebel, that earlier queen mother of Israel, standing so vulnerably at her window in 2 Kings 9, depicted there with goddess traces. The memory is shockingly reinforced by the violent imagery of the death awaiting Babylon, described so graphically in 17.16 and 18.8-9, and which 17.17 and 19.2 declare legitimated by God, a legitimation anticipated in 16.19 and again reinforced in 19.2.[31] Is there a goddess trace in Babylon's claim, albeit 'in her heart', that she is 'sitting enthroned as a queen' (18.7), and so challenging the one enthroned God? But it is her 'golden cup full of abominations' (17.4), and full indeed of earlier prophetic hate of Babylon that signals her fate.[32] The list of charges against her include bloodshed, fornication, sorcery and deception, and the descriptions are graphic, 'drunk with the blood of the saints and the blood of the witnesses to Jesus' (17.6), 'a dwelling place of demons, a haunt (or prison) of every foul and hateful bird and beast' (18.2). I wonder and hope that the woman of ch. 12 has already left her place in the wilderness for this is certainly not a place of much nourishment.

pp. 66-69, and Wolkstein and Kramer, *Inanna Queen of Heaven and Earth*. For Anat, see Neal H. Walls, *The Goddess Anat in Ugaritic Myth* (SBLDS, 135; Atlanta: Scholars Press, 1992). Malina and Pilch, *Social-Science Commentary*, p. 205, note that 'in the Ugaritic documents 'Anatu regularly decks herself out in crimson'.

30. As commentators note, the reference to the many waters may be a borrowing from Jer. 51.13.

31. Caroline Vander Stichele, 'Just a Whore: The Annihilation of Babylon According to Revelation 17.16', *Lectio Difficilior* 1 (2000), available online at <www.lectio.unibe.ch/>, notes that the Septuagint makes the connection with Jezebel sharper by using the same expression 'to eat someone's flesh'.

32. Rossing, *The Choice Between Two Cities*, p. 63, considers this 'a central symbol' in the judgment against Babylon. She cites the earlier texts (Ezek. 23.32-33; Jer. 25.15-16, 27-28; 51.7; Hab. 2.15-16; Isa. 51.22-23) on pp. 62-66. Rossing sees the combining of the cup imagery with the charge of prostitution as 'a daring and original image' which serves to link the oracles against the nations tradition with those of the 'evil woman/seductress'.

This is clearly the dangerous 'bitch-witch'.[33] This is a figure who is both seductive and desirable, as the kings of the earth have discovered, and abominably disgusting, and who clearly must be-got-rid-of. As I read the verses piled on verses against her the violent language of seduction and prostitution employed is all too recognizable: this Babylon is but the latest in the trail of the feminine abject, the verbally violated. Hosea's Gomer, Nahum's Nineveh, Isaiah's Tyre (Isa. 21) and Ezekiel's Jerusalem and Samaria (Ezek. 16 and 23) have all gone before her—bad women all, I have been told, and deserving of destruction.[34] The pile of abject bodies is high, traces of the goddess there for the sharp-eyed to discover. I am disturbed by what is being reaffirmed. I move on, realizing that the cumulative power of this imagery is carefully readying me to accept Great Babylon's fall, happening all in a day or one hour as it is hymned in ch. 18 (vv. 9-10) and to add my voice to the great satiric taunt song with its rich Isaian bass line (Isa. 14 and 47). In answer to the heavenly voice of 18.4, I may be ready to come out but I am certainly reneging at the *lex talionis* demands of vv. 6-7, and demanded in double measure in v. 6.

In this facing-backwards reading, I now only await the appearance of the good woman, whom the Israelite scribes have taught me to expect in their binary world of the good and the bad. She comes hard on the heels of the dispatched Other, the now burnt and eaten Babylon, and comes as the virgin bride of the Lamb (19.7), in her fine linen, bright and pure (19.8). Indeed she is even appearing in Babylon's fine linen and splendour.[35] At first glance this is Zion in whom God has long delighted (Isa. 62.2-5), of whom the great Isaiah scroll sang, and whom God long ago clothed in fine linen as well as adorned with gold and silver (Ezek. 16.10-13). And the seer is telling me that this fine linen is now the symbol of the 'righteous deeds of the saints' (v. 8). But the sinister beats of the binary counterpoint are continuing. Did the writer mean the marriage feast of 19.7 to be read as the counter to the

33. See Pippin, *Death and Desire*, p. 61. Bauckham, *The Climax of Prophecy*, pp. 347-48, sees the charges of deceiving through sorcery in 18.23 as seeking to portray Rome as a witch, much as the charge in Isa. 47.12.

34. See the discussion of cities and whores in Vander Stichele, 'Just a Whore'. Keller, *Apocalypse Now and Then*, p. 77, sums up the image as 'imperial patriarchy in drag'! Bauckham, *The Climax of Prophecy*, p. 346, sees the Isaiah text as the pivotal one because of the commercial connection: 'Tyre's commercial enterprise is compared with prostitution because it is association with other nations for the sake of profit'. Bauckham sees the economic reference as primary and so relates the religious connotations to this in that 'the political religion of Rome was the worst kind of false religion, since it absolutized Rome's claim of her subjects and cloaked her exploitation of them in the garb of religious loyalty' (p. 348). On a human level the strange woman of Proverbs fills the same role.

35. Rossing, *The Choice Between Two Cities*, p. 143, points to the parallel vocabulary between 19.7-8 and 18.12, 14.

funereal eating of the Whore? And is it to be read alongside the great supper
of God of vv. 17-18, in its graphic Ezekiel imagery?[36] I am discovering that
violence is never far from the positive in this work. Death comes to all the
powers of evil and those who are ensnared by them. The lake of fire will
consume them (20.14-15). It is against this background of violence that the
bride appears again. This time the seer himself has identified her as the new
Jerusalem (21.2), the word *new* recalling *the great* city that has been consumed and destroyed. But she is not only new, she is radiant (21.11), adorned
with precious jewels, recalling the description of the throne vision of ch. 4. I
hesitate at the notice that she has 'no need of sun or moon' (21.23). Is this
polemic? Is she absorbing or deconstructing the goddess-traces of the woman
clothed with the sun, since for her the glory of the male god is all sufficient?
Is it a case, as Catherine Keller puts it, of the style of the Sun Woman now
being 'passé: Miss New Jerusalem in her bijoux wears the "Last Word" in
fashion'?[37] But it is a fashion carefully devised out of familiar materials.
Viewed from one angle this is God's bride decked out in the glory of God
worn back in Isaiah (Isa. 60.19-20), with all the jewels promised by husband
God (Isa. 54.11-12); from another she is Wisdom, once again descending
from heaven to tent among Israel (Sir. 24.1-8),[38] but radiantly (Wis. 6.12)
refashioned as a city, and certainly not to be confused with the seductive,
but now burnt and consumed Strange Woman. But, as in Proverbs, she is a
Wisdom of God, for the throne of God, and of the Lamb, is there, out of
which flows the river of life (22.1-2). Now I am back in the garden of Eden,
in its freshly minted Ezekiel refurbishing, with the tree(s) of life growing on
either side of the river, with its fruit and healing leaves. Its familiarity is both
comforting and affirming. And as I listen to the Spirit and the Bride offering
the invitation of Wisdom herself (22.17), the familiar binary opposition is
spelt out in the warning: no share in the tree of life and the holy city for any
reader who fails to respect the integrity of the words of this book.

This is a collage of imagery, an intertextuality clearly employed to jar the
mind 'through dreams and nightmares'. In their refurbishment, familiar
female figures of the past, both human and divine, have become the tools for
a new work out of old material for a new purpose. Older dreams and nightmares are revamped as tools of an apocalyptic visioning. All this Tina Pippin
reads as fantasy, that literary genre which 'illuminates the real world' but
does so in such a way that 'the fictional nature of the fantastic destabilizes

---

36. Ezek. 39.17-20. Yarbro Collins, *The Combat Myth*, p. 225, also notes Isa. 34.1-7,
which she suggests has a fertility aspect. Keller, *Apocalypse Now and Then*, p. 76, suggests
that 'in terms of literary structure, these three feasts merge together… In the dreamlike
rapidity of the images, the wedding invitation merges with the vultures' feast.'

37. Keller, *Apocalypse Now and Then*, p. 82.

38. So Rossing, *The Choice Between Two Cities*, pp. 149-51.

the rational world'.[39] If this is so, the use of ancient motifs for an 'insider' affirmation of their own traditions will have been but one facet of the work. As a visionary writing aiming to destabilize the worldview of the imperium in the eyes of its readers, it must necessarily have been addressing its 'outsider' context in terms that would make this plainly understood. So, I will need to turn around and view the work again in its refurbished state as an overt expression of the political dreaming and visioning of this writer in his own contemporary location. Musa Dube has described decolonizing literary strategies as being 'at once a secret and a public code'. Where the secret code looks to the insider to decode the message, the public code openly faces the opposing worldview seeking 'to counteract the colonizer's claims and to subvert the colonizer's imperializing methods'. It is a case of using the masters' tools against the masters.[40] The challenge to the later reader is to recognize this strategy in action within the text. The fact that the Apocalypse is a collage of imagery and that images are inherently polyvalent only makes this all the more difficult. If, as I want to suggest, the apocalyptic picture is a composite, where the writer can be seen employing both strategies, looking back and providing an 'insider' work, but at the same time providing a 'double-faced' text that also faces the world of the imperium and subverts its own images,[41] then the book is to be read as an even more densely constructed intertextual mosaic. Not only will it be keeping ancient indigenous traditions alive, but at the same time it will be deconstructing those of the colonizers. In her earlier studies of the combat myth Adela Yarbro Collins talked of a fusion of traditions.[42] The challenge now is to detect the other side of this fusion. If each of these female figures is double-facing, I need to imagine that I am a reader from the 'other' side who will be quite naturally reaching for a Graeco-Roman key to interpret and decode. But if I now assume that I am reading a cross-cultural intertextuality, the question is: will I be able to detect and hear the Graeco-Roman echoes? Will I be able to detect traces of a political decolonizing drawing on the figures of 'the masters' to jar the mind 'through dreams and nightmares'?

I look again at the woman clothed with the sun and pursued by the dragon, and wonder afresh at her identity. Could she be Isis, addressed by Apuleius' banqueting Lucius as *regina caeli*, who with a mere nod of her moon-crowned

39. Pippin, *Death and Desire*, p. 95. Yarbro Collins' thesis, carefully set out in *The Combat Myth*, is that the work is structured on the pattern of the ancient combat myth, thus providing 'a proleptic experience of victory' (p. 234).

40. Dube, *Postcolonial Feminist Interpretation*, pp. 102-103.

41. Dube, *Postcolonial Feminist Interpretation*, p. 102.

42. Yarbro Collins, *The Combat Myth*, p. 58, and 'The History-of-Religion Approach to Apocalypticism and the "Angel of the Waters" (Rev 16.4-7)', *CBQ* 39 (1977), pp. 367-81 (367-68).

head rules the stars?[43] And who not only flew with two wings when she was attacked by Seth-Typhon, but also suckled her child in lonely solitary state.[44] Or could it be it Atargatis? As it was not only the Ephesian Artemis but also the Syrian Atargatis, and the Egyptian Isis who were linked with stars and planets, it is not so much a question of whether a Graeco-Roman goddess can be glimpsed hovering in the background, but which one might I be seeing moving clearly in the foreground. But more likely this is Leto, pursued by Python under orders to Hera as she was about to give birth but then rescued by the powers of Zeus and Poseidon.[45] But if this is Leto, is there a pointed anti-Artemis polemic here? It would be particularly pointed in Ephesus celebrated as the place of her birth and where Leto then concealed her children from Hera. The nativity scene even graced its coins. But where Leto gave birth to Artemis, as well as Apollo, the woman in ch. 12 gives birth to the son, and only the son, who, taken to God and God's throne, must surely be the Christian Son.[46] On the other hand, if the reference to the twelve of the twelve stars was not so much the tribes of Israel as the twelve signs of the Zodiac, then could this be Artemis herself, who wore the zodiac as a necklace and was acclaimed as Queen of the Cosmos.[47]

---

43. Apuleius, *Metamorphoses* 9.2, 5. Yarbro Collins, *The Combat Myth*, pp. 73-75, notes Isis' connections both with the moon, also mentioned in Plutarch, as well as the sun in Egyptian inscriptions. But the great Artemis of Ephesus was also called Queen of the Cosmos.

44. Yarbro Collins, *The Combat Myth*, p. 63, referring to Herodotus and the Metternich stele of 378 BCE. Although, as Aune, *Revelation 6–16*, pp. 673-74, notes, this detail found in a Egyptian Osiris hymn of c.1500 BCE is not included in the Herodotus text (2.156) and so questions its popularity in the first century CE.

45. Different versions of this myth have differing details. Yarbro Collins, *The Combat Myth*, pp. 61-70, makes a strong case, but concludes (p. 75) that here there may be 'a fusing of Leto and Isis traditions'. Aune, *Revelation 6–16*, p. 671, notes the discrepancies between the two, which he suggests are 'flaws' in her analysis. Harrington, *Revelation*, p. 129, argues for the Leto myth being the closest parallel, although combined with Gen. 3 and chaos traditions.

46. Certainly in its Christian reading. See Yarbro Collins, *The Combat Myth*, pp. 104-107, for a Jewish reading, taking the son as the messiah in line with Ps. 2.9. She also suggests (p. 190) that the Apollo myth is being used to set up an 'antithesis of Christ and Nero'. Richard E. Oster, 'Ephesus as a Religious Center under the Principate. I. Paganism before Constantine', in Wolfgang Haase (ed.), *Aufstieg und Niedergang der römischen Welt* Band II.18.3 (Berlin: W. de Gruyter, 1990), pp. 1661-1728 (1706), allows the possibility of this being a Christian adaptation of the myth.

47. Yarbro Collins, *The Combat Myth*, pp. 71-72. See also Oster, 'Ephesus as a Religious Center under the Principate', p. 1724. Yarbro Collins also notes (*The Combat Myth*, pp. 72-73), the association of the Syrian goddess Atargatis with the moon. See also Aune, *Revelation 6–16*, p. 681; Garrett, 'Revelation', p. 379. Rick Strelan, *Paul, Artemis, and the Jews in Ephesus* (Berlin: W. de Gruyter, 1996), pp. 113-14, considers the possibility of the

Although she was connected with childbirth, it was, however, as protector not birth-er. But if Leto's Artemis has no place here and she herself leaves the scene to be settled in the wilderness, the Son remains in heaven! And the myth is interrupted by the hymn from heaven (vv. 10-12), declaring that the authority of the Messiah/Christ has arrived even if the opposing forces are still rampaging down on earth. The challenge to the master's myth is clear.

What then of Babylon? Seated on a beast with seven heads and ten horns, there has to be a political message carefully encoded here. A Roman sestertius minted in 71CE with Dea Roma seated on her seven hills, her right foot touching the rivergod Tiber, most probably taken from a stock statue design,[48] would seem to provide the clue. And if the beast represents the power of the empire, then the vision of Babylon on its back may well, as Richard Bauckham suggests, be a way of visualizing 'Roman civilization, as a corrupting influence, rid[ing] on the back of Roman military power'.[49] The she-wolf suckling Romulus and Remus depicted alongside Roma on the coin neatly ties in the accusation of Mother of Whores for any Latin readers accustomed to using the word *lupa* for prostitutes.[50] But this is a prostitute who is doing very well from her trade, being kept in fine clothes and jewellery, in an enviable standard to which she has become accustomed.[51] The decolonizing sub-text asks: at whose cost? But if this is a key part of the decolonizing strategy of the writer, then indeed, as Tina Pippin writes, 'the idolatry of colonialism is tied with worship of the Goddess'.[52] So, here she is employed against herself as a means of attacking 'Rome's blasphemous self-glorification'.[53] 18.7 spells this out with the combination of glorifying and ruling assuming a presumptuous usurpation of the one God's glory. Is it the colonized insider or the colonizing outsider who is to be recognized among

woman being a parody of Artemis, the description 'dressed with the sun' referring to the gold of her statue, and concludes 'the suggestion is worth consideration'.

48. See Aune, *Revelation 17–22*, pp. 920-21. Aune (p. 923) suggests that ch. 17 is an *ekphrasis*, that is, a detailed description of a work of art. Not all agree that the referent here is Rome. G.K. Beale, *The Book of Revelation* (Grand Rapids: Eerdmans; Carlisle: Paternoster Press, 1999), p. 886, suggests 'the apostate church and unbelieving Israel' are included, while others such as J. Massyngberde Ford, *Revelation* (AB, 38; Garden City, NY: Doubleday, 1975), p. 285, propose Jerusalem.

49. Bauckham, *The Climax of Prophecy*, p. 343.

50. Aune, *Revelation 17–22*, p. 929.

51. Bauckham, *The Climax of Prophecy*, p. 346, reads 14.8, 17.2 and 18.3 as the peoples of the empire having been 'dazzled' by Rome's glory and 'seduced by the promised benefits of the *Pax Romana*'.

52. Pippin, *Death and Desire*, p. 56, following a quote from Yarbro Collins, that 'in Revelation idolatry is focused on a goddess, Roma'.

53. Yarbro Collins, *Crisis and Catharsis*, p. 123.

the weeping merchants who have benefited so well from Babylon's material wealth?[54] And yet as I gaze I wonder whether Babylon is so exclusively or securely tied to Rome. If Christian citizens of Ephesus were among the anticipated readership, might they not also be inclined to read Artemis here? Would a Graeco-Roman goddess whose 'cult and its activities epitomized the cultural and religious spirit of the city'[55] and 'whose credibility had stood the test of time'[56] not be posing a challenge to a Christian writer concerned with the dangers of assimilation? For in this section of the Graeco-Roman world, Artemis virtually was Ephesus, and while Rome's wealth may have ruled the empire, it was the temple of Artemis which functioned as the region's 'financial and banking pillar'.[57] This was a goddess with property, who took mortgages on other people's property, and had a considerable financial business working on her behalf. But whether it is Roma and/or Artemis pictured here the scene is typically carnivalesque and the graphic and grisly details of the death of Babylon, eaten by the ten horns and the beast and then burnt (17.16), halt me as I read and haunt my imagination.[58] The list in vv. 22-23 of what is to be lost in the downfall comes almost as a surprise, music and the daily tasks and joys of life will come to an end as the city falls. The cosmic vision stumbles for a moment and in the crack there is a glimpse of the ordinary earthly reality. But only for a moment.

For the smoke of the burning has barely settled before the bride of the Lamb is hymned. But who is this bride? If first-century readers brought up on two-women tales and Heracles' famed choice would now be ready and

54.   Bauckham, *The Climax of Prophecy*, p. 342, detects echoes of Ezekiel's prophecy against Tyre, which included a catalogue of merchandise (Ezek. 27.12-24) He suggests (p. 346) that this prophecy is used specifically to highlight Rome's economic exploitation, in that Tyre was the major trading centre of the its time. Bauckham had earlier (in 'Economic Critique of Rome', pp. 84-86), suggested that some of these merchants could well have been among the Christian readership, who would have read this 'with a salutary shock of recognition'.

55.   Oster, 'Ephesus as a Religious Center under the Principate', p. 1727. 'In a unique way, technically known as Neocorate, Artemis was involved in a reciprocal "give and take" with the civic self-image and urban needs of Ephesus'. In 'The Ephesian Artemis as an Opponent of Early Christianity', *Jahrbuch für Antike und Christentum* 19 (1976), pp. 24-44 (24), Oster argues that in Ephesus Artemis was 'by far the most formidable opponent to the Christian religion and the devotees of Christ'.

56.   Strelan, *Paul, Artemis, and the Jews in Ephesus*, p. 79.

57.   Strelan, *Paul, Artemis, and the Jews in Ephesus*, p. 76. See also Oster, 'The Ephesian Artemis', pp. 32-33, and 'Ephesus as a Religious Center under the Principate', pp. 1717-19, for discussions of the financial significance of Artemis.

58.   Pippin, *Death and Desire*, pp. 66-68, draws attention to the carnivalesque nature of the scene. As Garrett, 'Revelation', p. 381, comments, 'The objection that "Babylon" is only a metaphor, a symbol, does not eliminate the problem that the text creates for women readers'. Such divinely legitimated violence should be a problem for all readers.

waiting for the arrival of Virtue herself, then a Jerusalem, the Bride, 'adorned with purity' and dressed in white would be Virtue indeed.[59] Or did the writer assume the echo of Plato's *Republic* (9.13) for this ideal heavenly city? But in a world where cities each had their goddesses, this is surely a case of move over Roma, or move over Artemis, here comes virtuous Jerusalem, her 'radiance like a rare jewel' (21.11)! The repetition of 17.1-3 in 21.9-10 insists that I not miss the contrast. This is a city whose richness and splendour, with its gates of pearl and its street of gold (v. 21), is the glory of God—how can Artemis/Ephesus possibly compare? The number twelve is now explicit: twelve gates named for the twelve tribes of Israel and the twelve foundations for the twelve apostles of the Lamb—move over Artemis indeed. And no temple! For the city's temple is 'the Lord God, the Almighty, and the Lamb' (v. 22). So much for Ephesus' Artemisium![60] What earlier may have appeared as competing claims for the world's allegiance have now been shown not only as deadly but now as quite ephemeral, for in their place stands the new city from heaven. But a new city quite unrelated to the first earth, for that has passed away. This is a city without history, a discontinuity shocking in its completeness. I need to remember that I am suggesting that this is a counter-cultural decolonizing vision from the underside, for otherwise it brings uneasy memories of missionary attempts to block out, if not blot out, indigenous *whakapapa*, indigenous memories. The strictures of 22.18-19 would close down any further discussion, pulling the curtain down on the disclosing world of the apocalypse. And yet the call goes out, 'Come, Lord Jesus'. In this ambivalence the reader is left waiting.

So I am suggesting that a case can be made for the four female characters each having significant roles in a decolonizing text. While Jezebel, with her historical referent plays a smaller part in the negative Othering of this theo-political work, Babylon, the Great Whore, is, along with the Beast, one of the symbols of the imperialist power and therefore a most powerful negative female symbol. It is she who, in gender terms, stands tallest in this work. In political terms, as Tina Pippin writes, 'the cathartic experience of the reader at the death of the Whore is the ultimate release of a colonized people'.[61] A catharsis carefully prepared by the writer, for the charge of whoredom, with its strong canonical resonances, brings with it a whole cluster of accusations as wide ranging as false worship and the exploitative economics of a

59. Xenophon, *Memorabilia* 2.1.22, quoted by Rossing, *The Choice Between Two Cities*, p. 142. On pp. 18-40, Rossing notes the number of authors who employ or refer to the Heracles *topos*.

60. As Oster, 'The Ephesian Artemis as an Opponent', p. 31, notes, 'the most visually impressive manifestation of Artemis' close ties with the city of Ephesus and her pervasiveness in Ephesian culture was her temple'.

61. Pippin, *Death and Desire*, p. 28.

deceptive political domination.[62] As Tina Pippin's title indicates, there is
an entanglement of desirability and deathliness which works to promote a
hatred not only of colonizing powers, but sadly also of powerful and yet
desirable women. Of the two positive female figures who escape the death,
the Woman Clothed in Sun seemingly leaves the scene in ch. 12, while the
personified New Jerusalem is clearly marked as tied to the two main male
characters, God and the Lamb. While the charge may be levelled that male
figures are also threatened or destroyed in this apocalyptic fantasy world,[63]
the fact remains that it is Babylon who lingers longest in the memory. It
would appear that the feminine dimension of the divine, once represented
by the great female gods of the ancient world, has once again been carved up
and segmented into binary oppositions of good and evil, and even more
particularly, the sexually attractive becomes the whore while the most positive must be seen as the virginally pure. This feminine dimension is, of
course, an interesting feature in an early Christian work which would have
had no place at all for goddesses in its belief or worship systems. But if their
traces remain in the seer's rhetoric, it is, in the end, of little account, for
finally they are either destroyed or 'banished to the edges of the text',[64] for in
this work all has been in the service of God and the Lamb.

I do not wish to leave the discussion here. Tina Pippin has asked: 'is the
Apocalypse a desirable ending to Christian sacred scripture?'[65] I want to ask
what happens after that ending. Assuming that the eschatological Utopia
has not yet arrived, is there an ongoing afterlife for these mythical and gendered literary tropes? Are there similar traces of the supernatural feminine
to be unearthed in the literary works of our own time? I have followed the
suggestion that the Apocalypse may be read as a decolonizing work, the
writing of a minority people. I now wish to take the discussion a step further.
Here I am again following Musa Dube, and adopting one of her suggestions
for 'viable postcolonial feminist strategies of reading'. Namely,

> reading sacred and secular texts, ancient and contemporary texts…side by side,
> to highlight: (a) the ways in which they propound imperializing or decolo-
> nizing ideology; (b) their use of gender in the discourse of subordination and
> domination.[66]

---

62. Friesen, *Imperial Cults*, p. 205.
63. Friesen, *Imperial Cults*, p. 186, would maintain that *if* the work is to be regarded as
misogynist, then it should also be seen as 'misandrist and probably misanthropic'.
64. Pippin, *Death and Desire*, p. 72.
65. Pippin, *Death and Desire*, p. 21.
66. Dube, *Postcolonial Feminist Interpretation*, pp. 199-200. This is only a selection
from her much longer list. She also includes reading imperializing and decolonizing texts
side by side in this list.

As an intertextual reading of quite unrelated texts this is a significantly different understanding and use of intertextuality from that explored in the earlier section of this chapter. But it coheres with the thesis of Mikhail Bakhtin that 'a meaning only reveals its depths once it has encountered and come into contact with another, foreign meaning', at which point 'a light flash[es], illuminating both the posterior and the anterior, joining a given text to a dialogue'.[67] I am interested in the depths of meaning that may be revealed through this light, and the insights that may be gained, if I initiate a dialogue between this early Christian work of Apocalypse and a much later text written from the perspective of the colonized—or more accurately—the descendents of the colonized in Aotearoa New Zealand. Such a text is Witi Ihimara's novel, *The Matriarch*, published in 1986.[68] My decision to read these two works together takes seriously the fact that both currently hold a place in the discourse of the culture of Aotearoa New Zealand. So I am interested both in the web of related issues and imagery that links the two, and the effect that reading them together might have on the reader. For I am also taking note of George Aichele and Gary Phillips' statement, following Julia Kristeva, that 'readers are constantly made and "remade" through the intertextual process'.[69] When the fence around the Bible is taken down and conversation partners allowed from over or beyond the fence, a new and living contextual relationship between Bible and culture can thrive unfettered. It is, I suggest, an unnatural separation to keep our reading of the Bible, from which we gain much of our religious identity, quite apart from our reading of our own cultural canon of literature from which we gain much of our cultural identity.[70] Wherever our context might be, I am suggesting that we need to become participants in such intertextual readings, with all the insights that these afford.

If there was some unresolved debate about the readers of the Apocalypse, there is no debate about the intended readers of *The Matriarch*. Witi Ihimaera is recorded as saying 'I've always written for a Maori audience, I've never

67.   Mikhail M. Bakhtin, *Speech Genres and Other Late Essays* (ed. Caryl Emerson and Michael Holquist; trans. Vern W. McGee; Austin: University of Texas Press, 1986), pp. 7, 162.

68.   Witi Ihimaera, *The Matriarch* (Auckland: Heinemann, 1986).

69.   George Aichele and Gary A. Phillips, 'Introduction: Exegesis, Eisegesis, Inter-gesis', *Semeia* 69/70 (1995), pp. 7-18 (10). See also Mikhail M. Bakhtin, *Dialogic Imagi-nation: Four Essays by M.M. Bakhtin* (ed. Michael Holquist; trans. Caryl Emerson and Michael Holquist; Austin: University of Texas Press, 1981), p. 253, 'listeners or readers who recreate and in so doing renew the text—participate equally in the creation of the represented world in the text'.

70.   See Mieke Bal's thesis in, 'Religious Canon and Literary Identity', *Lectio Difficilior* 2 (2000), available online at <www.lectio.unibe.ch/>, that '*literariness* is the tool for identity formation'.

written for any other audience', although he qualifies that by adding 'it would be more accurate to say I write to a Maori kaupapa, which emphasizes an objective rather than an audience'.[71] So this too is a minority writing, a work from the political underside. As Ihimaera has written elsewhere, 'From a Maori perspective the two questions most at issue are: What is history and who owns it?'[72] His answer to the first is that 'the Maori definition of history would be one which included myth', which might provide a link with aspects of the female imagery I have been viewing in the biblical text. He follows his answer to the second, that 'nobody owns history or should be able to copyright it', with a strong statement that

> I believe that Maori people have every reason to be suspicious of the history that we are taught and which, to a certain extent, still determines the shape of our lives. Our duty is to confront history with our own... Each iwi, each hapu has a different or, rather, tribal, approach to their histories which are more parallel observations having parallel facts and parallel perceptions on the same factual events.[73]

His rider, that 'these are further informed by the holistic frameworks of the unreal as well as the real', makes an immediate connection with the world of the Apocalypse, where the metaphorical unreal was the medium for the political messages of the real.

While the work is titled *The Matriarch*, the story is the story of Tamatea Mahana's quest for self-discovery; the fictional narrator is the grandson, and it is through his eyes that we travel. Tina Pippin described the Apocalypse as a work that created 'space for these anxieties and hopes to roam freely', by which she meant anxieties and hopes for the future, the eschaton.[74] In another sense *The Matriarch* also works to provide space for anxieties and hopes, but for a more particular eschaton that centres on cultural identity and cultural relationships. But once again as I enter this work I find myself in an unfamiliar world. The book, fittingly described as a 'bricolage'[75] with its mixture of genres and its polyphony of voices, frequently crosses boundaries of time as well as the boundaries of the real and unreal. The past and the

---

71. Mark Williams, 'Witi Ihimaera: Interviewed by Mark Williams', in Elizabeth Alley and Mark Williams (eds.), *In the Same Room: Conversations with New Zealand Writers* (Auckland: Auckland University Press, 1992), pp. 219-36 (221). The *kaupapa* is the focus. *Kaupapa* has a wide range of meaning covering foundation, agenda and purpose.

72. Witi Ihimaera, 'A Maori Perspective', *Journal of New Zealand Literature* 9 (1991), pp. 53-54.

73. Ihimaera, 'A Maori Perspective', p. 54, where he also states that 'Indeed, there is no such thing as History. Rather there are many histories and, even within the Maori framework, this is acknowledged.'

74. Pippin, *Death and Desire*, p. 39.

75. By Alex Calder, 'The Matriarch, Witi Ihimaera—Two Responses', *Landfall* 161 (1986), pp. 79-86 (84).

present, the real and the unreal are constantly entangled. It is Musa Dube's identification of decolonizing strategies that provides me with a way of entry, although Ihimaera's own comments indicate that looking back and reaffirming the past is a natural element of his bricolage, 'For Maori people the past is not something behind us. It is before us, a long unbroken line of ancestors whose guidance must be accepted and to whom we are accountable'.[76] But it is not only human ancestors that are part of the living past; I listen as the grandson is told 'the spiritual and the physical are one and the same…when you walk the land you are in the company of gods'.[77] But who is Tama walking with? Is this just a grandmother? As I gaze at this dominating female figure, the matriarch of the title, Tama's fictional grandmother, I realize that she is not what she might seem, not what I might expect from a family narrative.[78] She herself is double-facing: Tamatea is told that the great goddess of death, Hine Nui Te Po has a mouth that is the mouth 'of a barracouta. Her eyes are flecked with greenstone.'[79] But a few pages on and it is his grandmother herself who appears as that very Hine Nui Te Po. Then at a *hui*[80] about Maori land issues, in the act of confronting an elder, angry that she has dared, as a woman, to speak in the capital city,

> her eyes were wide and unseeing… Within their depths a form was stirring. And the man, Timoti, saw it there…saw the goddess of death waiting to receive his life.[81]

And so 'the spider which had once been the matriarch fell upon him and with quick sickening, movements, began to feast upon him'.[82] A feasting, a potential death, with echoes of the Apocalypse, but with a reprieve. Her words to her grandson at the end of this episode are interesting to read together with the quote at the head of this chapter in mind:

> Remember the spider… It can so easily be done, when one walks so close to the border between the darkness and the light, to go too far onto the dark side.[83]

And this before one of the most dramatic scenes yet to come, when the matriarch releases hundreds of black spiders to fall from the ceiling and

---

76.   Williams, 'Witi Ihimaera: Interviewed by Mark Williams', p. 221.

77.   Ihimaera, *The Matriarch*, pp. 292-93.

78.   Although she is apparently based on the author's grandmother, as Ihimaera tells Paul Sharrad in 'Listening to One's Ancestors: An Interview with Witi Ihimaera', *Australian and New Zealand Studies in Canada* 8 (1992), pp. 97-105 (99).

79.   Ihimaera, *The Matriarch*, p. 233.

80.   A formal gathering where speeches are delivered.

81.   Ihimaera, *The Matriarch*, pp. 251-52.

82.   Ihimaera, *The Matriarch*, p. 258.

83.   Ihimaera, *The Matriarch*, p. 267.

weave their webs around an elder who is threatening the *mana*[84] of her grandson.[85] But if she is a figure of death, a fearsome figure of violence, even a 'witch-bitch',[86] in this work there is no opposing figure of life and peace. She, the matriarch, represents both. And as the bond between land and people is an integral part of the tradition, so she too is one with the land— the statement that 'Her voice struck the reverberating drum of the land' implying that she is to be understood as a very goddess of the land. If the generic term 'Apocalypse' implied a veiling, in this work the matriarch's veil is quite literally a pivotal image flagging this human/divine border crossing:

> Her face, veiled with black mesh, was mysterious. Her beauty was awesome. It shone out of her with a gleaming light that you could almost touch and feel. It vibrated and electrified the air.[87]

And 'Beneath the veil, shimmering like tears, were the pearls in her hair' which 'gleamed with brilliance'.[88] I begin to wonder whether she been borrowing the pearls of Babylon and Jerusalem. As I read I realize that I need to keep an eye on this veil, for as Judith Panny writes, it is used as a way of

> indicating the border between the real and the figurative. The lowering of the veil is the signal to view Artemis as an idea or a deity. The veil can also represent the morning mist that in Maori mythology links Sky and Earth, or it can suggest the transition from present time to an impression of timelessness in which there is no separation of past, present and future.[89]

It is the matriarch herself who is the affirmation of the spirituality of the culture, keenly felt to be denigrated by the *Pakeha*. For 'You, Pakeha, began taking away our culture', declares the narrator.[90] And as cultures are inevitably tied to political realities, so there is a particular earth-bound history to be addressed here too. This timeless matriarch is also, and very much, the human grandmother, whose story is the story of a quite specific historical time, born as she is 'into a world already colonized by the British Government'.[91] So her intervention at the land issues *hui*.

---

84. The honour or reputation.

85. Ihimaera, *The Matriarch*, pp. 290-91, 348-53.

86. So Atareta Poananga, 'The Matriarch: Takahia WahineToa: Trample on Strong Women. Part 2.' *Broadsheet* 46 (January–February 1987), pp. 24-29 (25), who sees the character as wholly negative.

87. Ihimaera, *The Matriarch*, p. 108.

88. Ihimaera, *The Matriarch*, p. 1.

89. Judith Dell Panny, *The Culture Within: Essays on Ihimaera, Grace, Hulme, Tuwhare* (Occasional Paper, 3; Palmerston North, NZ: International Pacific College, 1998), p. 6.

90. Ihimaera, *The Matriarch*, p. 74.

91. Ihimaera, *The Matriarch*, p. 46.

But, as in the Apocalypse, the second strategy of using the master's tools is also woven throughout this work, the two strategies working together as theme and counter-theme. The matriarch herself carries the names of Artemis Riripeti, Artemis interestingly echoing the great Artemis of Ephesus but functioning in this work as a significant reference to the world of European culture. *The Matriarch* may be written to a Maori *kaupapa*, but it is a *kaupapa* set in a *Pakeha* dominated world. So those of us who are *Pakeha* frequently hear ourselves addressed: 'For most assuredly *you*, Pakeha, began taking the land from us as you were signing your worthless Treaty'.[92] The anger of the colonized is palpable; the matriarch *hissed* to her grandson, '*listen to the groans of the Maori. Listen to the way in which the land and the people suffer under the yolk of Pharaoh*'.[93] But there is a counter-theme here too, explained by Witi Ihimarea in an interview: 'wherever I go now, I think of the world I'm in as being Maori, not European'. For him Maori culture will remain strong 'as long as we remember that we haven't become part of Pakeha history but it is has become part of ours'.[94] And so the work frequently goes off-shore to draw that *Pakeha* or European world into the ambit of the matriarch's story: the characters have ties to Venice, which is likened to Hawaiki,[95] the matriarch takes Tama to Rongapai, described as 'the Sistine Chapel of the Maori'.[96] The carrying of the long beam for the house of Rongapai is likened to the carrying of the Cross, as told in the Anglo-Saxon poem of 'The Dream of the Rood':

> The rood was raised on a hill just outside Jerusalem; the kahikatea was raised to be the long beam of the house called Rongapai, just outside Turanga.[97]

By this co-opting a significant point is being made. Despite the strong voice from below challenging the colonial history makers and would-be orderers of society, Ihimaera's aim is also to give

> dramatic expression to Maori life *from within*, without showing any need to cut off the sources of knowledge that are available to modern Maori as much as to modern Pakeha.[98]

In this work *Pakeha* and European references, including the biblical, are not so much subverting the coloniser's dominance as drawing the dominant culture into the world of the Maori.

92. Ihimaera, *The Matriarch*, pp. 73-74.
93. Ihimaera, *The Matriarch*, p. 233.
94. Williams, 'Witi Ihimaera: Interviewed by Mark Williams', p. 222.
95. Ihimaera, *The Matriarch*, p. 430.
96. Ihimaera, *The Matriarch*, p. 133.
97. Ihimaera, *The Matriarch*, p. 185.
98. Mark Williams, *Leaving the Highway: Six Contemporary New Zealand Novelists* (Auckland: Auckland University Press, 1990), p. 117.

Just as the reader is left waiting at the end of the Apocalypse in some ambivalence, so here in *The Matriarch* the book ends abruptly and enigmatically. At the end, the different worlds are still in view. Tama is in Venice but has a dream that his mother Tiana is struggling against the goddess Hine te Ariki about to take her away to oblivion. As he wakes, he interprets his mother's last-second reprieve as a call to return to Aotearoa, but the last sentences return to the dream where Tiana, with tears in her eyes, looks at her son 'with great despair'. The book ends with the words: 'I have never known my mother to cry'. What was the despair? Why the tears? As the reader, I am left wondering. The ambivalences that have been part of the very nature of this work remain unresolved. If Helen Tiffin is correct in her statement that a 'refusal of finality is characteristic of all post-colonial literatures',[99] then the lack of a satisfying closure in both these works is fitting.

What have I discovered in setting these two works together? The surprise in the Apocalypse reading was that goddess roots could still be heard behind the female figures, even the hope-filled image of the new Jerusalem as well as the hated Babylon. She, the feminine mysterium, long since denigrated in Israelite tradition, and part of the opposing forces of the Graeco-Roman world, proved to be a tool worth employing when a minority voice needed a powerful persuasive rhetoric. But the way in which she was used also followed a long biblical tradition, of pitting one powerful female figure against another. Babylon, as the foil to the hopes of the new Jerusalem, was but the last of such 'evil' women in the biblical line.[100] The woman clothed with the Sun, if she was to be viewed independently from the later Jerusalem bride, had already been removed to a safe keeping.[101] *The Matriarch* has not seen the need for such a confrontational rhetoric; the matriarch herself is the figure of the life-blood of the culture as well as of the deathly. The *Pakeha* Babylon is not defeated but incorporated, but most surprisingly perhaps, incorporated in the very figure of the matriarch. As Tama is told by his cousin,

> She had few peers, as a Maori woman of the taniwha line, in the Maori world... There was more—her accomplishments in the *Pakeha* world... Well, that part of her line is derived directly from the Thomas Halbert line.[102]

99.   Helen Tiffin, 'Recuperative Strategies in the Post-Colonial Novel', *Span* 24 (1987), pp. 27-45 (29), quoted by David Dowling, 'Historiography in Some Recent New Zealand Fiction', *Australian and New Zealand Studies in Canada* 2 (1989), pp. 37-62 (37).

100.   So Pippin, *Death and Desire*, p. 79, who adds, 'The Goddess is compartmentalized and stereotyped'. As she states on p. 74, 'Females with autonomous power bring death. Only those females who are connected with God—adorned for the honeymoon or with wombs for use by God...are safe.'

101.   See Pippin, *Death and Desire*, p. 76, who describes her as 'a goddess subdued, tamed and under control'.

102.   Ihimaera, *The Matriarch*, pp. 26-27.

The matriarch herself is part *Pakeha*! And she sings Italian opera! We hear her say to her grandson, of whom she has said, in biblical language, 'I have made him into a likeness as unto me',[103] 'You must grasp the tools of the Pakeha and understand them'.[104] But she adds the sharp warning, 'We must be alert, always alert, grandson, for the Pakeha shark. And we have to fight him in his courts, even his Parliament, if it is necessary.' And yet Tama himself embodies a much less confrontational Maori/Pakeha relationship. Although he has been brought up under his grandmother's eye in the rural world of the tribe, he is presented in the novel as a lawyer living and working in the professional world of the capital city, Wellington, and is married to a Pakeha wife. Striding both Maori and *Pakeha* cultures, like the author himself, he is part of a world in which biculturalism causes tensions but remains a possibility. The book itself explores this multi-dimensional possibility in its bricolage format, as it moves back and forth from myth to historical or parliamentary records, to the realism of the contemporary novel. It is hard to keep one's footing as the linear time of the narrator's contemporary world moves to the shifting time and space world of the matriarch. This might be understood in line with a further comment by Musa Dube, that 'The colonized do not reproduce the colonizer's literary forms. Rather, they interpolate them with various other literary genres unique to their contexts, thus subverting the master's tools and using them at the same time.'[105]

The ambiguities and ambivalences which abound in both works mirror the challenges of living in a world where two cultures meet, and meet most sharply for those on the underside of the power differential. The book of Revelation is a book of oppositions, the overthrow of Babylon is one of unrelieved violence, and yet in the world of the new Jerusalem the leaves of the tree of life are leaves of healing and 'nothing accursed will be found there anymore' (21.2-3). Setting *The Matriarch* as a dialogue partner allowed another possibility for the resolution of cultural threat and opposition to be heard. And yet the tension within the book, illustrated by differing viewpoints of the matriarch and her grandson, is not resolved. As the endings of both works imply, the conversations must continue. Is the way forward to be one of conflict and violence, with the only hope being endurance until death, or is it to be one of attempted accommodation of two cultures, each respected and each drawing the other into its own world in its own way? What, of course, has particularly interested me has been the place of the powerful feminine in this ongoing conversation. The fact that the issue of what we are to do with the powers of the goddess has travelled on into the postcolonial world sets this too as a conversation that has not come to an

103.   Ihimaera, *The Matriarch*, p. 103.
104.   Ihimaera, *The Matriarch*, p. 230.
105.   Dube, *Postcolonial Feminist Interpretation*, p. 103.

end, for it would seem that she cannot be denied, despite all attempts to denigrate her. Perhaps because, even when denigrated, 'the abject' is recognized, in Julia Kristeva's words, as 'edged with the sublime'.[106]

In the end there is no ending. Each work has been read in its own terms as an underside writing; applying a postcolonial lens to each I have been able to detect decolonizing strategies at work, and to watch the female figures being manipulated to fit both the gender and decolonizing requirements of their authors. So I have watched the Woman Clothed with the Sun being pursued, rescued and left in the wilderness, her usefulness over once the Son has been born and taken to the Throne; I have watched and turned my head away from the violence meted out to the too powerful Babylon, and tried to keep Bride Jerusalem in focus, in her rapid city-turn, before the light of God and the Lamb blotted her from sight. I have watched Artemis Riripeti in giddy wonderment, not sure how to reconcile the life-giving and potentially death-dealing aspects of this goddess/human. Applying a postcolonial lens has been a salutary reminder that I read and watch, not only as a woman, but from my place as a reader within the still-dominant *Pakeha* culture. Reading both works together and with this awareness has indeed revealed depths of meaning for me. If it is true that

> [t]he text-fabric is never finished. It is a cloth with loose ends; a tissue which varies in transparency, color and text-ure[107]

then perhaps this is all the truer of intertextual and inter-cultural readings.

---

106. Julia Kristeva, *Powers of Horror: An Essay on Abjection* (New York: Columbia University Press, 1982), p. 11.

107. David Blumenthal, *Facing the Abusing God: A Theology of Protest* (Louisville, KY: Westminster/John Knox Press, 1995), p. 60, quoted by Keller, *Apocalypse Now and Then*, p. 32.

CONCLUSION

I began this exploration with a brief gaze at the Wisdom and Eve figures with their traces of the feminine divine and ended with the new Jerusalem, descending from heaven as the city-bride. Between these boundary marks I came down to earth and kept my eye, for the most part, focused on the more earthly human biblical women. But they were women of the texts, women as the writers wished me to see them and as my own presuppositions and interests led me to view them. As I have watched the characters in their narratives and pondered over what I have been seeing, and what has been happening within the parameters of the texts themselves, differing texts and differing methodological approaches have raised differing issues. In Chapters 1 and 7 I decided to follow Sarah entering Canaan, a silent figure so soon to become a silenced supposed sister carrying the vulnerability of Israel with her into an unwittingly violating Egypt. In this first portrayal, at the beginning of the Israel's own narrative, the Sarah both of the entry into Canaan and the descent into Egypt was a disturbingly passive female origin figure and clearly a pawn of the writer's own interests. Certainly in the two scenes of the conflicted and conflicting trio of Sarah, Abraham and Hagar each woman had an assertive moment or two, but both were soon silenced, for despite the encouraging message of the angel of God in Genesis 16 and the divine rescue in ch. 21, Hagar was left in the wilderness with her child while Sarah was abandoned by the text as the Abraham cycle continued. Were these the women ancestors as those early biblical writers, or perhaps more particularly those early Israelite editors, imagined them, or wished them to be? Was this a case of 'projecting onto woman what man desires most', which Esther Fuchs has long seen as an ideological strategy carried by the biblical narrative?[1]

Another aspect of this has led to further pondering. If this was a Persian era narrative, as the suggestion I have been following proposes, then it is interesting to consider how these women compare with those in Israel's other origin accounts. Assuming Genesis is a late work, then it is possible that some of the canonically later narratives may well have been earlier traditions. This raises some interesting questions. Has the quick thinking

---

1. Esther Fuchs, 'The Literary Characterization of Mothers and Sexual Politics in the Hebrew Bible', in Yarbro Collins (ed.), *Feminist Perspectives on Biblical Scholarship* (Atlanta: Scholars Press, 1985), pp. 117-36 (130).

Canaanite Rahab, that rescuer of Israelite spies and pivotal accomplice in Israel's entry to the land, now been replaced/displaced by this vulnerable, silent and passive Sarah, who has instead to be rescued herself by the God of plagues? Rahab may have been an unwitting player in the theological struggles occasioned by the angst of a sixth-century exile and its accompanying problems of theodicy, but she stands out as a woman of initiative and cunning enterprise in marked contrast to this canonically earlier, but now probably later penned, matriarch. Ironies multiply in the contrasts. For one of the ironies of the Rahab narrative lies in the fact that a woman who was openly available for violation becomes the protected, in return for having protected the would-be Yahwistic violators of both her land and body; Sarah in contrast moved from protection to being the exploited in a land doubly removed from being her own. But if it is also possible that the Genesis beginnings could be dated later than those of the Exodus, Sarah's silent acquiescence would also contrast markedly with the enterprising initiatives of the women who birthed the Exodus narrative, those shrewd quick-thinking midwives, and its celebrator, the daringly outspoken Miriam. If so, setting Miriam and Rahab aside for a silent Sarah and dispatched Hagar would be a disturbing strategy. But on closer viewing there are notable similarities between the women in all three origin tales. In each scenario there is a problem: Genesis is promising descendents but Sarai is barren (11.30), Miriam is party to the rescue of the baby Moses, but later challenges his very god-given authority (Num. 12), while in Joshua the spies, protected by Rahab, have set out from Shittim, the very place where Israel fell sexually into the arms of the women of Moab, which resulted in the sin of worshiping the Baal of Peor, resulting in turn in the deaths of many Israelites (Num. 25.1-5). Irony has balanced irony: a barren wife setting out with the promise of descendents; a sister rescuing a brother only to attempt to displace him; spies leaving the place of prostitution for the house of a Canaanite prostitute. Above each hovered divine displeasure, barren wombs a sign of that, as so many biblical women knew well, so too the whiteness of the scaly skin hinting of God-sent death, while mention of prostitute resonates with echoes of other texts where metaphorical prostitution carried the full force of the sin of violation of Yahweh's covenant.[2]

In the end, of course, Sarah's silence and acquiescence benefits Abraham, Moses has divine defense in Numbers 12 and Joshua is the recognized hero of Jericho. But one of the questions underlying this study is to what extent we are to watch the biblical women through the frames assigned by their rhetorical movers. Although, even if we strictly adhere to this the reading task will still be fraught with difficulty for so often the biblical characters move in ambiguity. Was Sarah, for example, a willing partner in Abram's move, or

    2. Hawk, *Every Promise Fulfilled*, p. 61.

the reluctant and doubting wife as Maitland and Diski suggest? Was she Abram's Sarai or Pharaoh's in Egypt?

But I myself have been quite deliberately choosing and changing the frames for these readings. Just as over centuries scribes, editors, scholars, and creative imaginers have all taken these female characters and images and shaped them to fit their own careful construals, so I have been suggesting that for women and for (post)colonial readers there is a need to scrutinize them afresh and read them again with care. My choice of critical frames for reading and writing about these biblical women and female images has been governed by my own experience of the tensions of a gendered and post-colonial world. So, applying a postcolonial lens, it was clear to me that Sarah, for example, in that canonically first entry to the land, was a Sarah clearly enmeshed in a discourse of land claims. Rahab, just as clearly, was a figure colluding in the entry to others' land and seemingly prepared to assimilate within the invaders' culture, while Jezebel was consigned to the dung-heap because she chose to remain resolutely 'other'. In these readings I was also conscious of Musa Dube's call to examine such texts for their imperializing influence, which makes such open-eyed rereadings an impera-tive for (post)colonial women readers—although even a postcolonial reading may end with an uneasy question. Was Sarah, for example, a colonizer or, in gender terms, the silently colonized? Although Sarah's earliest storytellers might have wondered at the reading companions who have journeyed with her, occupying places next to her in my collage of voices in Chapter 7, so be it. Sarah, Hagar, Rahab and the others are simply dead figures of the past if they do not keep journeying with others. Setting Sarah and Hagar's stories in a textual equivalent of a visual collage to be read alongside the writings of other women's histories, as well as fictioning imaginers and contemporary scholars, provides yet another performative context in which past and present understandings can be heard together, allowing fresh insights and connections.

Jezebel occupied more than one chapter, and even then she could not be contained in the space allotted. She is the archetypal example of the woman the Deuteronomists did not want in their ranks, but she straddled Israelite traditions too, bearing some of the marks of the sages' Strange/Outsider Woman. With Otherness the key, redactional and intratextual tools pro-vided a way of detecting the writers' strategies to paint her in dangerously and deathly Other guise. But her own death, chillingly echoed in that of Babylon in the Apocalypse, raised even more disturbing questions. I quoted Danna Fewell and David Gunn's term 'visceral hostility' and tried to under-stand the violence of this presentation. Certainly she provided an example of what Julia Kristeva describes as the 'abject'. But why? Was it simply because she was an Asherah worshiping Phoenician? The outlawed feminine

divine was hovering again. Or was it rather the fact that she was a Phoenician woman exercising power as queen mother that was so unacceptable?
The descriptions of her appearance required some sharp gender analysis, with
glances not only back to ancient Israel, and further back to the ancient Near
East, but also sideways to the psychoanalytical insights of Freud, Lacan and
Kristeva. Reading the encounter between Jesus and the Canaanite woman
with Rahab and Jezebel still in mind resulted in an uneasy response. On the
one hand Jesus could be seen 'unlearning his privilege' but there were still
those dogs! In these chapters I have been attempting to understand something of the interests that have shaped the writings, and are encoded within
them, but I have also been taking seriously the view, expressed by Guardiola-
Sáenz, that 'a cultural text...should be read not just for the history it reflects,
but also for the history it has made'.[3] So, if the Rahab story is heard persuading the reader that the good Canaanite is not just the Canaanite who
delivers enemy spies and works for the destruction of her own people, but
the one who leaves behind her Canaanite identity and adopts the belief
system of the winning or dominant power, a question has to be asked of the
message that has been passed on to generations of readers. Just as Tina
Pippin asks, 'What have we done with the story of Jezebel? Is her story continually recolonized, reopened, the brief scenes of her life re-enacted and
reinscribed?'[4] For if so, it is now readers' lives which will be at stake.

In the last chapter I chose to set the Apocalypse of John of Patmos beside
Witi Ihimaera's *The Matriarch*, noting their very different approaches to the
power of the feminine, and in particular the traces of the goddess in their
respective traditions. The choice of the Apocalypse was carefully considered,
for as the last book of the Christian canon it assumes a certain importance as
its last word. That the canon ends on such an oppositional view of the feminine, the new Jerusalem over against the cursed Babylon, is disturbing. I
began this study with a mention of my earlier reading of the Wisdom figure.
Throughout the first nine chapters of the book of Proverbs her poems are
interspersed with warnings against the seductive, honey-lipped Outsider
Woman, and in ch. 9 Wisdom has her deathly counterpart *Kesilut*—so this
splitting of the feminine into the good and the bad has a long biblical
tradition. Eve has suffered a similar fate in the hands of later tradition
responsible for setting a good Eve against a bad. Was she the one responsible
for our knowing good and evil, for our sense of discernment, without which
we would have remained as amoral beasts of the field? Or was she the one
tricked by the satanic serpent, and therefore responsible for evil coming into
the world, as Ben Sira and the writer of the later *Vita* of Adam and Eve

3. Guardiola-Sáenz, 'Borderless Women and Borderless Texts', p. 71.
4. Tina Pippin, 'Jezebel Re-Vamped', in Brenner (ed.), *A Feminist Companion to Samuel and Kings*, pp. 196-206 (206).

would have it? Interpreters as well as writers leave their marks on the biblical women to influence the generations of readers that follow; contemporary interpreters are attempting to provide ways forward in resolving this binary divide of the good and bad woman. Claudia Camp suggests that the two faces of Wisdom and the Strange Woman be read together in trickster mode as 'a single paradoxical entity', the trickster who 'teases the either/or logic of apocalypse toward a more sustainable Wisdom',[5] or the entity that speaks out for herself in the *Nag Hammadi* Thunder poem.[6] A similar resolution as that employed in the contemporary postcolonial work of Witi Ihimaera. These current possibilities serve as a reminder that the biblical binary opposition was not and need not be the last word or the end of the matter. As I applied Musa Dube's questions to the Apocalypse and *The Matriarch*, what was striking about both these works, written in very different styles and genres and from vastly different times and world situations, was that similar post-colonial strategies could be detected in each. Here again, as in ch. 7, the collage approach provided a way for a viewing in which ancient and present voices could be seen together, their agreements and their differences plainly in view leaving me as the reader free to wander in front of both, knowing that each was part of our present and each needed to be acknowledged. At the same time this was a viewing with the sharp questions of the postcolonial critics ringing in the ears. Not a place for the politically neutral or the ethically unaware.

At the same time I have been wondering as I have read and reread these texts whether my own critical frames have been covering over what might yet be celebrated in these chosen biblical texts. I am mindful that Paul Ricoeur has talked of every society possessing, or being part of, 'a socio-political *imaginaire*', which 'can function as a rupture or a reaffirmation'. While he aligns the reaffirming task with the maintenance of the master narratives, he sees the rupture as 'a symbolic opening towards the future'.[7] So I wonder whether, if I move back to the biblical texts and read them again for signs of rupture, it might be possible to read them differently. Certainly in

5. Keller, *Apocalypse Now and Then*, pp. 305-306, 309, referring to Claudia V. Camp, 'Wise and Strange: An Interpretation of the Female Imagery in Proverbs in Light of Trickster Mythology', *Semeia* 42 (1988), pp. 14-36.

6. 'For I am the first and the last / I am the honored one and the scorned one / I am the whore and the holy one / I am the wife and the virgin / I am the mother and the daughter… / I am the barren one and many are her sons / I am she whose wedding is great / And I have not taken a husband… / I am the silence that is incomprehensible / And the idea whose remembrance is frequent / I am the voice whose sound is manifold / And the word whose appearance is multiple' ('The Thunder, Perfect Mind' [6.2], quoted by Keller, *Apocalypse Now and Then*, p. 308).

7. Paul Ricoeur, 'The Creativity of Language', in Mario J. Valdes (ed.), *A Ricoeur Reader: Reflection and Imagination* (Toronto: University of Toronto Press, 1991), pp. 463-81 (475).

my reading of Hagar there was the transformative possibility of the wilderness, understood as the liberative borderline. If I return to the book of Ruth and consider again Ruth's act on the threshing floor where she comes so close to being seen as the sexual foreign stereotype, I could read this as the subversive act of rupture in allowing a Moabite to become an ancestor of David. And indeed, as I noted in Chapter 2, the rupture as regards acceptance of difference was enshrined for Israel in the priestly manual of Leviticus (Lev. 19.34) where it was underlined with the divine formula: 'I am Yahweh, your God'. Just as in its vision of the divinely-ordered future the Isaiah scroll sang of bringing the *ben nekar* to God's holy mountain (Isa. 56.6-7).[8] Interpreting Ruth in this way would be both the more traditional and more positive reading, but the message of rewards for assimilation is not so easily silenced once it has been heard. If I return and listen again to Jesus and the Canaanite Syrophoenician woman, shutting out all disturbing echoes, I might simply hear a rupturing of the cultural barriers, splintering as they talk. For she is demanding that the discourse of the master narrative be opened up to include 'Others' in its centre, and he, albeit after notable hesitation and sharp rebuttal, eventually agrees; a rupture indeed. But my readings have alerted me to the multi-voiced nature of the biblical texts, and to the double-sided potential of rupture. For not only is there a rupture that opens towards a hoped-for and celebratory future, but there is also the rupture that is potentially harmful and divisive. So, while those texts that are clearly and undisputedly anticipatory of hope-filled possibilities must indeed be kept in full view, my hope would be that biblical studies with its careful and rigorous analytical reading strategies would have a challenging and disturbing role in any programme that would use the Bible as warrant for unequal, lopsided and unhealthy political practices.

I conclude mindful of Laurel Richardson's questions, asked of her sociology colleagues:

> How does our writing, including this writing, reproduce a system of domination and how does it challenge that system? For whom do we speak and to whom do we speak, with what voice, to what end, using what criteria?[9]

Her statement that 'People live by stories...if the available narrative is limiting, people's lives are limited, textually disenfranchised' makes the sharp connection with this study.[10] With what voice has this been written? I

---

8. See also Isa. 66.18-21, although, as Jon D. Levenson, 'The Universal Horizon of Biblical Particularism', in Brett (ed.), *Ethnicity and the Bible*, pp. 143-69 (162), notes of the historical realities, 'the degree of integration of a foreigner into ancient Israel remains shrouded in obscurity'.

9. Laurel Richardson, *Fields of Play: Constructing an Academic Life* (New Brunswick, NJ: Rutgers University Press, 1997), p. 57.

10. Richardson, *Fields of Play*, p. 58.

have attempted to write in my own voice, as a woman and as the descendent of settlers in a postcolonial society. To what end have I written? I have an interest in the constructs of gender, and in the understandings of identity and difference. As a reader of biblical texts I have a concern for the ways in which these texts may be heard. I have a fear that the faces of Rahab, Jezebel and Babylon and others may still be lingering below the surface of later and even contemporary texts, refusing final erasure and so adding their warrant to gender and ethnic assumptions and prejudice that continue to bring ongoing harm to women readers. I have an interest in the ways in which the feminine dimension of the divine refuses to be erased, despite the many attempts to achieve this. In the end what matters is that these biblical writings spur those of us who read them and study them to further conversations, with the appropriate interpretive lenses, reminding us that 'gender', 'identity' and 'difference' are always, and must always be, under negotiation.

POSTLUDE

And so I saw them there before me—characters lying in wait, lifeless, flat objects, folded into themselves like collapsed cardboard cartons. But as I watched there was a flurry of light and the sound of pages being opened very gently. The characters quietly stretched themselves and flesh rounded itself on their bodies. Then it was all activity. Eve was standing up with what seemed to be a little small-footed animal beside her with a long body and sharp eyes. It almost seemed as if they were deep in conversation. But soon she was handing around apples—or were they apricots? Breakfast time on fresh grass. It was difficult to see the trees, they kept hazily disappearing into a mist that was springing up. At times they didn't look like trees at all, more like large female forms that were bending down to the ground and covering it with their fruit, so much fruit that the women who were springing to life, one after another, could barely gather it all. Eve too began to grow taller and almost merge into the trees, as she kept calling to the others to come and eat. Jezebel came at once. At first I wasn't sure what she was doing, she seemed to be hugging the tree and then talking to it as if there was some conversation to be had with a tree. But others came and took what they wanted and then went off. Sarah and Hagar were taking care of their children which was no easy matter as they were in and out of the trees tricking each other and laughing loudly together. The Syrophoenician woman's daughter was wistfully watching them, not yet quite energetic enough for their play. Rahab was talking about getting her house in order again after her last unexpected guests, and Jezebel was planning on planting out her vegetable garden, bequeathed by a kindly Naboth. A woman sitting out in the full sun, almost clothed with it, was preferring a wilderness plot, hoping to share it with Hagar. They went off to consult with Jerusalem about the irrigation they would need. But even as the day began to clear in the bright sunshine, the treelike figures remained in a surrounding haze, spreading their branches out as if they would protect all the women and children enjoying the peace and each other's company. Not that it was entirely peaceful with Ishmael and Isaac sporting all over the place.

Then suddenly there was a rumbling—pages were being turned again but not so gently. Other characters were coming to life. I was now in a room full of scrolls, codices and books. The place was abuzz with chatter, groups in deep conversation and some with loud voices attempting to drown others.

The name Eve rang out and there were nods all round. Jesus ben Sira spoke out, 'From a woman sin had its beginning and because of her we all die'. The muttering continued and became angrier. I heard the names of Jezebel and Babylon joined to those of Eve, although others were pointing to the faithfulness of Rahab and the beauty of Sarah. John of Patmos was waving his finger and warning anyone who would listen that his words were to be taken... I missed the final word. Was it as gospel or as warning? I looked back to the garden—just glimpsed through the windows. The women were scattering, running into the trees for shelter, but they too were disappearing, almost shrivelling into nothingness, apart from one apple tree whose bark was now growing gnarled and twisted. Eve too seemed shrunken, treading on a snake in her haste and getting bitten on the heel. I watched as she was taken off by a none-too-happy Adam who seemed to have emerged from a hidden space somewhere in the garden. Naboth came out to reclaim his vegetable patch, and a pack of wild dogs was to be seen snapping at the feet of Jezebel who was now clinging desperately to her tree. She was saying to anyone who would listen that it was no use relying on Ahab to come to her rescue. But it was an act of sheer desperation on her part for a gang of foresters had already arrived and were attacking the tree with electric saws, apparently on official order to chop it down along with most of the others. Only indigenous trees were to be saved and most of these growing in the garden had been classified as foreign imports. Hagar and the sun-bathed woman were deciding that their wilderness patch was the safer place for them and Hagar seemed relieved to be away from Sarah who was now telling some libellous story about her and Abraham. The Syrophoenician woman was trying to keep her distance from the dogs, but it was with difficulty—they kept snapping at her as if they would bring her down to their level. Jerusalem remained out in the open. It almost seemed as if the sun had melted into her with a brightness that caught the spots of a remaining dew so that she sparkled in the light. Rahab was watching apparently equally unperturbed and at ease, but keeping at a distance. Then, as I watched, Jesus/God entered, embraced Jerusalem and went off for a long feasting with Adam, Abraham and Rahab in attendance. The mention of feasting had obviously upset Jezebel and Babylon. The others had all drifted away out of sight.

Then there was a loud clicking, as if there many books all being opened and shut not once but a great many times. The room with the scrolls and codices was still there, but the readers had changed. The conversation was as loud as before, but the readers kept lifting small figures of the women I had been watching out of the scrolls and from the pages of the books. As they held them up the faces of the women kept changing depending on where the readers were standing and behind each of the reader's chairs was a blackboard on which was written the agenda for which the women were to be used. But other people kept arriving so that the boards kept shifting, their programmes continually being overwritten by others. On some I saw the words 'imperializing' and 'silencing' being written in fresh chalk, at first in small letters but increasing in size at each new chalking. Arguments were heard from groups in corners of the room and cries for judicial commissions to hear cases: was Jezebel guilty of Naboth's death or not? Was Rahab to keep her place among the faithful in Israel? Who was to be held responsible for the death of Babylon? Crowds of people were gathering at the windows, some eager to read the latest blackboard messages, others clearly concerned for their own safety and wellbeing, both in the crush itself and in what they might hear relayed to them by the front-runners. But as I gazed in some wonderment at this scene, I heard another gentle murmuring of voices and turned to see the biblical women themselves watching from the sidelines. Some were smiling secretly to themselves, others were comforting those who appeared to have been hurt. Very quietly they turned and left the room and headed back to the garden, leaving the door open. I think they were still wanting to hear what the next readers would be saying.

BIBLIOGRAPHY

Ackerman, Susan, 'The Queen Mother and the Cult in Ancient Israel', *JBL* 112 (1993), pp. 385-401.

—*Warrior, Dancer, Seductress, Queen: Women in Judges and Biblical Israel* (New York: Doubleday, 1998).

Ackroyd, Peter R. 'Goddesses, Women and Jezebel', in Averil Cameron and Amélie Kuhrt (eds.), *Images of Women in Antiquity* (Detroit: Wayne State University Press, rev. edn, 1993), pp. 245-59.

Ahlström, Gösta W., *The History of Ancient Palestine from the Palaeolithic Period to Alexander's Conquest* (ed. Diana Edelman; JSOTSup, 146; Sheffield: Sheffield Academic Press, 1993).

Aichele, George, and Gary Phillips, 'Introduction: Exegesis, Eisegesis, Intergesis', *Semeia* 69/70 (1995), pp. 7-18.

Albertz, Rainer, *History of Israelite Religion in the Old Testament Period. II. From the Exile to the Maccabees* (trans. J. Bowden; London: SCM Press, 1994).

—'In Search of the Deuteronomists: A First Solution to a Historical Riddle', in T. Römer (ed.), *The Future of the Deuteronomistic History* (Leuven: Leuven University Press, 2000), pp. 1-17.

Alexander, T.D., 'Are the Wife/Sister Incidents of Genesis Literary Compositional Variants?', *VT* 42 (1992), pp. 145-53.

Alter, R., *The Art of Biblical Narrative* (New York: Basic Books, 1981).

Amit, Yairah, *History and Ideology: An Introduction to Historiography in the Hebrew Bible* (trans. Yael Lotan; The Biblical Seminar, 60; Sheffield: Sheffield Academic Press, 1999).

Anderson, Janice Capel, 'Matthew: Gender and Reading', *Semeia* 28 (1983), pp. 3-27.

Anonymous, 'The New System of Colonization—Australia and New Zealand', *The Phrenological Journal and Magazine of Modern Science* 11 NS 1 (1838), pp. 247-60.

Appadurai, Arjun, 'Disjuncture and Difference in the Global Cultural Economy', *Public Culture* 2 (1990), pp. 1-24.

Armour, Ellen T., *Deconstruction, Feminist Theology, and the Problem of Difference: Subverting the Race/Gender Divide* (Chicago: Chicago University Press, 1999).

Ashley, Kathleen M., 'Interrogating Biblical Deception and Trickster Theories: Narratives of Patriarchy or Possibility?', *Semeia* 42 (1988), pp. 103-15.

Aune, David E., *Revelation 6–16* (WBC, 52B; Nashville: Thomas Nelson, 1998).

—*Revelation 17–22* (WBC, 52C; Nashville: Thomas Nelson, 1998).

Bagnall, A.G., and G.C. Petersen, *William Colenso, Printer, Missionary, Botanist, Explorer, Politician: His Life and Journeys* (Wellington, NZ: A.H. & A.W. Reed, 1948).

Bakhtin, Mikhail, *Dialogic Imagination: Four Essays by M.M. Bakhtin* (ed. Michael Holquist; trans. Caryl Emerson and Michael Holquist; Austin: University of Texas Press, 1981).

—*Problems of Dostoevsky's Poetics* (ed. and trans. Caryl Emerson; Minneapolis: University of Minneapolis Press, 1984).

—*Rabelais and His World* (trans. Helene Iswolsky; Cambridge, MA: MIT Press, 1984).

—*Speech Genres and Other Late Essays* (ed. Caryl Emerson and Michael Holquist; trans. Vern W. McGee; Austin: University of Texas Press, 1986).

Bal, Mieke, 'Introduction', in Bal, Crewe and Spitzer (eds.), *Acts of Memory*, pp. i-xvii.

—'Metaphors He Lives By', *Semeia* 61 (1993), pp. 185-207.

—'Religious Canon and Literary Identity', *Lectio Difficilior* 2 (2000), available online at <www.lectio.unibe.ch/>.

Bal, M., J. Crewe and L. Spitzer (eds.), *Acts of Memory: Cultural Recall in the Present* (Hanover, NH: University Press of New England, 1999).

Barclay, John M.G., *Jews in the Mediterranean Diaspora: From Alexander to Trajan (323 BCE–117 CE)* (Edinburgh: T. & T. Clark, 1996).

Barker, Margaret, *The Revelation of Jesus Christ* (Edinburgh: T. & T. Clark, 2000).

Barr, James, *The Garden of Eden and the Hope of Immortality* (London: SCM Press, 1992).

Bauckham, Richard, *The Climax of Prophecy: Studies on the Book of Revelation* (Edinburgh: T. & T. Clark, 1993).

—'Economic Critique of Rome in Revelation 18', in Loveday Alexander (ed.), *Images of Empire* (JSOTSup, 122: Sheffield: JSOT Press, 1991), pp. 47-90.

Beach, Eleanor Ferris, 'The Samaria Ivories, Marzeah and Biblical Texts', *Biblical Archaeologist* 56 (1992), pp. 130-39.

Beale, G.K., *The Book of Revelation* (Grand Rapids: Eerdmans; Carlisle: Paternoster Press, 1999).

Beare, F.W., *The Gospel according to Matthew* (Oxford: Basil Blackwell, 1981).

Becking, Bob, and Marjo C.A. Korpel (eds.), *The Crisis of Israelite Religion* (Leiden: E.J. Brill, 1999).

Becking, Bob, Meindert Dijkstra, Marjo C.A. Korpel and Karel Vreizen (eds.), *Only One God? Monotheism in Ancient Israel and the Veneration of the Goddess Asherah* (The Biblical Seminar, 77; London: Sheffield Academic Press, 2001).

Begg, C.T., 'Foreigner', in *ABD*, II, pp. 829-30.

Belich, James, *Making Peoples: A History of the New Zealanders From Polynesian Settlement to the End of the Nineteenth Century* (Auckland: Penguin Books New Zealand, 1996).

—*The New Zealand Wars and the Victorian Interpretation of Racial Conflict* (Auckland: Auckland University Press, 1989).

Bhabha, Homi K., *The Location of Culture* (London and New York: Routledge, 1994).

Binney, Judith, *Redemption Songs: A Life of Te Kooti Arikirangi Te Turuki* (Auckland: Auckland University Press, 1995).

Bird, Phyllis A., 'The Harlot as Heroine: Narrative Art and Social Presupposition in Three Old Testament Texts', *Semeia* 46 (1989), pp. 119-39.

—' "To Play the Harlot": An Inquiry into an Old Testament Metaphor', in Peggy L. Day (ed.), *Gender and Difference in Ancient Israel* (Minneapolis: Fortress Press, 1989), pp. 75-94.

Blumenthal, David, *Facing the Abusing God: A Theology of Protest* (Louisville, KY: Westminster/John Knox Press, 1995).

Boer, Roland, 'Remembering Babylon: Postcolonialism and Australian Biblical Studies', in Sugirtharajah (ed.), *The Postcolonial Bible*, pp. 24-48.

Boesak, Allan A., *Comfort and Protest: The Apocalypse from a South Africa Perspective* (Philadelphia: Westminster Press, 1987).

Bourdieu, Pierre, *Outline of a Theory of Practice* (Cambridge: Cambridge University Press, 1977).

Bourdieu, Pierre, and Terry Eagleton, 'Doxa and the Common Life', in Slavoj Žižek (ed.), *Mapping Ideology* (London/New York: Verso, 1994), pp. 265-77.

Bowman, Richard G., and Richard W. Swanson, 'Samson and the Son of God or Dead Heroes and Dead Goats: Ethical Readings of Narrative Violence in Judges and Matthew', *Semeia* 77 (1997), pp. 59-73.

Boyd, Mary, *City of the Plains: A History of Hastings* (Wellington, NZ: Victoria University Press for Hastings City Council, 1984).

Brah, Avtar, 'Re-framing Europe: Engendered Racisms, Ethnicities and Nationalisms in Contemporary Western Europe', *Feminist Review* 45 (1993), pp. 9-28.

Bredin, Mark R.J., 'Gentiles and the Davidic Tradition in Matthew', in Athalya Brenner (ed.), *A Feminist Companion to the Hebrew Bible in the New Testament* (The Feminist Companion to the Bible, 10; Sheffield: Sheffield Academic Press, 1996), pp. 95-111.

Brenner, Athalya (ed.), *A Feminist Companion to Samuel and Kings* (The Feminist Companion to the Bible, 5; Sheffield: Sheffield Academic Press, 1994).

Brett, Mark G., *Genesis: Procreation and the Politics of Identity* (Old Testament Readings; London and New York: Routledge, 2000).

—'Interpreting Ethnicity: Method, Hermeneutics, Ethics', in *idem* (ed.), *Ethnicity and the Bible*, pp. 3-22.

Brett, Mark G. (ed.), *Ethnicity and the Bible* (Leiden: E.J. Brill, 1996).

Bright, John, *A History of Israel* (London: SCM Press, 2nd edn, 1972).

Bronfen, Elisabeth, 'From Omphalos to Phallus: Cultural Representations of Femininity and Death', *Women: A Cultural Review* 3 (1992), pp. 145-58.

—*Over Her Dead Body: Death, Femininity and the Aesthetic* (Manchester: Manchester University Press, 1992).

—*Powers of Horror: An Essay on Abjection* (trans. Leon S. Roudiez; New York: Columbia University Press, 1982).

Bronfen, Elisabeth, and Sarah Webster Goodwin (eds.), *Death and Representation* (Baltimore, MD: The Johns Hopkins University Press, 1993).

Brooke-Rose, Christine, 'Woman as a Semiotic Object', in Suleiman (ed.), *The Female Body in Western Culture*, pp. 305-16.

Brooten, Bernadette J., 'Early Christian Women and their Cultural Context: Issues of Method in Historical Reconstruction', in Yarbro Collins (ed.), *Feminist Perspectives on Biblical Scholarship*, pp. 65-91.

Brown, R.E., *The Birth of the Messiah: A Commentary on the Infancy Narratives in Matthew and Luke* (Garden City, NY: Doubleday, 1977).

—'Rachab in Matthew 1.5 Probably is Rahab of Jericho', *Bib* 63 (1982), pp. 79-80.

Brueggemann, Walter, *Genesis* (Interpretation; Atlanta: John Knox Press, 1982).

Burkill, T.A., 'Historical Development of the Story of the Syro-Phoenician Woman', *NovT* 9 (1967), pp. 161-77.

Burrows, R., 'Journal, 27 April 1845', in *Extracts from a Diary kept by the Rev. R. Burrows During Heke's War in the North, in 1845* (Auckland, 1886), p. 32.

Butler, Trent C., *Joshua* (WBC, 7; Waco, TX: Word Books, 1983).

Caird, G.B., *The Language and Imagery of the Bible* (London: Gerald Duckworth, 1980).

Calder, Alex, 'The Matriarch, Witi Ihimaera—Two Responses', *Landfall* 161 (1986), pp. 79-86.

Camp, Claudia V., *Wisdom and the Feminine in the Book of Proverbs* (Bible and Literature Series, 11; Sheffield Sheffield: Almond Press, 1985).

—'1 and 2 Kings', in Newsom and Ringe (eds.). *The Women's Bible Commentary*, pp. 96-109.

—*Wise, Strange and Holy: The Strange Woman and the Making of the Bible* (JSOTSup, 320; Gender, Culture, Theory, 9; Sheffield: Sheffield Academic Press, 2000).

Campbell, Antony F., and Mark A. O'Brien, *Unfolding the Deuteronomistic History: Origins, Ugrades, Present Text* (Minneapolis: Augsburg Fortress, 2000).

Carroll, Robert P., 'The Myth of the Empty Land', *Semeia* 59 (1992), pp. 79-93.

—'Textual Strategies and Ideology', in Philip R. Davies (ed.), *Second Temple Studies 1: Persian Period* (JSOTSup, 117; Sheffield: JSOT Press, 1991), pp. 108-24.

Cassuto, U., *A Commentary on the Book of Genesis* (trans. L. Abrahams; Jerusalem: Magnes Press, 1964).

Clément, Catherine, and Julia Kristeva, *The Feminine and the Sacred* (trans. Jane Marie Todd; New York: Columbia University Press, 2001).

Cogan, Mordechai, and Hayim Tadmor, *II Kings* (New York: Doubleday, 1988).

Colebrook, Claire, *New Literary Histories: New Historicism and Contemporary Criticism* (Manchester: Manchester University Press, 1997).

Colenso, William, 'Autobiography—Typescript 88-103-1/01', in *Further Papers* (ed. A.G. Bagnall; Alexander Turnbull Library, n.d.).

—'Letters from his Wife, Elizabeth 88-103-1/22' (Alexander Turnbull Library, 1843–99).

Comaroff, John, 'Reflections on the Colonial State, in South Africa and Elsewhere: Factions, Fragments, Facts, and Fictions', *Social Identities* 4 (1998), pp. 317-58.

Cross, Frank Moore, *Canaanite Myth and Hebrew Epic: Essays in the History of the Religion of Israel* (Cambridge, MA: Harvard University Press, 1973).

—'A Response to Zakovitch's "Successful Failure of Israelite Intelligence"', in Niditch (ed.), *Text and Tradition*, pp. 99-104.

Culley, Robert, 'Stories of the Conquest: Joshua 2, 6, 7 and 8', *HAR* 8 (1984), pp. 25-44.

Daube, David, *The Exodus Pattern in the Bible* (London: Faber & Faber, 1963), pp. 23-38.

Davidson, Allan K., and Peter J. Lineham, *Transplanted Christianity: Documents Illustrating Aspects of New Zealand Church History* (Palmerston North: Department of History, Massey University, 3rd edn, 1995).

Diski, Jenny, *Only Human: A Comedy* (London: Virago Press, 2000).

Donaldson, Laura, 'The Sign of Orpah: Reading Ruth Through Native Eyes', in Brenner (ed.), *Ruth and Esther*, pp. 130-44.

Dowling, David, 'Historiography in Some Recent New Zealand Fiction', *Australian and New Zealand Studies in Canada* 2 (1989), pp. 37-62.

Dozeman, Thomas B., 'The Wilderness and Salvation History in the Hagar Story', *JBL* 117 (1998), pp. 23-43.

Dube, Musa W., *Postcolonial Feminist Interpretation of the Bible* (St Louis, MI: Chalice Press, 2000).

Dube, Musa W., and Jeffrey L. Staley, 'Descending from and Ascending into Heaven: A Postcolonial Analysis of Travel, Space and Power in John', in *idem* (eds.), *John and Postcolonialism*, pp. 1-10

Dube, Musa W., and Jeffrey L. Staley (eds.), *John and Postcolonialism: Travel, Space and Power* (The Bible and Postcolonialism, 7; London: Sheffield Academic Press, 2002).

Dennis C. Duling, 'Matthew's Plurisignificant "Son of David" in Social Science Perspective: Kinship, Kingship, Magic, and Miracle', *Biblical Theology Bulletin* 22 (1992), pp. 99-116.

Edelman, Diana, 'Ethnicity and Early Israel', in Brett (ed.), *Ethnicity and The Bible*, pp. 25-55.

Elsmore, Bronwyn, *Like Them that Dream: The Maori and the Old Testament* (Tauranga: Tauranga Moana, 1985).

—*Mana from Heaven: A Century of Maori Prophets in New Zealand* (Tauranga: Moana Press, 1989).

Enloe, Cynthia, *Bananas, Beaches and Bases: Making Feminist Sense of International Politics* (Berkeley, CA: University of California Press, 1989).

Eskenazi, Tamara C., and Eleanore P. Judd, 'Marriage to a Stranger in Ezra 9–10', in Eskenazi and Richards (eds.), *Second Temple Studies 2*, pp. 266-85.

Eskenazi, Tamara C., and Kent H. Richards (eds.), *Second Temple Studies 2: Temple and Community in the Persian Period* (JSOTSup, 175; Sheffield: JSOT Press, 1994).

Exum, J. Cheryl, *Fragmented Women: Feminist (Sub)versions of Biblical Narratives* (JSOTSup, 163; Sheffield: JSOT Press, 1993).

—'Who's Afraid of the "Endangered Ancestress"?', in Exum and Clines (eds.), *The New Literary Criticism*, pp. 91-113.

Exum, J. Cheryl, and David J.A. Clines (eds.), *The New Literary Criticism and the Hebrew Bible* (JSOTSup, 143; Sheffield: JSOT Press, 1993).

Felder, Cain Hope, 'Race, Racism, and the Biblical Narratives', in *idem* (ed.), *Stony the Road We Trod*, pp. 127-45.

Felder, Cain Hope (ed.), *Stony the Road We Trod: African American Biblical Interpretation* (Minneapolis: Fortress Press, 1991).

Fenshaw, F.C., 'A Few Observations on the Polarisation Between Yahweh and Baal in 1 Kings 17–19', *ZAW* 92 (1980), pp. 227-37.

Fewell, Danna Nolan, 'Changing the Subject: Retelling the Story of Hagar the Egyptian', in Athalya Brenner (ed.), *Genesis* (The Feminist Companion to the Bible, Second Series, 1; Sheffield: Sheffield Academic Press, 1998), pp. 182-94.

—'Imagination, Method, and Murder: Un/Framing the Face of Post-Exilic Israel', in Timothy K. Beal and David M. Gunn (eds.), *Reading Bibles, Writing Bodies: Identity and the Book* (New York: Routledge, 1997), pp. 132-52.

Fewell, Danna Nolan, and David M. Gunn, 'Boaz, Pillar of Society: Measures of Worth in the Book of Ruth', *JSOT* 45 (1989), pp. 45-59.

—*Gender, Power and Promise: The Subject of the Bible's First Story* (Nashville: Abingdon Press, 1993).

'"A Son is Born to Naomi!": Literary Allusions and Interpretation in the Book of Ruth', *JSOT* 40 (1988), pp. 99-108.

Fleras, Augie, and Paul Spoonley, *Recalling Aotearoa: Indigenous Politics and Ethnic Relations in New Zealand* (Auckland: Oxford University Press, 1999).

Fontaine, Carole R., 'The Deceptive Goddess in Ancient Near Eastern Myth: Inanna and Inaras', *Semeia* 42 (1988), pp. 84-102.

—*Smooth Words: Women, Proverbs and Performance in Biblical Wisdom* (JSOTSup, 356; London: Sheffield Academic Press, 2002).

Ford, J. Massyngberde, *Revelation* (AB, 38; Garden City, NY: Doubleday, 1975).

Friedman, Susan Stanford, 'Beyond White and Other: Relationality and Narratives of Race in Feminist Discourse', *Signs* 21 (1995), pp. 1-49.

Friesen, Steven J., *Imperial Cults and the Apocalypse of John: Reading Revelation in the Ruins* (Oxford: Oxford University Press, 2001).

Frymer-Kensky, Tikva, *In the Wake of the Goddesses: Women, Culture, and the Biblical Transforamtion of Pagan Myth* (New York: Free Press, 1992).

Fuchs, Esther, 'For I Have the Way of Women: Deception, Gender, and Ideology in Biblical Narrative', *Semeia* 42 (1988), pp. 68-83.

—'The Literary Characterization of Mothers and Sexual Politics in the Hebrew Bible', in Yarbro Collins (ed.), *Feminist Perspectives on Biblical Scholarship*, pp. 117-36 (repr. in *Semeia* 46 [1989], pp. 151-66).

Gaines, Janet Howe, *Music in the Old Bones: Jezebel through the Ages* (Carbondale and Edwardsville: Southern Illinois University Press, 1999).

García-Treto, Francisco, 'The Fall of the House: A Carnivalesque Reading of 2 Kings 9 and 10', *JSOT* 46 (1990), pp. 47-65.

Garrett, Susan R., 'Revelation', in Newsom and Ringe (eds.), *The Women's Bible Commentary*, pp. 377-82.

Gelder, Ken, and Jane M. Jacobs, *Uncanny Australia: Sacredness and Identity in a Postcolonial Nation* (Melbourne: Melbourne University Press, 1998).

Girard, René, 'Introduction', in James G. Williams, *The Bible, Violence, and the Sacred: Liberation from the Myth of Sanctioned Violence* (San Francisco: HarperSanFrancisco, 1991), pp. vii-x.

—*Violence and the Sacred* (trans. Patrick Gregory; Baltimore, MD: The Johns Hopkins University Press, 1977).

Gnuse, Robert Karl, 'The Emergence of Monotheism in Ancient Israel: A Survey of Recent Scholarship', *Religion* 29 (1999), pp. 315-36.

—*No Other Gods: Emergent Monotheism in Israel* (JSOTSup, 241; Sheffield: Sheffield Academic Press, 1997).

Goldberg, David Theo, 'Heterogeneity and Hybridity: Colonial Legacy, Postcolonial Heresy', in Schwartz and Ray (eds.), *A Companion to Postcolonial Studies*, pp. 72-86.

Goodman, Felicitas, *Where the Spirits Ride the Wind: Trance Journeys and Other Ecstatic Experience* (Bloomington: Indiana University Press, 1990).

Gordon, Cyrus H., 'Ugaritic *RBT/RABITU*', in Lyle Eslinger and Glen Taylor (eds.), *Ascribe to the Lord: Biblical and Other Studies in Memory of Peter C. Craigie* (JSOTSup, 67; Sheffield: JSOT Press, 1988), pp. 127-32.

Grace, Patricia, *Cousins* (Auckland: Penguin Books New Zealand, 1992).

Gray, John, *I and II Kings* (London: SCM Press, 3rd rev. edn, 1977).

Greenblatt, Stephen, *Marvellous Possessions: The Wonder of the New World* (Oxford: Clarendon Press, 1991).

Grimshaw, M.P., '"Fouling the Nest": The Conflict between the "Church Party" and Settler Society during the New Zealand Wars 1860–1865' (unpublished PhD dissertation; University of Otago, Dunedin, New Zealand, 1999).

Grosby, Steven, *Biblical Ideas of Nationality Ancient and Modern* (Winona Lake, IN: Eisenbrauns, 2002).

Grosz, Elizabeth, *Volatile Bodies: Toward a Corporeal Feminism* (Bloomington: Indiana University Press, 1994).

Guardiola-Sáenz, Leticia A., 'Borderless Women and Borderless Texts: A Cultural Reading of Matthew 15.21-28', *Semeia* 78 (1997), pp. 69-81.

Gunkel, Hermann, *Genesis* (Göttingen: Vandenhoeck & Ruprecht, 1964).

Habel, Norman C., *The Land is Mine: Six Biblical Land Ideologies* (Minneapolis: Fortress Press, 1995).

Hadley, Judith M., *The Cult of Asherah in Ancient Israel and Judah: Evidence for a Hebrew Goddess* (Cambridge: Cambridge University Press, 2000).

Hamerton-Kelly, Robert G. (ed.), *Violent Origins* (Stanford, CA: Stanford University Press, 1987).

Hamilton, V.P., *The Book of Genesis: Chapters 1–17* (The New International Commentary on the Old Testament; Grand Rapids: Eerdmans, 1990).

Harrington, Wilfrid J., OP, *Revelation* (Sacra Pagina Series, 16; Collegeville, MN: Liturgical Press, 1993).

Hauser, Alan J., 'Yahweh Versus Death—The Real Struggle in 1 Kings 17–19', in Alan J. Hauser and Russell Gregory (eds.), *From Carmel to Horeb: Elijah in Crisis* (JSOTSup, 85; Sheffield: The Almond Press, 1990), pp. 11-89.

Hawk, L. Daniel, *Every Promise Fulfilled: Contesting Plots in Joshua* (Louisville, KY: Westminster/John Knox Press, 1991).

—'The Problem with Pagans', in Timothy K. Beal and David M. Gunn (eds.), *Reading Bibles, Writing Bodies: Identity and the Book* (London/New York: Routledge, 1997), pp. 153-63.

Hayes, John H., and J. Maxwell Miller, *Israelite and Judaean History* (Philadelphia: Westminster Press, 1977).

Heard, R. Christopher, *Dynamics of Diselection: Ambiguity in Genesis 12–36 and Ethnic Boundaries in Post-Exilic Judah* (Atlanta: Society of Biblical Literature, 2001)

Hoglund, Kenneth, *Achaemenid Imperial Administration in Syria-Palestine and the Missions of Ezra and Nehemiah* (Atlanta: Scholars Press, 1992).

hooks, bell, *Yearning: Race, Gender, and Cultural Politics* (Boston, MA: South End Press, 1990).

Huie-Jolly, Mary, 'Maori "Jews" and a Resistant Reading of John 5.10-47', in Dube and Staley (eds.), *John and Postcolonialism*, pp. 94-110.

Humphries-Brooks, Stephenson, 'The Canaanite Women in Matthew', in Levine (ed.), *A Feminist Companion to Matthew*, pp. 138-56.

Hutcheon, Linda, 'Circling the Downspout of Empire', in Ian Adam and Helen Tiffin (eds.), *Past the Last Post: Theorizing Post-Colonialism and Post-Modernism* (Calgary: University of Calgary Press, 1990), pp. 167-89.

Ihimaera, Witi, 'A Maori Perspective', *Journal of New Zealand Literature* 9 (1991), pp. 53-54.

—*The Matriarch* (Auckland: Heinemann, 1986).

Irigaray, Luce, *Elemental Passions* (trans. Joanne Collie and Judith Still; London: Athlone Press, 1992).

James, Bev, and Kay Saville Smith, *Gender, Culture and Power: Challenging New Zealand's Gendered Society* (Auckland: Oxford University Press, 1989).

Jameson, Fredric R., 'A Conversation with Fredric Jameson', *Semeia* 59 (1992), pp. 227-37.

Jobling, David, 'Ruth Finds a Home: Canon, Politics, Method', in Exum and Clines (eds.), *The New Literary Criticism*, pp. 125-39.

—'A Bettered Woman: Elisha and the Shunammite in the Deuteronomic Work', in Fiona C. Black, Roland Boer and Erin Runions (eds.), *The Labour of Reading: Desire, Alienation, and Biblical Interpretation* (Atlanta: Scholars Press, 1999), pp. 177-92.

Jobling, David, Tina Pippin and Ronald Schleifer, 'Part III. The Conscience of the Bible: Introduction', in idem (eds.), *The Postmodern Bible Reader*, pp. 249-64.

Jobling, David, Tina Pippin and Ronald Schleifer (eds.), *The Postmodern Bible Reader* (Oxford: Basil Blackwell, 2001).

Johnston, Anna, and Alan Lawson, 'Settler Colonies', in Schwartz and Ray (eds.), *A Companion to Postcolonial Studies*, pp. 360-76.

Jones, Gwilym H., *1 and 2 Kings* (2 vols.; Grand Rapids: Eerdmans, 1984).

Jones, Siân, 'Identities in Practice: Towards an Archaeological Perspective on Jewish Identity in Antiquity', in Jones and Pearce (eds.), *Jewish Local Patriotism*, pp. 29-49.

Jones, Siân, and Sarah Pearce (eds.), *Jewish Local Patriotism and Self-Identification in the Graeco-Roman Period* (JSPSup, 31; Sheffield: Sheffield Academic Press, 1998).

Keel, Othmar, *Goddesses and Trees, New Moon and Yahweh: Ancient Near Eastern Art and the Hebrew Bible* (JSOTSup, 261; Sheffield: Sheffield Academic Press, 1998).

Keel, Othmar, and Christoph Uehlinger, *Gods, Goddesses, and Images of God in Ancient Israel* (Minneapolis: Fortress Press, 1998).

Keller, Catherine, *Apocalypse Now and Then: A Feminist Guide to the End of the World* (Boston: Beacon Press, 1996).

Kelsey, Jane, 'From Flagpoles to Pine Trees: Tino Rangatiratanga and Treaty Policy Today', in Paul Spoonley, David Pearson and Cluny Macpherson (eds.), *Nga Patai: Racism and Ethnic Relations in Aotearoa/New Zealand* (Palmerston North: The Dunmore Press, 1996), pp. 177-201.

Kidd, José Ramírez, *Alterity and Identity in Israel* (Berlin: W. de Gruyter, 1999).

Kingsbury, Jack Dean, *Matthew as Story* (Philadelphia: Fortress Press, 1986).

Kramer, Samuel Noah, 'The Weeping Goddess: Sumerian Prototypes of the *Mater Dolorosa*', *Biblical Archaeologist* 46 (1983), pp. 69-80.

Kratz, R.G., *Die Komposition der erzählenden Bücher des Alten Testaments. Grundwissen der Bibelkritik* (UTB 2157 M; Vandenhoeck & Ruprecht, 2000).

Kristeva, Julia, 'Bakhtin, le mot, le dialogue at le roman', *Critique* 33 (1967), pp. 438-65.

—*New Maladies of the Soul* (trans. Ross Guberman; New York: Columbia University Press, 1995).

—*Powers of Horror: An Essay on Abjection* (trans. Leon S. Roudiez; New York: Columbia University Press, 1982).

—*Strangers to Ourselves* (trans. Leon S. Roudiez; New York: Columbia University Press, 1991).

Kwok Pui-lan, *Discovering the Bible in the Non-Biblical World* (Maryknoll, NY: Orbis Books, 1995).

Landry, Donna, and Graham MacLean, *The Spivak Reader: Selected Works of Gayatri Chakravorty Spivak* (London: Routledge, 1996).

Landy, Francis, 'On Metaphor, Play and Nonsense', *Semeia* 61 (1993), pp. 219-37.

Larkin, Katrina J.A., *Ruth and Esther* (OTG; Sheffield: Sheffield Academic Press, 1996).

Larner, Wendy, and Paul Spoonley, 'Post-Colonial Politics in Aotearoa/New Zealand', in Stasiulis and Yuval-Davis (eds.), *Unsettling Settler Societies*, pp. 39-64.

Leaney, A.R.C., *The Jewish and Christian World 200BC to AD200* (Cambridge Commentaries on Writings of the Jewish and Christian World 200 BC to AD 200, 7; Cambridge: Cambridge University Press, 1984).

Lemche, Niels Peter, *Ancient Israel: A New History of Israelite Society* (The Biblical Seminar, 5; Sheffield: JSOT Press, 1988).

—*The Canaanites and their Land: The Tradition of the Canaanites* (JSOTSup, 110; Sheffield: JSOT Press, 1990).

Levenson, Jon D., 'The Universal Horizon of Biblical Particularism', in Brett (ed.), *Ethnicity and the Bible*, pp. 143-69.

Levine, Amy-Jill, '"Hemmed in on Every Side": Jews and Women in the Book of Susanna', in Athalya Brenner (ed.), *A Feminist Companion to Esther, Judith and Susanna* (The Feminist Companion to the Bible, 7; Sheffield: Sheffield Academic Press, 1995), pp. 303-23.

Levine, Amy-Jill, with Marianne Blickenstaff (eds.), *A Feminist Companion to Matthew* (The Feminist Companion to the New Testament and Early Christian Writings, 1; Sheffield: Sheffield Academic Press, 2001).

Lionnet, Françoise, *Postcolonial Representations: Women, Literature, Identity* (Ithaca, NY: Cornell University Press, 1995).

Loader, William, 'Challenged at the Boundaries: A Conservative Jesus in Mark's Tradition', *JSNT* 63 (1996), pp. 45-61.

Long, Burke O., *1 Kings with an Introduction to Historical Literature* (Grand Rapids: Eerdmans, 1984).

Luther, Martin, *Lectures on Genesis: Chapters 6–14*, in Jaroslav Pelikan (ed.), *Luthers' Works*, II (St Louis: Concordia, 1960), pp. 291-96.

Lutz, Helma, Ann Phoenix and Nira Yuval-Davis, 'Introduction: Nationalism, Racism and Gender—European Crossfires', in *idem* (eds.), *Crossfires: Nationalism, Racism and Gender in Europe* (London: Pluto Press, 1995), pp. 1-25.

Luz, Ulrich, *Matthew 1–7: A Commentary* (trans. Wilhelm C. Linss; Edinburgh: T. & T. Clark, 1989).

—*The Theology of the Gospel of Matthew* (trans. J. Bradford Robinson; Cambridge: Cambridge University Press, 1995).

Lyke, Larry L., *King David with the Wise Woman of Tekoa: The Resonance of Tradition in Parabolic Narrative* (JSOTSup, 255; Sheffield: Sheffield Academic Press, 1997).

Mack, Burton, 'Introduction: Religion and Ritual', in Hamerton-Kelly (ed.), *Violent Origins*, pp. 1-70.

Maitland, Sara, *A Book of Spells* (London: Michael Joseph, 1987).

Malina, Bruce J., and John J. Pilch, *Social-Science Commentary on the Book of Revelation* (Minneapolis: Fortress Press, 2000).

Matthews, Victor H., and Don C. Benjamin, 'Introduction: Social Sciences and Biblical Studies', *Semeia* 68 (1994), pp. 7-21.

McClintock, Anne, 'The Angel of Progress: Pitfalls of the Term "Postcolonialism"', in Francis Barker, Peter Hulme and Margaret Iversen (eds.), *Colonial Discourse/ Postcolonial Theory* (Manchester: Manchester University Press, 1994), pp. 253-66.

McCreesh, T.P., 'Wisdom as Wife: Proverbs 31:10-31', *RB* 92 (1985), pp. 25-46.

McEvenue, Sean E., 'A Comparison of Narrative Styles in the Hagar Stories', *Semeia* 3 (1975), pp. 64-80.

McEwan Humphrey, Edith, *The Ladies and the Cities: Transformation and Apocalyptic Identity in Joseph and Aseneth, 4 Ezra, the Apocalypse and the Shepherd of Hermes* (JSPSup, 17; Sheffield: Sheffield Academic Press, 1995).

McKenzie, John L., *The World of the Judges* (Englewood Cliffs, NJ: Prentice–Hall, 1966).

McKinlay, Judith E., 'Dead Spots or Living Texts? A Matter of Biblical Reading', *Pacifica* 5 (1992), pp. 1-16.

—*Gendering Wisdom the Host: Biblical Invitations to Eat and Drink* (JSOTSup, 216; Gender, Culture, Theory, 4; Sheffield: Sheffield Academic Press, 1996).

—'Rahab: A Hero/ine?', *BibInt* 7 (1999), pp. 44-57.

McLeod, Rosemary, 'We're all right, mate', *Sunday Star Times* (4 June 2000), p. A9.

Meyers, Carol, *Discovering Eve: Ancient Israelite Women in Context* (New York and Oxford: Oxford University Press, 1988).

—'Gender Roles and Genesis 3.16 Revisited', in C.L. Meyers and M. O'Connor (eds.), *The Word of the Lord Shall Go Forth: Essays in Honor of David Noel Freedman in Celebration of his Sixtieth Birthday* (Winona Lake, IN: Eisenbrauns 1983), pp. 337-54.

Minh-ha, Trinh T., *Woman, Native, Other: Writing Postcoloniality and Feminism* (Bloomington: Indiana University Press, 1989).

Miscall, Peter D., 'Isaiah: New Heavens, New Earth, New Book', in Danna Nolan Fewell (ed.), *Reading Between Texts: Intertexuality and the Hebrew Bible* (Literary Currents in Biblical Interpretation; Louisville, KY: Westminster/John Knox Press, 1992), pp. 41-56.

—'Notes and Readings: Elijah, Ahab and Jehu: A Prophecy Fulfilled', *Prooftexts* 9 (1989), pp. 73-83.

Mohanty, Chandra Talpade, 'Introduction: Cartographies of Struggle—Third World Women and the Politics of Feminism', in Chandra Talpade Mohanty *et al.* (eds.), *Third World Women and the Politics of Feminism* (Bloomington: Indiana University Press, 1991), pp. 1-47.

Moi, Toril (ed.), *The Kristeva Reader* (Oxford: Basil Blackwell, 1986).

Montgomery, James A., *The Books of Kings* (Edinburgh: T. & T. Clark, 1951).

Moor, J.C. de, 'Ugarit and Israelite Origins', in J.A. Emerton (ed.), *Congress Volume: Paris, 1992* (Leiden: E.J. Brill, 1995), pp. 205-38.

Moore, Rick Dale, *God Saves: Lessons from the Elisha Stories* (JSOTSup, 95; Sheffield: JSOT Press, 1990).

Moruzzi, Norma Claire, 'National Abjects: Julia Kristeva on the Process of Political Self-Identification', in Kelly Oliver (ed.), *Ethics, Politics, and Difference in Julia Kristeva's Writing* (New York: Routledge, 1993), pp. 135-49.

Myers, William, 'The Hermeneutical Dilemma of the African American Biblical Student', in Felder (ed.), *Stony the Road We Trod*, pp. 40-56,

Na'aman, Nadav, 'Prophetic Stories as Sources for the Histories of Jehoshaphat and the Omrides', *Bib* 78 (1997), pp. 53-173.

Nadar, Sarojini, 'A South African Indian Womanist Reading of the Character of Ruth', in Musa W. Dube (ed.), *Other Ways of Reading: African Women and the Bible* (Atlanta: Society of Biblical Literature; Geneva: WCC Publications, 2001), pp. 159-75.

Napier, B.D., 'The Omrides of Jezreel', *VT* 9 (1959), pp. 366-78.

Nelson, Richard D., *First and Second Kings* (Interpretation; Louisville, KY: John Knox Press, 1987).

Newsom, Carol A., *The Book of Job: A Contest of Moral Imaginations* (Oxford: Oxford University Press, 2003).

Newsom, Carol A., and Sharon H. Ringe (eds.), *The Women's Bible Commentary* (Louisville, KY: Westminster/John Knox Press, 1992).

Niditch, Susan, *Ancient Israelite Religion* (Oxford: Oxford University Press, 1997).

—*War in the Hebrew Bible* (Oxford: Oxford University Press, 1993).

Niditch, Susan (ed.), *Text and Tradition: The Hebrew Bible and Folklore* (Atlanta: Scholars Press, 1990).

Noll, K.L., *Canaan and Israel in Antiquity: An Introduction* (The Biblical Seminar, 83; London: Sheffield Academic Press, 2001).

Noth, Martin, *Überlieferungsgeschichtliche Studien* (Tübingen: Niemeyer Verlag, 1943).

O'Day, Gail R., 'Surprised by Faith: Jesus and the Canaanite Woman', in Levine (ed.), *A Feminist Companion to Matthew*, pp. 114-25.

Olyan, Saul M., *Asherah and the Cult of Yahweh in Israel* (SBLMS, 34; Atlanta; Scholars Press, 1988).

—*Rites and Rank: Hierarchy in Biblical Representations of Cult* (Princeton, NJ: Princeton University Press, 2000).

Orange, Claudia, *The Treaty of Waitangi* (Wellington: Allen & Unwin New Zealand, 1987).

Oster, Richard E., 'The Ephesian Artemis as an Opponent of Early Christianity', *Jahrbuch für Antike und Christentum* 19 (1976), pp. 24-44.

—'Ephesus as a Religious Center under the Principate. I. Paganism before Constantine', in Wolfgang Haase (ed.), *Aufstieg und Niedergang der römischen Welt* II.18.3 (Berlin: W. de Gruyter, 1990), pp. 1661-28.

Ottoson, Magnus, 'Rahab and the Spies', in Herman Behrens *et al.* (eds.), *Dumu-E2-Dub-Ba-A: Studies in Honor of Ake W. Sjöberg* (Philadelphia: Occasional Publications of the Samuel Noah Kramer Fund, 1989), pp. 419-27.

Panny, Judith Dell, *The Culture Within: Essays on Ihimaera, Grace, Hulme, Tuwhare* (Occasional Paper, 3; Palmerston North, New Zealand: International Pacific College, 1998).

Parker, Simon B., 'Jezebel's Reception of Jehu', *Maarav* 1 (1978), pp. 67-78.

Patte, Daniel, 'Critical Biblical Studies from a Semiotics Perspective', *Semeia* 81 (1998), pp. 3-26.

Peckham, Brian, 'Phoenicia and the Religion of Israel: The Epigraphic Evidence', in Patrick D. Miller, Jr, Paul D. Hanson and S. Dean McBride (eds.), *Ancient Israelite Religion* (Philadelphia: Fortress Press, 1987), pp. 79-99.

Penchanksy, David, 'Up for Grabs: A Tentative Proposal for Doing Ideological Criticism', *Semeia* 59 (1992), pp. 35-41.

Perkinson, Jim, 'A Canaanite Word in the Logos of Christ; or the Difference the Syro-Phoenician Woman Makes to Jesus', *Semeia* 75 (1996), pp. 61-85.

Person, Raymond F., Jr, *The Deuteronomic School: History, Social Setting and Literature* (Studies in Biblical Literature, 2; Atlanta: Society of Biblical Literature, 2002).

Phillips, Gary A., and Danna Nolan Fewell, 'Ethics, Bible, Reading As If', *Semeia* 77 (1997), pp. 1-21.

Pippin, Tina, *Death and Desire: The Rhetoric of Gender in the Apocalypse of John* (Literary Currents in Biblical Interpretation; Louisville, KY: Westminster/John Knox Press, 1992).

—'Jezebel Re-Vamped', in Brenner (ed.), *A Feminist Companion to Samuel and Kings*, pp. 196-206.

Poananga, Atareta, '*The Matriarch*: Takahia WahineToa: Trample on Strong Women. Part 2', *Broadsheet* 46 (January–February 1987), pp. 24-29.

Pokorny, P., 'From a Puppy to a Child: Problems of Contemporary Biblical Exegesis Demonstrated from Mark 7.24-30/Matt 15.21-28', *NTS* 41 (1995), pp. 321-37.

Polzin, Robert, '"The Ancestress of Israel in Danger" in Danger', *Semeia* 3 (1975), pp. 81-98.

—*Moses and the Deuteronomist: A Literary Study of the Deuteronomic History* (New York: Seabury Press, 1980).

Porter, Frances, and Charlotte MacDonald (eds.), '*My Hand Will Write What My Heart Dictates*': *The Unsettled Lives of Women in Nineteenth-Century New Zealand as Revealed to Sisters, Family and Friends* (Auckland: Auckland University Press with Bridget Williams Books, 1996).

Prior, Michael, C.M., *The Bible and Colonialism: A Moral Critique* (The Biblical Seminar, 48; Sheffield: Sheffield Academic Press, 1997).

Pritchard, Elizabeth A., 'Feminist Theology and the Politics of Failure', *Journal of Feminist Studies in Religion* 15/2 (1999), pp. 50-72.

Provan, Iain W., *1 and 2 Kings* (OTG, 11; Sheffield: Sheffield Academic Press, 1997).

Quin, J., 'Is Rahab in Matthew 1.5 Rahab of Jericho?', *Bib* 62 (1982), pp. 225-28.

Reis, Pamela Tamarkin, 'Hagar Requited', *JSOT* 87 (2000), pp. 75-109.

Rendtorff, Rolf, 'The *Ger* in the Priestly Laws of the Pentateuch', in Brett (ed.), *Ethnicity and the Bible*, pp. 77-87.

Resseguie, James L., *Revelation Unsealed: A Narrative Critical Approach to John's Apocalypse* (Leiden: E.J. Brill, 1998).

Rhoads, David, 'Jesus and the Syro-Phoenician Woman in Mark: A Narrative-Critical Study', *JAAR* 62 (1994), pp. 343-76.

Rich, Adrienne, 'When We Dead Awaken: Writing as Re-vision', in idem, *On Lies, Secrets, and Silence: Selected Prose 1966–1978* (New York: W.W. Norton, 1979), pp. 33-49.

Richardson, Laurel, *Fields of Play: Constructing an Academic Life* (New Brunswick, NJ: Rutgers University Press, 1997).

Ricoeur, P., 'The Creativity of Language', in Mario J. Valdes (ed.), *A Ricoeur Reader: Reflection and Imagination* (Toronto: University of Toronto Press, 1991), pp. 463-81.

—*The Rule of Metaphor: Multi-Disciplinary Studies of the Creation of Meaning in Language Texts* (trans. R. Czerny et al.; London: Routledge & Kegan Paul, 1978).

Ringe, Sharon H., 'A Gentile Woman's Story', in Letty Russell (ed.), *Feminist Interpretation of the Bible* (Oxford: Basil Blackwell, 1985), pp. 65-72.

—'A Gentile Woman's Story, Revisited: Rereading Mark 7.24-31', in Amy-Jill Levine (ed.), *A Feminist Companion to Mark* (The Feminist Companion to the New Testament and Early Christian Writings, 2; Sheffield: Sheffield Academic Press, 2001), pp. 79-100.

—'Places at the Table: Feminist and Postcolonial Biblical Interpretation', in Sugirtharajah (ed.), *The Postcolonial Bible*, pp. 136-51.

Rofé, Alexander, 'The Vineyard of Naboth: The Origin and Message of the Story', *VT* 38 (1988), pp. 89-104.

Roncace, Mark, 'Elisha and the Woman of Shunem: 2 Kings 4.8-37 and 8.1-6 Read in Conjunction', *JSOT* 91 (2000), pp. 109-27.

Ross, Cathy, 'More than Wives?' (draft of PhD dissertation, Auckland University, 2002).

Rossing, Barbara R., *The Choice Between Two Cities: Whore, Bride, and Empire in the Apocalypse* (HTS, 48; Harrisburg, PA: Trinity Press International, 1999).

Rowlett, Lori, 'Inclusion, Exclusion and Marginality in the Book of Joshua', *JSOT* 55 (1992), pp. 15-23.

Said, Edward W., *Culture and Imperialism* (London: Chatto & Windus, 1993).

— 'Zionism from the Standpoint of its Victims', in David Theo Goldberg (ed.), *Anatomy of Racism* (Minneapolis: University of Minnesota Press, 1990), pp. 210-46.

Sarna, Nahum, 'Naboth's Vineyard Revisited (1 Kings 21)', in idem (ed.), *Studies in Biblical Interpretation* (Philadelphia: The Jewish Publication Society of America, 2000), pp. 271-80.

Scarry, Elaine, *Resisting Representation* (New York: Oxford University Press, 1994).

Schaberg, Jane, 'A Feminist Experience of Historical-Jesus Scholarship', in William E. Arnal and Michel Desjardins (eds.), *Whose Historical Jesus?* (Canadian Corporation for Studies in Religion/Corporation Canadienne des Sciences Religieuses; Ontario: Wilfred Laurier University Press, 1997), pp. 146-60.

Schroer, Sylvia, *Wisdom Has Built her House: Studies on the Figure of Sophia in the Bible* (Collegeville, MN: Liturgical Press, 2000).

Schüssler Fiorenza, Elisabeth, *In Memory of Her* (New York: Crossroad, 1983).

Schwartz, Henry, and Sangeeta Ray (eds.), *A Companion to Postcolonial Studies* (Oxford: Basil Blackwell, 2000).

Schwartz, Regina M., *The Curse of Cain: The Violent Legacy of Monotheism* (Chicago: University of Chicago Press, 1997).

Schweickart, Patrocinio P., 'Reading Ourselves: Toward a Feminist Theory of Reading', in Elizabeth A. Flynn and Patrocinio P. Schweickart (eds.), *Gender and Reading* (Baltimore: The John Hopkins University Press, 1986), pp. 31-62.

Scott, J.C., *Domination and the Arts of Resistance: Hidden Transcripts* (New Haven: Yale University Press, 1990).

Scott, J. Martin C., 'Matthew 15.21-28: A Test-Case for Jesus' Manners', *JSNT* 63 (1996), pp. 21-44.

Segovia, Fernando F., 'Biblical Criticism and Postcolonial Studies: Toward a Postcolonial Optic', in Sugirtharajah (ed.), *The Postcolonial Bible*, pp. 49-65.

—*Interpreting Beyond Borders* (The Bible and Postcolonialism, 3: Sheffield: Sheffield Academic Press, 2000).

—'Notes toward Refining the Postcolonial Optic', *JSNT* 75 (1999), pp. 103-14.

Sharp, Andrew, *Justice and the Maori: The Philosophy and Practice of Maori Claims in New Zealand Since the 1970s* (Auckland: Oxford University Press, 2nd edn, 1997).

Sharrad, Paul, 'Listening to One's Ancestors: An Interview with Witi Ihimaera', *Australian and New Zealand Studies in Canada* 8 (1992), pp. 97-105.

Shields, Mary, 'Subverting a Man of God, Elevating a Woman: Role and Power Reversals in 2 Kings 4', *JSOT* 58 (1993), pp. 59-69.

Siebert-Hommes, Jopie, 'The Widow of Zarephath and the Great Woman of Shunem: A Comparative Analysis of Two Stories', in Bob Becking and Meindert Dijkstra (eds.), *On Reading Prophetic Texts: Gender-Specific and Related Studies in Memory of Fokkelien van Dijk-Hemmes* (Leiden: E.J. Brill, 1996), pp. 231-50.

Sim, David C., 'Christianity and Ethnicity in the Gospel of Matthew', Brett (ed.), *Ethnicity and the Bible*, pp. 171-95.

Smelik, K.A.D., 'The Literary Function of 1 Kings 17.8-24', in C. Brekelmans and J. Lust (eds.), *Pentateuchal and Deuteronomistic Studies* (Leuven: Leuven University Press, 1990), pp. 239-43.

Smith, J.Z., 'What a Difference a Difference Makes', in J. Neusner and E.S. Frerichs (eds.), *'To See Ourselves as Others See Us': Christians, Jews, 'Others' in Late Antiquity* (Chico: Scholars Press, 1985).

Smith, Mark S., *The Early History of God: Yahweh and the Other Deities in Ancient Israel* (San Francisco: Harper & Row, 1990).

—*The Origins of Biblical Monotheism: Israel's Polytheistic Background and the Ugaritic Texts* (Oxford: Oxford University Texts, 2001).

Smith-Christopher, Daniel L., 'Ezra and Isaiah: Exclusion, Transformation, and Inclusion of the "Foreigner" in Post-Exilic Biblical Theology', in Brett (ed.), *Ethnicity and the Bible*, pp. 117-42.

—'The Mixed Marriage Crisis in Ezra 9–10 and Nehemiah 13: A Study of the Sociology or the Post-Exilic Judaean Community', in Eskenazi and Richards (eds.), *Second Temple Studies 2*, pp. 243-65.

Soggin, J. Alberto, *An Introduction to the History of Israel and Judah* (trans. John Bowden; Valley Forge, PA: Trinity Press International, 1993).

Soja, Edward W., 'Thirdspace: Expanding the Scope of the Geographical Imagination', in Doreen Massey, John Allen and Philip Sarre (eds.), *Human Geography Today* (Cambridge: Polity Press, 1999), pp. 260-78.

—*Thirdspace: Journeys to Los Angeles and Other Real-and-Imagined Places* (Oxford: Basil Blackwell, 1996).

Soskice, Janet Martin, *Metaphor and Religious Language* (Oxford: Clarendon Press, 1985).

Spivak, Gayatri Chakravorty, 'Can the Subaltern Speak?', in Cary Nelson and Lawrence Grossberg (eds.), *Marxism and the Interpretation of Culture* (Urbana: University of Illinois Press, 1988), pp. 271-313.

—*The Post-Colonial Critic: Interviews, Strategies, Dialogues* (ed. Sarah Harasym; New York: Routledge, 1990).

Stanton, Graham N., *A Gospel for a New People: Studies in Matthew* (Louisville, KY: Westminster/John Knox Press, 1992).

Stasiulis, Daiva, and Nira Yuval-Davis, 'Introduction: Beyond Dichotomies—Gender, Race, Ethnicity and Class in Settler Societies', in *idem* (eds.), *Unsettling Settler Societies*, pp. 1-38.

Stasiulis, Daiva, and Nira Yuval-Davis (eds.), *Unsettling Settler Societies: Articulations of Gender, Race, Ethnicity and Class* (London: Sage Publications, 1995).

Stern, Ephraim, 'Religion in Palestine in the Assyrian and Persian Periods', in Bob Becking and Marjo C.A. Korpel (eds.), *The Crisis of Israelite Religion* (Leiden: E.J. Brill, 1999), pp. 245-55.

Stratton, Beverly J., *Out of Eden: Reading, Rhetoric, and Ideology in Genesis 2–3* (JSOTSup, 208; Sheffield: JSOT Press, 1995).

Streete, Gail Corrington, *The Strange Woman: Power and Sex in the Bible* (Louisville, KY: Westminster/John Knox Press, 1997).

Strelan, Rick, *Paul, Artemis, and the Jews in Ephesus* (Berlin: W. de Gruyter, 1996).

Sugirtharajah, R.S., 'A Postcolonial Exploration of Collusion and Construction in Biblical Interpretation', in *idem* (ed.), *The Postcolonial Bible*, pp. 91-116.

—'Textual Cleansing: A Move from the Colonial to the Postcolonial Version', *Semeia* 76 (1996), pp. 7-19.

Sugirtharajah, R.S. (ed.), *The Postcolonial Bible* (The Bible and Postcolonialism, 1; Sheffield: Sheffield Academic Press, 1998).

Suleiman, Susan Rubin, 'Introduction', in *idem* (ed.), *The Female Body in Western Culture*, pp. 1-4

Suleiman, Susan Rubin (ed.), *The Female Body in Western Culture* (Cambridge, MA: Harvard University Press, 1986).

Thompson, Leonard, 'A Sociological Analysis of Tribulation in the Apocalypse of John', *Semeia* 36 (1986), pp. 147-74.

Tiffin, Helen, 'Recuperative Strategies in the Post-Colonial Novel', *Span* 24 (1987), pp. 27-45.

Tigay, J., *You Shall Have No Other Gods: Israelite Religion in the Light of Hebrew Inscriptions* (HSS, 31; Atlanta: Scholars Press, 1986).

Tompkins, Jane, 'Me and My Shadow', in Linda Kauffman (ed.), *Gender and Theory: Dialogues on Feminist Criticism* (Oxford: Basil Blackwell, 1989), pp. 121-39.

Trible, Phyllis, 'Exegesis for Storytellers and Other Strangers', *JBL* 114 (1995), pp. 3-19.

—'The Odd Couple: Elijah and Jezebel', in Christina Büchmann and Celina Spiegel (eds.), *Out of the Garden: Women Writers on the Bible* (New York: Fawcett Columbine, 1994), pp. 166-79.

—*Texts of Terror* (Philadelphia: Fortress Press, 1984).

Tucker, Gene M., 'The Rahab Saga (Joshua 2)', in James M. Efird (ed.), *The Use of the Old Testament in the New and Other Essays: Studies in Honor of William Franklin Stinespring* (Durham, NC: Duke University Press, 1972), pp. 66-86.

Ussishkin, David, 'Jezreel, Samaria and Megiddo: Royal Centres of Omri and Ahab', in J.A. Emerton (ed.), *Congress Volume: Cambridge, 1995* (VTSup, 66; Leiden: E.J. Brill, 1997), pp. 351-64.

Van Dijk-Hemmes, Fokkelien, 'The Great Woman of Shunem and the Man of God: A Dual Interpretation of 2 Kings 4.8-37', in Brenner (ed.), *A Feminist Companion to Samuel and Kings*, pp. 218-30.

—'Sarai's Exile: A Gender-Motivated Reading of Genesis 12.20–13.2', in Athalya Brenner (ed.), *A Feminist Companion to Genesis* (The Feminist Companion to the Bible, 2; Sheffield: Sheffield Academic Press, 1993), pp. 222-34.

Van Houten, Christiana, *The Alien in Israelite Law: A Study of the Changing Legal Status of Strangers in Ancient Israel* (JSOTSup, 107; Sheffield: JSOT Press, 1991).

Van Seters, John, 'Creative Imagination in the Hebrew Bible', *Studies in Religion/Sciences Religieuses* 29 (2000), pp. 395-409.

Van Wolde, Ellen, 'Texts in Dialogue with Texts: Intertextuality in the Ruth and Tamar Narratives', *BibInt* 5.1 (1997), pp. 1-28.

Vander Stichele, Caroline, 'Just a Whore: The Annihilation of Babylon According to Revelation 17.16', *Lectio Difficilior* 1 (2000), available online at <www.lectio.unibe.ch/>.

Vawter, Bruce, *On Genesis: A New Reading* (Garden City, NY: Doubleday, 1977).

Wainwright, Elaine, 'The Gospel of Matthew', in Elisabeth Schüssler Fiorenza (ed.), *Searching the Scriptures. II. A Feminist Commentary* (New York: Crossroad, 1994), pp. 635-77.

—*Shall We Look for Another? A Feminist Rereading of the Matthean Jesus* (Maryknoll, NY: Orbis Books, 1998).

—*Towards a Feminist Critical Reading of the Gospel According to Matthew* (Berlin: W. de Gruyter, 1991).

Wall, Melanie, 'Stereotypical Constructions of the Maori "Race" in the Media', *New Zealand Geographer* 53.2 (1997), pp. 40-45.

Walls, Neal H., *The Goddess Anat in Ugaritic Myth* (SBLDS, 135; Atlanta: Scholars Press, 1992).

Walsh, Jerome T., *1 Kings* (Berit Olam: Studies in Hebrew Narrative and Poetry; Collegeville, MN: Liturgical Press, 1996).

—'Methods and Meanings: Multiple Studies of 1 Kings 21', *JBL* 111 (1992), pp. 193-211.

Warrior, R.A., 'Canaanites, Cowboys and Indians', *Christianity and Crisis* 29 (1989), pp. 261-65.

Washington, Harold C., 'Violence and the Construction of Gender in the Hebrew Bible: A New Historicist Approach', *BibInt* 5 (1997), pp. 324-63.

Weeks, Stuart, *Early Israelite Wisdom* (Oxford: Clarendon Press, 1994).

Weems, Renita J., 'Reading Her Way through the Struggle: African American Women and the Bible', in Felder (ed.), *Stony the Road We Trod*, pp. 57-77.

Weisman, Ze'ev, *Political Satire in the Bible* (Atlanta: Scholars Press, 1998).

Wendt, Albert, *The Mango's Kiss* (Auckland: Vintage Books, 2003).

Westermann, Claus, *Genesis 12–36: A Continental Commentary* (trans. John J. Scullion; Minneapolis: Fortress Press, 1995).

White, Hugh C., *Narration and Discourse in the Book of Genesis* (Cambridge: Cambridge University Press, 1991).

Williams, Mark, *Leaving the Highway: Six Contemporary New Zealand Novelists* (Auckland: Auckland University Press, 1990).

—'Witi Ihimaera: Interviewed by Mark Williams', in Elizabeth Alley and Mark Williams (eds.), *In the Same Room: Conversations with New Zealand Writers* (Auckland: Auckland University Press, 1992), pp. 219-36.

Wilson, Robert R., 'Genealogy, Genealogies', in *ABD*, II, pp. 929-32.

Wolkstein, Diane, and Samuel Noah Kramer, *Inanna Queen of Heaven and Earth: Her Stories and Hymns from Sumer* (New York: Harper & Row, 1983).

Yarbro Collins, Adela, *The Combat Myth in the Book of Revelation* (HDR, 9; Missoula, MT: Scholars Press, 1976).

—*Cosmology and Eschatology in Jewish and Christian Apocalypticism* (Leiden: E.J. Brill, 1996).

—*Crisis and Catharsis: The Power of the Apocalypse* (Philadelphia: Westminster Press, 1984).

—'The History-of-Religion Approach to Apocalypticism and the "Angel of the Waters" (Rev 16.4-7)', *CBQ* 39 (1977), pp. 367-81.

Yarbro Collins, Adela (ed.), *Feminist Perspectives on Biblical Scholarship* (Atlanta: Scholars Press, 1985).

Yee, Gale A., '"She is Not My Wife and I am Not Her Husband": A Materialist Analysis of Hosea 1–2', *BibInt* 9 (2000), pp. 345-83.

Young, Robert J.C., *Colonial Desire: Hybridity in Theory, Culture and Race* (New York: Routledge, 1995).

Zakovitch, Yair, 'Humor and Theology or the Successful Failure of Israelite Intelligence: A Literary-Folkloric Approach to Joshua 2', in Niditch (ed.), *Text and Tradition*, pp. 75-98.

Zlotnick, Helena, 'From Jezebel to Esther: Fashioning Images of Queenship in the Hebrew Bible', *Bib* 82 (2001), pp. 477-95.

INDEXES

INDEX OF REFERENCES

INDEX OF AUTHORS

Siebert-Hommes, J. 59, 63
Sim, D.C. 103
Smelik, K.A.D. 60
Smith, J.Z. 22, 65
Smith, M.S. 2, 57, 58, 141
Smith-Christopher, D.L. 28, 29, 71
Soggin, J.A. 74
Soja, E.W. 134-36
Soskice, J.M. 5
Spivak, G.C. 77, 139
Spoonley, P. 19, 31, 33, 35
Staley, J.L. ix
Stanton, G.N. 100
Stasiulis, D. 20, 23, 30, 114
Stern, E. 89
Stratton, B.J. 11
Streete, G.C. 26, 84, 87
Strelan, R. 148, 150
Sugirtharajah, R.S. ix, 20, 108, 112
Suleiman, S.R. 79
Swanson, R.W. 93

Tadmor, H. 64, 82, 84
Thompson, L. 138
Tiffin, H. 158
Tigay, J. 4
Tompkins, J. 13
Trible, P. 59, 68, 71, 133
Tucker, G.M. 42, 44

Uehlinger, C. 141
Ussishkin, D. 73, 74

Vander Stichele, C. 144, 145
Van Dijk-Hemmes, F. 9-11, 62
Van Houten, C. 24
Van Seters, J. 69
Van Wolde, E. 54
Vawter, B. 12

Wainwright, E. 98-102, 104, 108, 109
Wall, M. 19
Walls, N.H. 144
Walsh, J.T. 67, 68, 70, 71, 73
Warrior, R.A. 33
Washington, H.C. 81
Weeks, S. 4
Weems, R.J. 48
Weisman, Z. 80
Wendt, A. 77, 78
Westermann, C. 132
White, H.C. 10
Williams, M. 154, 155, 157
Wilson, R.R. 100
Wolkstein, D. 141, 144

Yarbro Collins, A. 138, 141-43, 146-49
Yee, G.A. 74
Young, R.J.C. 131, 132
Yuval-Davis, N. 20, 23, 30, 114, 120

Zakovitch, Y. 40-42
Zlotnick, H. 69, 74

CPSIA information can be obtained at www.ICGtesting.com
Printed in the USA
BVOW020406210911

271767BV00002B/28/A